PILGRIMAGE of Desire

An Explorer's Journey Through the Labyrinths of Life

Alison Gresik

Reunion Road Press
VANCOUVER, BC

I have tried to recreate events, locales, and conversations from my memories of them. In order to maintain the anonymity of individuals and places, in some instances I have changed their names, and I may have changed some identifying characteristics and details such as physical properties, occupations, and places of residence.

This book is not intended as a substitute for the medical advice of physicians. The reader should regularly consult a physician in matters relating to his/her health and particularly with respect to any symptoms that may require diagnosis or medical attention.

Every effort has been made to contact copyright holders; in the event of an inadvertent omission or error, please notify the publisher.

Reunion Road Press
Suite 202 – 1965 West 4th Avenue
Vancouver, BC, V6J 1M8
www.reunionroadpress.com

Cover design by Michelle Farinella
Editing by Brenda Leifso
Book Layout ©2017 BookDesignTemplates.com

Library and Archives Canada Cataloguing in Publication

Gresik, Alison, 1973-, author
     Pilgrimage of desire : an explorer's journey through the labyrinths
of life / Alison Gresik.

Includes bibliographical references.
Issued in print, electronic and audiobook formats.
ISBN 978-0-9938306-4-8 (bound).--ISBN 978-0-9938306-5-5 (pbk.).--
ISBN 978-0-9938306-0-0 (mobi).--ISBN 978-0-9938306-1-7 (epub).--
ISBN 978-0-9938306-2-4 (pdf).--ISBN 978-0-9938306-3-1 (MP3)

     1. Gresik, Alison, 1973--Mental health. 2. Gresik, Alison, 1973--
Travel. 3. Depressed persons--Canada--Biography. 4. Authors,
Canadian (English)--20th century--Biography. I. Title.

PS8563.R484Z53 2014   C813'.54   C2014-907644-4
                           C2014-907645-2
                           C2014-907646-0

Contents

For Shawn,
Lia & Nico

My beloved fellow pilgrims

The center and the beginning are the same.

–MICHAEL MEADE

Prologue

As a kid, I was a quiet rebel. One Saturday morning, my little sister and I crept downstairs to watch cartoons and lifted a bottle of Flintstones vitamins from the cupboard to snack on. Eyes glued to the TV, we crunched Fred and Wilma between our teeth, feeling the technicolour powder explode against our cheeks, huffing the fruity chemical fumes from the emptying bottle. At six years old, I knew we were only supposed to eat one vitamin a day, but I thought the rule was stupid: why would they make them taste so good if you weren't supposed to eat them?

When my parents discovered us and freaked out, I somehow convinced them that my sister Melody had eaten every last Bamm Bamm and I was an innocent onlooker. Poor Mel had to go to the hospital to drink ipecac while I got off scot-free. The rule might be stupid, but I didn't want to lose my good-girl image, which had the power to make Mom and Dad believe me when I was obviously lying!

By Grade 5, my quiet rebellion had turned me into a misfit wallflower. During the class Christmas party, while everyone else listened to Michael Jackson songs and argued about whether Julie was actually going out with Eric or just really liked him a lot, I sat perched on a counter in the back corner and read an entire book. I couldn't be bothered to pretend that I cared about who had a new T shirt or who had asked for a ghetto blaster from Santa. What mattered to me was reaching a hundred thousand points in the reading contest, and I didn't mind if I had a sore butt and cookie crumbs on my shirt and everyone thought I was weird. In fact, I found most of school so boring that I was quite happy when my parents pulled me out to teach me at home. Disappearing from Welborne Public was my stealthy rebellion against the coming trials of middle school, and I spent three years practicing recorder and learning to sew instead of playing the social pariah.

When I went back to school for Grade 9, I relished being different. While the other kids on the bus wore pegged jeans and Tretorn sneakers and OP tees with jams, I started my first day in a turquoise shirt-dress with matching hair bow. I thought Def Leppard and the Beastie Boys were vulgar and listened to oldies music on my pink Walkman: "Can't Get Next to You," "Tears of a Clown," "Sugar Pie Honey Bunch." My intro English paper described the creative process of novelist P.G. Wodehouse, and my teacher was rather dumbfounded that I had read the entire *Jeeves* series by the age of thirteen.

Towards the middle of high school, though, my skirt-wearing, Motown-loving routine was getting lonely, and I was ready to try fitting in. I got a perm, contact lenses, and my first pair of jeans and thought I would be all set.

I'm sure it helped that I no longer looked like a boarding school prat (seriously, my favourite outfit was a navy jumper and puffed-sleeve blouse). But actually making friends happened when I showed people what was under the surface. I started exchanging letters with the cutest guy in class — sheets of ballpoint handwriting folded into tiny squares and slipped into pockets and locker vents. This boy had written me off as a shy nerd who beat his times in typing class, but through our secret correspondence, he fell in love with a girl who was funny and passionate about everything from science fiction to feminism. After hiding for years, I was so happy to be truly seen.

I still had no time for nonsensical rules, shallow obsessions, and a monochrome world where everyone copied everyone else. But I didn't get loud and indignant about it like the metalheads who wore black and smoked cigarettes (although, to be fair, I was at a Christian high school, so even our rebels weren't that rebellious.) I just carried on below the radar, keeping up my grades and feigning a horror of sex to my parents while I made out with my boyfriend on the sly.

What I desired was a life where I could explore the furthest reaches of my ideals — truth, equality, freedom — without getting hung up on dogma and tradition. I wanted to write stories that captured people's beautiful contradictions, the places where ordinary and extraordinary intersected. I wanted to take all the brains and love inside me and make something that really mattered, something subversive and different.

But instead of going there directly, I took the long way around. Somewhere along the line, I fell for my own façade and became addicted to the approval of grown-ups and the sense of control and safety that came from following the rules.

In my twenties, the path I followed looked nothing like a rebel's. I was married to my high-school boyfriend. I had a good-paying corporate job as a technical writer and put money in my retirement savings. Shawn and I took an after-hours position supervising a university residence so we could pay our student loans and save a down payment for a house. I volunteered at my Anglican church, running the worship music program and leading a home group. Whenever someone asked for something, I gave: editing Shawn's grad school papers, chairing committees for our cohousing group, coordinating mailings for an environmental newspaper. I had *good girl* down to a science.

Meanwhile, I was unhappy with my frustrated progress in building a writing career. Four years after I finished my creative writing degree and published my first book, I had only produced a handful of short stories. Many of my mornings, which were supposed to be set aside for time at the keyboard, got swallowed by meetings, interviews, and chores. Resentment boiled in my blood whenever I had to sacrifice my own work for something else, but I tried to keep the lid on.

In the urban design world, planners have a name for the natural paths that develop along the shortest or easiest route between two points: they're called *desire lines* (from the French, *chemins du désir*). You've probably seen examples in parks and on campuses — someone takes a diagonal across the quad, and others follow until a dirt track snakes clearly through the lawn, marking the path of least resistance.

In my adult life, I had become a person dutifully walking the sidewalks, going blocks out of my way to stay on sanctioned concrete and keeping to the protocol of a helpful, responsible citizen. In my heart, though, I longed to make my own desire lines, cutting across the grass straight toward the objects of my affection, following foot-worn paths or tramping out new ones.

Eventually my psyche rebelled in the only way I would listen, bowling me over with a body slam of depression. At night, I huddled on the couch, paralysed with anxiety, while my mind raced in obsessive thoughts that made me want to crawl out of my skin. The energy I needed to keep up with my commitments leached away. Holding myself together in front of other people took monumental strength. But I was afraid to be alone too — petrified of taking a shower because it meant there was no protection from the onslaught of my despair.

Worst of all was the loss of desire. The doctors call it *anhedonia*, a lack of interest in enjoyable activities, and it's a significant clinical symptom in the diagnosis of depression. In that state, I couldn't imagine anything to look forward to. Things I used to love no longer gave me pleasure — food was just something to fill my stomach, and conversations with friends were dreary ordeals. For months, I couldn't muster the interest to read a single book. Writing was completely out of the question. And when there's nothing to want, to reach for, why get out of bed? Why go on living when nothing feels good?

So many creative people I know are in the same quandary — pulled in two by these selves at odds, the good girl and the rebel. One craves order and action, always looking outward to see who she can serve and please. The other wants spontaneity and stillness, curling around her inner world to protect and savour the richness there. Both impulses are essential: action and reflection, yang and yin, the in-and-out breath that sustains life. But with one stampeding over the other, I was pulled off course, down thoroughfares I had never wanted to visit.

In the core of my being, where the wise and sane part of me still resided, I knew that *depressed* was not how I was meant to be. Despite the self-loathing voice inside that said, *You're weak! You're broken! You're pathetic!*, I knew I had so much to give. I didn't want to waste my life, caught in the riptide of these two conflicting forces. I had no choice but to look at the damage my good-girl act was doing to me and begin to change my course, degree by degree. After all, I still wanted to make something of myself that mattered — to other people, yes, and also to me.

Ten years later, I am on an airplane with my husband and children, flying to Hong Kong. The house we saved up for has been sold. The furniture I picked out so carefully, thinking it would shield me from existential angst, is gone. The unhappiness that dogged me in my twenties has disappeared. I am healthy and strong and filled to the brim with desire.

We have set out on an open-ended trip around the world — my tall, wise-cracking sweetheart Shawn, our feisty five-year-old daughter Lia, our goofy boy Nico, who's nearly four, and me.

In a nod to Joni Mitchell, we've named our adventure *Operation Hejira* after her 1976 folk jazz album. *Hejira*, meaning "journey," was written on a car trip Mitchell made from Maine to Los Angeles. For me, Hejira is not just about the "urge for going" but the urge to turn the journey into art.

After a summer in Grosse Pointe, Michigan, living down the road from family, we'll spend the winter in Penang, Malaysia and the spring in France and Holland. Shawn's looking forward to visiting his Dutch relatives and bicycling the provinces. Lia is enraptured at the thought of swimming outdoors all winter. Nico is just happy that he's finally on an airplane!

And me? I want to spend my year telling the story of this journey and the journey to the journey. How did I go from being a despondent mess to being strong and brave enough for Operation Hejira? (Believe me, this endeavour is taking more strength and bravery than I've needed in a long time.) How did I get the nerve to do something risky that takes me far away from the family and friends I love just for the thrill and challenge? And how am I going to build writing and coaching careers in the midst of an itinerant life — with two young dynamos to take care of?

Operation Hejira has me firmly pointed in the direction of my desires. I crave the colour of travel, the simplicity of two suitcases, and the chance to work less and see more. I long for adventures with Shawn and the kids and a view of the ocean as I write. I'm counting on desire to carry me when the road is rough.

When I was depressed, I lost track of the compass heading toward my own yearnings and got hopelessly mired in dread. Looking inside myself, I saw a big frown and a long sigh, but no joy. And I learned, on the slow road of healing, that two avenues continually led me back into the way of desire.

WHOLENESS. Bringing my neural chemistry back into balance. Rediscovering a God who nurtured me instead of judging me. Learning to pull on the same side as my husband rather than forcing myself to win or surrender. Making peace between my right and left brain, my adult self and my inner child, my light and shadow. Positioning my identity as a writer and artist in the centre instead of on the fringes and bringing all of my other roles— mother, daughter, wife, friend, coach — into orbit around.

DESIGN. Deciding to live for my *own* life purpose, instead of someone else's. Taking time to go inside and discover what I truly want without discounting it as selfish or something to be earned with good behaviour. Setting intentions and goals to create the life I envision and earmarking my time and energy to accomplish them. Making big changes (like quitting my job, selling the car, having kids, starting a coaching business) when the time is right.

With Operation Hejira, my cover as a conventional good girl has been completely blown. I'm not following the North American middle class rules for career-building and property ownership and spending Christmas with both sets of parents. Now is the time to get noisy about my defiant streak so that other quiet rebels can see a different way forward.

Some people leap and let the journey change them. I seem to change a lot beforehand: surveying the terrain, outfitting myself for what lies ahead, and striking out when I'm ready. In the last ten years, I've covertly acquired the courage and self-possession I need to make a public break from the status quo. And I hope that, by showing you the paths I've taken and where they've led, you may be able to embark on your own pilgrimage of desire.

Quiet Rebel

"Deep down, beneath the pleasant demeanor and quiet competence, in the invisible self that nobody knew, I was a rebel to the very center. ... But I was a patient rebel. I watched. I listened. I learned. I plotted. I did not want to rebel in some symbolic way. I had no interest in a futile act of defiance that would lead to my destruction. ... There is great power in harboring a single goal. With my words and actions, I excelled at my daily tasks. But with my thoughts I planned my coup."
— Brandon Mull, *Fablehaven: Keys to the Demon Prison*

Rebel may seem like a strong word to describe a girl who handed in all her homework on time, who once returned a romance book to the Christian bookstore because her mother didn't approve. A woman who has never kissed anyone but her own husband, who has only smoked a single cigarette as research for a short story.

In my upbringing, *rebellious* was the worst thing you could be. Rebellious meant that you didn't honour your parents and you rejected the community. A rebellious child was obstinate, dangerous, and out of control.

In current culture, the word *rebel* is associated with punk rockers and anarchists. Graffiti artists and high school dropouts and members of armed uprisings. A rebel is not usually a petite woman with one hole pierced demurely in each ear and no experience with light weaponry.

Gretchen Rubin, author of *Better Than Before*, would say that I'm a questioner rather than a rebel. I don't flout all the rules from traffic laws to New Year's resolutions. Instead, I question norms in my family culture, religion, the academy, the government and capitalism, especially where I see injustice, waste, and suffering. Therapy taught me to question even my own thoughts.

But I still toe the line when it makes sense to me. I pay my taxes and try to return my library books on time, and I don't touch my smartphone while I'm driving since I got that ticket.

Even so, I'm going to keep my moniker of *quiet rebel*. A quiet rebel follows the rules to provide cover while she's plotting her escape. She focuses her rebellious energy on the things that matter most to her. And she wins more converts with persuasion than with fists in the air. Quiet rebels, unite!

PART 1: OTTAWA

1 Lighter by the Minute

I'm wearing a kitchen apron overtop of my high-tech rain jacket —
coins go in one pocket, bills in the other. Three carloads of stuff are
spread on tarps next to me: downhill skis, snowmobile boots, a
Christmas tree skirt, an inflatable mattress, a clothes steamer. The
sloping verge of schoolyard I rented for the Great Glebe Garage Sale
faces a busy corner, and from 6:30 in the morning until 3:30 in the
afternoon, a constant flow of gawkers, browsers, and buyers moves
slowly by my display, scanning for something valuable or interesting
and asking, "How much?" "Will you take five bucks?" "What *is* that?"

I flit around the tarp, bargaining, talking up the wares, and making
change. Every so often I take a wad of twenties from my apron and
stuff it into a zippered jacket pocket. I rearrange the books in totes
along the sidewalk, flip price tags right-side up, and explain that the
tiny slow cooker is great for chocolate fondue and hot dip.

I'm so happy, it's almost obscene.

The Glebe is one of the more affluent downtown neighbourhoods
in Ottawa, and every year on the last Saturday in May, people come in
swarms to snag bargains from the endless blocks of tables and yard

sales. We are getting our condo ready to start showings, and the garage sale comes at just the right time to clear out the clutter so the place looks open and spacious.

I've been worried about the forecast, which predicted rain storms all day, but some friends assured me that the weather wouldn't dampen the foot traffic, and they were right. Thankfully the rain is holding to an occasional misty spray that doesn't threaten any merchandise except the paperbacks.

A young hippy-ish woman buys my hardcover copy of *The 4-Hour Workweek* by Tim Ferriss for $2. "Be careful," I say. "That book is dangerous. I read it four years ago and now my husband has quit his job and we're selling everything to travel around the world."

She grins at me. She has no idea.

While I unload the contents of our closets on the Saturday morning crowds, Shawn is performing his own feats of preparation: meeting our real estate agent to spackle holes in the wall before the house gets listed, renting a steam cleaner for the carpets, bringing more boxes of stuff for me to sell. Somewhere in there he drops Lia at Chinese school, but Nico putters around with him all morning. They bring me a hamburger for lunch, but I hardly have time to eat with all the selling going on.

Every time Shawn comes by, we exult in how much has sold, the growing stash of bills in my pocket, how he won't have to pack up all this stuff and take it home again. Someone even bought the giant wall map of Europe! We feel lighter by the minute. Our dream is going to come true.

Ten years ago, Operation Hejira wasn't even a glimmer on the horizon. The most ambitious trip we could muster was a few hours' drive to the Lac Brome region of Quebec. The location sounds idyllic —

just the two of us and the duck confit, a fancy hotel, a golf course, and a water park in the foothills of the Appalachians. In fact, it was an emergency vacation suggested by our couples therapist as we sat, dazed, on her chintz couch.

Our therapist, Connie, was a solicitous maiden-aunt type with a South African accent; I had coaxed Shawn into her office because we were coming off a tough year in our university residence job and dealing with some challenging family stuff. I had just started medication for depression, but the drugs hadn't kicked in yet. We were deep in shock from my diagnosis and everything it meant for our future.

I had some time off from work and was planning a solo trip to upstate New York to research a novel I'd been working on. I wasn't looking forward to the trip because I was depressed and couldn't look forward to anything. But I wanted to go — if only to prove to myself that I still had a toehold on my identity and work as a writer.

I'm sure we looked like a couple of miserable, burned-out wretches — because we were. "Why don't you go away *together*?" Connie said with gentle concern.

Well, if there's one thing Shawn and I know how to do, it's travel. So we found a tourist destination, booked a room, and drove off in the July sun.

Unfortunately, a beautiful setting does not automatically cure unhappiness. I spent the first afternoon lying on a chaise lounge by the pool, trying not to pass out from anxiety and panic. All my senses were telling me *Life is wonderful! Birds are singing! Blue sky, warm air!* And at the same time, I felt like if I moved, I would die. Some part of me was convinced that I was in mortal danger.

We tried visiting the water park, but I was spooked by the crowds and clung to Shawn like an invalid. When I finally worked up the nerve to go down a slide, I encountered a sign — *Pas de lunettes* — and had to use my foggy brain to decide what to do with my prescription sunglasses. Finally I took them off and put them in Shawn's bathing suit pocket. When we reached the bottom, we felt sick at the discovery that my expensive eyewear had disappeared (duh) in the cascade of water and happy swimmers. I had to stumble through the rest of the day half-blind, squinting in the sun.

Later, I bought a sun visor so we could go golfing. My anxiety started to relent, and I faked a little vacation cheer so Shawn would have a good time. But at the end of nine holes, over milkshakes and burgers, we confessed our fears to each other. What if I didn't get better? What if I lived with depression all my life? What if I couldn't handle having children?

We didn't have answers then. All we could do was hold each other and keep going.

The sun visor I had settled so resolutely on my brow that weekend is now disappearing down the street with a new owner. I'm happy to see it go — don't need any mementoes of that particular trip; my memories will do just fine.

I relish the conversations as people poke through our things and occasionally claim something for their own. One woman with a greying ponytail discovers my old copy of Adobe Creative Suite, which includes all kinds of design software: Photoshop, Illustrator, GoLive, Acrobat. Without my employee discount, the software would have cost over $500; today's price tag reads $35. The woman asks me all kinds of questions: How much has the software changed? If she learns on these versions, will her skills transfer to the newer release? I answer as best I can, and she decides to go for it.

"Do I dare bargain you down?" she asks. "Will you take thirty dollars?"

"Sure!" I say. She's so excited, I would be happy just to give it to her.

Once the purchase has been made, she leans closer to confide in me. "I've been wanting to get this Creative Suite, but it's so expensive, and I didn't know where the money was going to come from. I'm a single mom, so things are tight. To find this today — I hope you don't mind me saying, but you are an answer to prayer!"

My eyes well up as I feel God smiling down on us like a matchmaker. I'm honoured to know that this software, which has been sitting on my shelf unused for years, is such a treasure to her.

A girl about four years old with long brown hair decides to buy our toy doctor's kit. She and her mother open it up to look at all of the instruments inside — stethoscope, blood pressure cuff, tweezers, needle. The girl gives me a twoonie and then pipes up, "I can sing with no words!"

Now this I have to hear. I get down on her level and say, "Please show me, I'd love that."

She composes herself, closes her lips, and hums a careful tune. So pleased with herself. My heart overcome by the look on her face.

"Thank you," I say, and she skips off.

I tuck the moment away with all the others, connections that flare bright and brief as matches.

I discovered my depression in a glass of wine.

The condition is no stranger to me. When I was thirteen, my mother had a baby, developed fibromyalgia, and lost her mother to cancer, all in the space of a year. No surprise that she got swallowed by this sludgy black pool — sleeping all the time, never smiling, living in her housecoat. I'd watched her go up and down over the years as she tried meds and health remedies and prayer, often rallying during the summer but sinking down again by Christmas.

I always thought of myself as immune. The cheerful, optimistic one in the family. Even when I fell into a funk in university and had a few sessions with my family doctor, she attributed my mood to the fact that I hadn't found a summer job yet. Once I got hired as an admin assistant, I dusted off my hands and put that period behind me. Or so I imagined.

For much of the winter before our trip to Lac Brome, the signs were there, but I wasn't putting them together. A dread of the coming day made it nearly impossible to get out of bed. I couldn't concentrate at my tech writing job. I had mornings for writing but I wasn't making progress on my novel. I worried constantly about my younger brother, who was being bullied at school. My stomach dropped when the phone rang with news of another problem in our residence. I struggled to keep up with my long and intimidating to-do list. Shawn avoided me because I was such a bummer.

Back then, we didn't cook for ourselves during the school year. Cafeteria privileges were one of the perks of our university job, and we got to visit with students over plates heaped with pasta salad and meatloaf. But in the summer, we went back to having dinner alone in our Glengarry House apartment with the cinder block walls and industrial carpeting, and we could enjoy a little Rioja with our lasagne.

This one night in June, we had our glass of wine, and I noticed that I felt better. A lot better. I made a few tough phone calls, cleared away paperwork, had a pleasant conversation with Shawn. I savoured the sense of buoyancy.

By the end of the night, I knew. If having a drink made that big a change in my mood, there was no question. I was depressed. The realization devastated me — I was more depressed about being depressed than anything else. Instead of being immune, I was weak. Vulnerable. Sick.

Rather than try to write the next morning, I went to Bikram yoga class for the heat and sweat, the chance to turn off my thoughts and follow someone else's instructions. My trembling, burned-out state reminded me of the morning after a fever has broken; I was past the crisis, but I still had a long recovery ahead of me.

That afternoon I made an appointment to see my family doctor and bought David D. Burns' book, *The Feeling Good Handbook*, on the advice of a psychologist friend. My desire to be in control, to fix everything, was both my downfall and my salvation. I wasn't going to waste any time wallowing — better to jump right into the work of getting well. Thanks to my mother, I knew the symptoms and the treatment, right down to which antidepressant I should start taking. I planned to get an A+ in mental health.

That's where I was at when we went to Quebec. I was waiting for the meds to take effect. I could see nothing good in the months ahead. I mourned for my place as the strong one in my family and feared being hobbled for life by faulty brain chemistry.

And yet, a vital part of me, more primal than my desire to fix everything, was determined not to give up. I had to get better. I had to be able to write again.

Someone buys my old copy of *Feeling Good* for a dollar. I hope it does make him feel good. For me, the book was a valuable introduction to cognitive behavioural therapy: the idea that I didn't have to believe all the thoughts in my head and that I could choose thoughts that made me feel better. A simple practice that revolutionized my life.

I'm letting go of my modest-but-lovingly-curated library. Once I fantasized about a whole room in my house filled with books and one of those rolling ladders to access the highest shelves. I actively collected — saved textbooks from university, stocked up at used bookstores, bought copies of books I had already read and loved just to have them around.

Now my dream is to have an empty house so my family can pick up and travel wherever we want. Books are heavy, cumbersome, and costly to move and store. I found that I rarely touched the volumes in my house — they seemed to have a static, dull energy, whereas the books that arrived on hold for me at the library were more attractive and precious for being temporary. So most of our collection is making its way into the hands of new readers. Shawn's political theory and history texts, my Canadian lit, self-help, and writing books. People are so discriminating as they study what's on offer, finding one or two volumes that are just right, and I love getting to meet the new owners.

I'm thrilled when a pack of students hovers around my *Gateway to the Great Books* set — ten pristine volumes with coloured spines, filled with excerpts from classic literature. I've had them since I was a kid, but hardly ever cracked them open. I had tried to sell the set to a used bookstore or donate it to a high school, but found no takers.

A guy in the middle finally makes a decision and hoists the Pampers box holding the books, bringing it over for payment. I take his $30 and then say, "Before you go, I have to tell you the story of these books. Okay?"

He nods and smiles as if to say, *Sure, crazy lady.*

"When I was ten or eleven, my parents bought a leather-bound set of the *Encyclopaedia Britannica*. And while they were talking to the salesman, I was salivating over these Great Books: *Robinson Crusoe, The Jungle Book, Dr. Jekyll and Mr. Hyde*. Then just before he left, the salesman said he was so impressed with my literary interests at such a young age that he would give me this *Gateway to the Great Books* if I wrote him a letter of recommendation. So that's what I did. Now you know the story and you can take them home with you."

The guy balances the box on his forearms and leaves with his friends. I wonder whether he will ever actually read the books. I did make a good start, getting through most of *Robinson Crusoe* nestled in my blue beanbag chair. Now I could download any one of those books for free and read it on my computer. Words have become weightless.

In 2002, the same year that I was diagnosed with depression, creativity coach Eric Maisel published a book about why creative people are prone to unhappiness and how they can find their way back to joy. In *The Van Gogh Blues*, he writes:

> "Creators have trouble maintaining meaning. Creating is one of the ways they endeavor to maintain meaning. In the act of creation, they lay a veneer of meaning over meaninglessness and sometimes produce work that helps others maintain meaning. This is why creating is such a crucial activity in the life of a creator: It is one of the ways, and often the most important way, that she manages to make life feel meaningful. Not creating is depressing because she is not making meaning when she is not creating."

There were some obvious external causes of my breakdown: lack of sleep and exercise; high-stress situations with family and at the residence; the anxiety of a possible layoff at my software job. But underneath those causes were other questions: Why did I put myself in those situations? Why did I think it was necessary to overwork myself? Why did I assume responsibility for so many people? And the upshot of all that martyrdom was that I didn't have enough time, energy, and mental space left for the work that was most significant to me — writing.

I'm glad I started treatment with medication. I needed the boost of selective serotonin reuptake inhibitors to give me respite from that suffocating bleakness, so I could do the work of therapy: seeing and resolving old patterns, changing my thoughts and my life. But I do believe that my misery was of the existential kind that Maisel describes — I was not creating the way I wanted to, and that made me feel like my life wasn't worth living. Medication wasn't going to dispense with my need for meaning. To recover from unhappiness long-term, I had to rearrange my life so I could write to my heart's content.

Shawn is the gardener in our family, and he has some beloved houseplants he's been nurturing for many years. His pride and joy is a majestic jade grown large with thick glossy leaves. Since we displayed the gorgeous, healthy plant on the corner of our garage sale lot, everyone has been remarking on it, but one bohemian couple goes into raptures. They chat for some time in lavish appreciation of the beautiful specimen.

"Where will we put it?" he asks at last.

"What about the dining room?" she says.

They debate options. They're in no rush; this is a pleasant question to puzzle out.

"We keep it in an east window," I say. "Jade likes indirect sun."

"I know!" the woman exclaims. "I'm going to put it in my studio!"

Our jade is going to an artist. How perfect. They happily pay the full price of $35, a bargain compared to what a plant like that would garner in a florist's shop, and process triumphantly down the sidewalk, holding their prize high.

I file the story away to share with Shawn later. He'll be happy to know that his jade is in good hands.

Near the end of the day, an older couple scrutinizes our guidebooks and travel books, picking up *A Hiker's Guide to Alberta* and a few others from our time in Calgary. When they come to settle up, they tell me about their daughter in Edmonton who has inherited their bent for adventuring. I share our Hejira plans and they ask, "Where are you going first?"

"We'll be in Malaysia for the winter," I say.

The woman's dark eyes widen and she says, "I was born in Penang! It's my favourite place in the world. You're going to have a wonderful time."

"Penang! That's where we're staying!" I say. "We can't wait to see it."

Chills run through my body. What are the chances that a woman born on the other side of the world would come by my garage sale stand and tell me so? A serendipitous grace note to the day.

Back home, I count out the bills and make stacks of coins, subtract the float and *voila*, we cleared $863.55! That's a nice haul, but the greater return was in seeing the delight on people's faces when they found something they really wanted.

I'm feeling good about our progress until I look around at all the other stuff left in our house. Sixteen hundred square feet of furniture, toys, books, clothes, dishes, artwork, and miscellaneous junk. Possessions collected over fifteen years of marriage.

We still have a long way to go.

About the Flow Exercises

"Hope is like a road in the country; there was never a road, but when many people walk on it, the road comes into existence."
— Lin Yutang

Sharing my story is a way of inviting you to create a road of hope with me. Hope beckons in our desires: the ones we walk toward and the ones we discover on the journey. The hope for happiness, for a life of truth and beauty, for the deep satisfaction of being ourselves.

The flow exercises I've designed for each chapter of this book are steps along the road of hope. So are the resources I've listed at the end of the book under Further Reading. They all provide ways to move closer to what you long for by clearing away the brambles in your path. I encourage you to join me by doing the exercises and sharing what comes out of them. I'd love to hear from you — details for how to get in touch are in the Afterword. My pilgrimage is that much more meaningful in the companionship of others.

Flow Exercise: Handrail

Janice, the therapist who walked me out of the thickets of sadness, lived a few blocks from our university residence. Every two weeks we sat in her daisy-yellow study and I hugged a pillow on my lap while we teased apart my misery. I loved her soft voice and how she always wore purple so that you couldn't help but know it was her favourite colour.

Janice introduced me to the concept of intention. In the years since, my relationship with intention has expanded into a way of life, but Janice kept things simple for me in my despair-addled state.

"Think of your intention as a handrail," she said. "When you need to steady yourself, you can reach out and let it guide you." Since I felt tottery and fragile as I put my life and health back together, that image was perfect for me. I needed to stop grasping at whatever handrail presented itself, and instead choose the one that would lead me where I wanted to go.

I took my time creating my new intention. The process felt good because the task was so well-defined and personal, and because I had Janice to share it with when I was finished. So I would mull over ideas while I walked to work and washed dishes. It seemed that my unhappy state was marked by three things: self-deception, self-abuse, and anhedonia. I told myself things that weren't true, I neglected my needs or actively punished myself, and I took little delight from what the world offered.

The antidote was also three-fold. Here's the intention I wrote to show Janice:

Every day I will
Create art that tells the truth
Make choices that honour myself and God
Enjoy the pleasures of life
So that I may experience myself as joy.

Write your own intention, a handrail that will guide you true every day throughout your life along the lines of your desires. You could begin by inverting the negative states that you want to leave behind. You could invoke the qualities that mark your favourite days. Let the process be simple and take its own time. You will know when you have found the rail that fits your hand perfectly.

2 The Alchemy of Telling

"For the most trivial event to become an adventure, all you have to do is start telling about it."
— Jean-Paul Sartre, *Nausea*

Preparations continue morning, noon, and night. One day I paint the front hallway — the first time I've ever wielded a roller! The next day Shawn and I meet with a lawyer to draw up our will. The following day brings a trip to the children's hospital for Nico's speech therapy. Then I'm packing for the World Domination Summit in Portland, a conference for people who want to live a remarkable life in a conventional world. I can hardly fathom how everything is getting done, and yet it is.

In the midst of all the busyness, I am writing. At 5:25 a.m., the clock radio plays a peppy alarm that Shawn has learned to sleep through, and I half-roll, half-fall off my side of the bed and onto my feet. I scrounge for socks and a sweatshirt to keep me warm (they don't have to be clean) and pad downstairs, laptop tucked under my arm. I'm still sleepy, a good frame of mind for writing — the inner critic snuggles deeper under the silk comforter and lapses back into unconsciousness while the dreamer and I begin work undisturbed. I turn on the software that disables networking on my computer so the Internet won't distract me. I set it for sixty minutes, a comforting guarantee that I'll have all that time for myself, typing and staring into space while the sentences of my draft grow like fractals under my fingers.

I stumbled into writing almost by accident. I was a precocious reader — my mother says I started with the Sears catalogue at eighteen months old and never looked back. Books substituted for playmates; they didn't quarrel or boss me or make fun of the big words I liked to use. Instead they offered up their riches willingly: McGurk mysteries for the taking at the library, *The Tower of Geburah* wrapped in paper for Christmas, and Grace Livingston Hill romances hidden in musty basement boxes. I could gorge myself as much as school and chores allowed, and the only complaint I heard came from my parents. *Put that down. Get your nose out of there. You're being antisocial.* I'm sure I seemed distant and even rude sometimes, besotted with narrative and unable to focus my eyes on the world in front of me.

But I idolized authors so much that it never occurred to me that I could become one. When I was ten, a teacher-friend saw me reading *The Secret Garden* and asked, "Have you ever thought of writing one of those yourself?"

I was at a bit of a loss. He might as well have asked, "Would you like to be a unicorn when you grow up?"

"I don't know anything about Victorian England," I said.

"You could write something from the present day," my friend suggested.

I considered how dull and random my life was compared to the books I read. I couldn't imagine having the magic to turn my twentieth-century suburban Canadian world into a story that would be as fascinating as *Island of the Blue Dolphins, I Am David,* or *The Pushcart War.* To me, authors were alchemists conjuring gold out of thin air, and I was a mere mortal. So I never wrote anything beyond school assignments, notes to friends, and overwrought journal entries.

Of course, writing was there for me the whole time, waiting for me to realize that the stories I had to tell were just as important as everyone else's and that I could learn the skill needed to tell them. One day in university, I got caught up in describing my loneliness in a letter to Shawn, who went to school a few hours away. I found myself using imagery and descriptive language, creative line breaks, all the literary flourishes I'd been absorbing in English classes.

At the end of the evening, as I read back over my ink-covered foolscap, I realized I had written a poem.

And I noticed how much I enjoyed creating something. Taking the base metals of my emotions and my life as a sophomore and polishing them into a piece of art. In that moment, I was hooked.

My plan for the future had been to teach high school English, which seemed the most practical way to apply my love for literature. But I never liked the circularity of teaching — you get educated so you can educate others so they can educate others, *ad infinitum.* Writing my first poem, I realized that I didn't have to sit on the sidelines, studying other people's work. I could contribute my own.

Soon I had abandoned my teaching plans and enrolled in every writing class available. Ah, the early days when I had no idea what I was doing and blithely charged forward anyway. I wrote concrete poetry about bathroom graffiti, a sonnet about watching *Hamlet,* and a pretty dreadful short story called "Miss Information Booth." But I had fun. Writing engaged my brain *and* my emotions, and it gave me a challenge I could work at in solitude before presenting my creations to the world.

All that changed when I arrived in Calgary for a graduate program in creative writing. That's where I learned to suffer for my art.

The pain started gradually. I wrote my first story for the workshop class with oblivious enthusiasm, the act of creation still seeming miraculous. But the night of our first critique, I went home and cried myself to sleep — and it wasn't even my piece being workshopped! I had thought revision meant changing a few words here and there, and I was horrified at the idea of scrapping dozens of pages and starting over from square one.

My supervisor, Aritha van Herk, didn't pull any punches about what worked in our stories and what we had to throw out and do again. After the gentle nurturing of my undergrad professors, her brusque manner and sky-high standards left me tongue-tied and questioning whether I could hack it at this level. I was dazzled by the clever and imaginative contributions of my fellow students and fell back into childhood doubts about whether my life stories could ever be interesting.

For two years, I laboured over my graduate thesis, a collection of linked short stories set in a Presbyterian church community. The environment kicked my perfectionism into high gear, and the inner critic was never far from my ear, making me question every word and phrase so that my drafts were slow and torturous. I did everything I could to avoid writing. I slept in until nine or ten in the morning. My schedule filled with volunteer work and activities. I served on the chaplaincy committee and worked on the church newsletter. I took temporary secretarial gigs to earn extra money. Our small apartment was kept neat as a pin, and I wasted hours on the free cable TV.

I once spent two entire days on the couch, catatonic, because I couldn't face the manuscript. Aritha turned out to be a softie underneath and talked me back from the edge, but the work remained an excruciating grind. The moments when I enjoyed myself were few and far between. In the end, my fear of not graduating won out over my fear of writing, but the cost was high. I had become hopelessly mired in resistance.

I have to pause for a moment and send some compassion to my younger self, who just wanted to be a writer and tried so damn hard that she tied herself in knots. She hadn't yet learned that the more tightly she clung and the harder she wrestled, the more elusive was the tantalizing flow she'd tasted in the early days.

I admire her doggedness — she really was like a puppy that had a rope between her teeth and was not letting go come hell or high water. Little did she know that no one else had the power to take her writing away from her — she only had to step forward and *give her writing to herself.* She could have relaxed knowing that she had her whole lifetime to devote to her craft, that there was no hurry to publish or succeed, that she could take time to explore genres and play with subject matter to find her literary home.

For whatever reason, though, I couldn't hear or take in that truth at the time. Looking at my journals in the years after grad school, I see myself trying to solve the problem of disappointment in my writing life by applying more discipline, more systems and accountability. I set monthly goals for number of words written in my journal, number of books read, percentage of possible hours worked on my manuscripts, and then evaluated myself on how much I had accomplished. I had a constant sense of being behind and falling short of my own expectations.

And people tried to get the message through to me. One therapist pointed out that things were all or nothing with me — I was either completely writing or completely not writing. She wanted me to learn that there was a difference between doing something well and doing it perfectly. So maybe I didn't write four hours in a morning, but progress was still being made. She didn't think I should be so obsessed with productivity.

But even as she explained these quite reasonable perspectives, I was secretly sure that she was wrong. If I settled for two hours of writing instead of four, how would I ever finish a novel? This therapist, this *non-writer*, was trying to tempt me into becoming a slacker, like a doctor persuading an anorexic to eat, and I wasn't falling for it. I nodded along in session, and then went right back to my spreadsheets and tallies at home.

If only I could have stepped back and seen that I was running to stand still — churning on a ridiculously ambitious project, a novel with four separate story lines and multiple point-of-view characters. I was reading scads of background material on comic, tragic, and epic forms, and writing sheaves of detailed notes while having no idea of the overall scope of the book (the first chapter alone came out to twelve thousand words). I needed to just chill out and experiment, get in touch with what kinds of books turned me on, but I was terrified that if I stepped off the treadmill, I'd never get back on again. I'd be one of those pathetic writers who gets a degree and then disappears into mundane life.

So I kept the pressure on until the burden became too heavy to bear. One of the last straws came when life began to imitate art. For my novel, I was writing about a boy who was being bullied, and then my younger brother Ben started to confide in me about the rough treatment he was getting at the hands of his classmates. I had many worried nights and long conversations with Ben and my parents about what could be done. The strain of hauling myself out of the manuscript and trying to right real-life wrongs was more than I could handle and started the downhill slide that ended with me in the doctor's office a few months later.

I gave up trying to write for a year after the depression diagnosis. My creative engine had been leaking oil for so long that I'd driven it into the ground and my imagination was completely seized.

I still wrote a few things — journal entries, a lecture for the Wheaton College writing conference. But I stopped *trying*: striving to be productive during my mornings off, tracking the number of hours I wrote each month, fretting about how long it would take to finish my next book at this pace. Laying down my writing burden now came as a guilty relief, as though I had a doctor's note to excuse me from a gruelling competition.

One story did have a deadline: my contribution to an anthology about friendship that our writing group was putting together. Most of the other members had finished their stories, and since I joined later, I needed to come up with a draft as soon as possible. I toiled away on one idea, but I couldn't get it to coalesce.

One May morning, I was making lacklustre progress with my story, so I decided to go for a walk in the neighbouring arboretum. Amid the yellow willows and emerald grass, my mind drifted to Rika, the miniature dachshund puppy that my parents got for my brother Ben to keep him company now that they had pulled him out of school. I had just met Rika, a tiny, wriggling bundle of affection, and instantly fell for her. Her bounty of joy was such a contrast to my unhappiness.

I wondered as I walked, almost academically, how one could put Rika in a story. This dog was so impossibly loving, so good, that you'd need something terrible to offset the sweetness.

You would have to kill her, I thought. But how?

You would have to drown her.

At that moment, the devastating image appeared in my mind of a boy holding his sopping and lifeless puppy. I began to cry. There was nothing I could do with the scene, the emotion, except get it down in black and white. I rushed back to my computer and typed out a draft as fast as I could, about a page and a half, sobbing uncontrollably the whole time and for an hour afterward. I was shattered by grief for the boy and his dog, and for myself, to have this dark tragedy come up from inside. Two lines held the truth of the whole story for me:

"Holding her wet limp body, matted fur, in his hands, he felt the familiar things: sorrow, anger, hatred. These were easier to bear than love."

I saw, dimly, that Rika's love was painful to me because I did not believe I was worthy of it. For a long time, I had been refusing myself the basic necessities of proper food, rest, and exercise, as well as the pleasures of writing time, so I could fulfill my obligations. My habits of self-denial had taught me that I didn't deserve to be cared for.

At the same time, having this story come through my imagination was powerful proof that I was a writer and that I was not blocked. I found this knowledge comforting. I put the piece aside, certain that I would never show it to anyone. Leaving the puppy dead at the end spoke of a hopelessness that I could not allow myself to succumb to.

But the story continued to work on me. A few days later, in the middle of watching a hockey game with Shawn, I bolted upright on the couch and announced: "Resurrection!" That's what I still believed in, that was how I could transform the piece from despair to a kind of reprieve. Love and life must win out — for my characters and, I hoped, for me.

I rewrote the ending and decided to submit it as my friendship story for the anthology. I worried that the puppy's revival after the boy's attempted drowning was too cowardly or sentimental. My fellow writers, however, read the ending ironically, and felt, along with the relief of the puppy's recovery, the ominous sense that neither character was out of danger.

That's where I was too — relieved that my depression had been recognized and treated, but knowing that I was still vulnerable and facing a long and tangled path ahead. My drive to write, which made life so difficult when it came up against my stoic need to please, was also what would save me. The flow of that story through me was like a shot of adrenaline to a stopped heart, and I needed more.

My desire for more writing time is part of what makes Operation Hejira so attractive now. I dream of living in a small apartment, somewhere warm and cheap, where we can afford to eat out and hire a housekeeper. With our monthly expenses cut down, I won't have to work as much. I fantasize about an empty calendar and a simple routine that allows lots of time at my writing desk.

Between me and my dream stands a mile-long list of tasks and many cubic feet of stuff to dispose of. We leave in one month. Will someone buy our bedroom set before then? Will anyone come to our good-bye parties? Can I pry Lia and Nico away from their mountain of stuffed animals? And where the hell did I put my birth certificate?

And yet, I am writing now in the morning hours before everyone wakes up, before I have to make French toast and spot-clean Lia's favourite pink shirt and find the medical receipts for Shawn to send to our insurance company. My mother drives to Ottawa on Tuesdays to spend time with her grandkids while I work at the library. I write in the evenings, surrounded by dirty dishes and piles of the kids' artwork. I'm proud of myself for having learned to write in the middle of life, primed and ready to let the words flow at the drop of a hat. Creating is a powerful ward against my existential angst.

Flow Exercise: Open Hand

For years, I dreamed of the life of a writer, the whole kit and caboodle. I wanted hard-backed books I could hold in my hand, with my name on the spine. I wanted to put my signature on the title page. I wanted to visit primary school classrooms and talk to children about reading. I wanted an antique desk and a view of wildflower meadows from my writing shed in the backyard. I wanted to judge literary contests and win the Governor General's Award. I wanted an agent who would auction my manuscripts to eager publishing houses. I wanted to travel to Morocco for research. I wanted a librarian to lovingly preserve my literary archives. I certainly wanted other writers to admire me.

I wanted so hard and so much that I choked on my desire.

Martha Beck, the life coach who practically invented life coaching, says in her article "The Formula for Happiness" that "intense yearning is a form of attachment that can actually stop the thing you desire from reaching you." I know what she means. When all of me was flooded with longing, there was no room for anything else to enter. My brain raced with schemes for fixing my life so I could write, my throat closed when I heard of a fellow author getting an award or a publishing deal, and my heart ached with regret as each month and year passed with no finished book in sight.

Beck goes on to say, "Recognize that yearning is loving something before you believe in it. The same may be said of jealousy, envy, disappointment and even despair. To love something deeply without believing it can be true is enormously painful."

In the wake of my breakdown, I needed to let go of writing so I could clear space within myself for it to come back to me. This was a scary prospect — if I didn't write, was I still a writer? Without my word counts and publications, did I matter? I entered this time of no-writing without those answers, trusting that my writing would come around to me again.

(Spoiler alert: it did.)

Find a small object — a marble, a rock, a ping-pong ball — that can represent one great yearning of your life that hasn't come to you yet. Play with the object in your hand: roll it around, cup it in your palm, squeeze it tight and balance it gently.

Bring to mind the phases of your relationship to this yearning. When did you grasp it with all your strength? When did you loosen your grip? What made you shift your hold? What changed in your feelings when you clung or released? What happened to bring the object of your desire closer or push it further away?

With your beautiful object resting in your palm, let your heart well up with love for the thing you desire. Don't try to put this love into words, just feel it spread through your body, warm and tender. The pure power of this love is where you will find the belief that what you want can be true. Notice how your faith grows when you hold your desire with an open hand.

3 The Thread of Travel Caught in Our Hearts

I'm crossing the condo parking lot, pulling a little red suitcase on my way to the airport, when I hear frantic tapping on glass. Ah yes, in the twenty seconds since I walked out the door, I've forgotten to wave and blow kisses at Lia and Nico, who have crowded into the bay window of our kitchen. Lia has her fingers folded into the shape of the ASL sign for "I love you," and Nico's face has crumpled into tears. He often cries when I leave, but I remind myself that he'll be okay in a few minutes. I see Shawn scoop him up to comfort him.

I'm headed to the World Domination Summit in Portland, Oregon — a conference of rebellious, entrepreneurial, globe-trotting creative souls who, like Shawn and me, are striking out from the conventional routes and making their own desire lines. I can't wait to meet other coaches, travelers, artists, and seekers who will understand exactly why we're leaving our life in Ottawa behind.

This weekend is a bookmark trip — a term I find in an in-flight magazine article about bibliotherapy that I page through on the way to Portland. A bookmark trip marks the place where one part of your life story ends and another begins. I like the symbolism, but in practical terms I couldn't be away at a worse time. We just listed the house for sale, and Shawn has to manage the showings himself while making sure that Nico and Lia don't trash the place. Oh, and he's presenting a paper at a conference on Saturday. Meanwhile, I'll be eating gourmet *macarons* and overstuffed gyros from Portland's famous food carts while meeting fascinating people for three kid-free days. Once upon a time I wouldn't have dared ask Shawn to cover like this while I indulged myself. But I've become bolder, and he's grown more generous.

We barely had a chance to nod in passing at our fifteenth wedding anniversary a few days ago. Usually, we celebrate at an expensive restaurant. But this year we don't have the time for a night like that, and I suspect we'd be too frazzled to enjoy it anyway. We joke that, instead of dinner out, we're going on a year-long trip around the world.

Come to think of it, Operation Hejira as an homage to our marriage is not so far off the mark. Our romance started on the road at age sixteen, when we spent a week biking around eastern Ontario with our high school class. Slapping at mosquitos as we shared our first kiss, the smell of sunscreen and sweat on our skin. Watching each other settle into sleeping bags across the hay barn. From this trip on, the thread of travel seemed to catch and entwine as our hearts came together, and now we couldn't separate our love from our wanderlust if we tried.

Camping was the best way to spend time together without parents around, so we planned canoe trips with friends in Algonquin and Frontenac Provincial Parks. Card games by the campfire and stargazing after sunset were heightened by stolen moments alone in the dark before we went off to our separate tents. I loved Shawn's obsession with maps and the way he wasn't afraid to work hard: portaging our gear, rigging tarps, and digging in with a paddle. And everyone teased me the time that Shawn gashed his shin open on a rock and I whipped off my shirt to make a tourniquet.

We logged many miles on a bus every March Break, touring Ontario and the northeastern States with a performing arts group. Each night saw us couchsurfing with various billets, and we would trade stories about the luxurious or bizarre accommodations the next morning — Shawn's best score was a hot tub in a suburban mansion while I managed to catch chicken pox from the kids in one family I stayed with.

At university in different towns, we took turns hitching rides with other students for weekend visits until Shawn got his first car, a sky-blue Chevette hatchback with manual transmission. We explored the area around Hamilton, hiking the Niagara Escarpment and touring the art gallery in Dundas, taking late-night walks through the downtown streets. I can see now how our taste in travel was developing: we liked to stumble on out-of-the-way spots, we'd rather go deep into one place than wide across many, and we were suckers for natural beauty that required a little effort to enjoy.

After graduation, when we were finally married and free to travel overnight without a chaperone, the whole world opened up to us. We splurged on a longer-than-usual honeymoon: two weeks in Newfoundland, starting on the east coast in St. John's and driving clear across the island to Cornerbrook. Early June was still off-season, and many times we had an entire bed-and-breakfast establishment to ourselves. We took boat tours to watch sea birds nesting and circle around icebergs, met a children's author doing class visits, slept in a bed reclaimed from the San Francisco earthquake, and befriended one host's four-pound teacup poodle. We heard about village politics and nosy neighbours who point out that you haven't done your spring cleaning because your curtains haven't come down. Despite the sad fact that our whole first roll of film got chewed up by the camera, I still have many vivid snapshots of that trip in my head.

After a few newlywed months in Toronto, we packed the Chevette full of boxes and drove west for a week until we reached Calgary —

my first real road trip. Shawn had spent summers driving all over the States with his parents and brothers and sister, hanging out in the back of a station wagon and helping set up a hard-top camper when they stopped for the night. But my summer vacations had been stationary, parked at the family cottage in the Muskokas. I adored the long days of our pre-grad-school trip across the country, with the landscape of northern Ontario and the prairies sliding past the window. We plunged gratefully into KOA swimming pools after baking in the car all day, cooked over our camp stove, and paused long enough for a round of golf in Saskatchewan that included moose sightings on the course.

It's easy to remember the happy moments of our travels, like the Rocky Mountain peaks that welcomed us as we drove into Calgary — they stand out among the humdrum days. But Shawn and I have also had some of our biggest fights over travel and what it meant for our money and my writing.

In February 2002, a few months before my breakdown, we were planning a trip to Culebra during our precious Reading Week vacation. Shawn had come across this hidden gem of a tropical island off Puerto Rico while combing through travel recommendations on the Internet, and we couldn't wait to go snorkelling and lie on the beach, far away from the frigid Ottawa winter — that is, until my pre-trip anxiety kicked in.

A few days before we left, I was obsessing over whether our vacation would be ruined because we had decided to save money by renting bikes instead of a jeep. I worried that the guesthouse where we were staying was too far from town, and that we'd be exhausted trying to get around the island, and that I hadn't planned the right food to cook in our little kitchen, and that we'd have too much luggage for the puddle-jumper that would fly us between Culebra and San Jose. Heck, I was consumed with regret that I'd chosen to have my toenails painted deep pink instead of a dark iridescent fuchsia.

The long and short of it was that I felt guilty for going — for enjoying myself when the students we supervised were broke and couldn't travel, when my parents rarely went somewhere warm for the winter, when other people had to cover for me while I was away. I was also afraid that Culebra wasn't going to be perfect. What if we had to bike up and down hills through the rain? What if they confiscated my carefully prepared dehydrated food at the border? What if I didn't like snorkelling or wasn't good at it or got too tired?

And why were we wasting our money if Culebra wasn't going to be perfect? The trip was costing several thousand dollars, which I calculated would have bought me a month and a half of full-time writing, away from my job. Why was I applying for writing grants when we were blowing a big wad on a single week's escapades?

You can imagine how well these questions went over with Shawn. My angst ballooned as our departure date approached, and the night before our flight, Shawn made me tell him why I was so mopey. My confession triggered a disastrous fight as we tried to pack: me moaning and crying about my hang-ups, Shawn fuming that I was spoiling a trip he had lovingly planned and was looking forward to so much.

Once I had spilled all of my fears about Culebra and wept out an apology for dumping this on Shawn at the last minute, there was nothing left to do but salvage our week together. We weren't going to cancel now — everything was already paid for. As we dug out T-shirts and shorts from the back of our closet and wedged packages of granola around our snorkel fins and masks, I tried to set aside my worries and focus on what I knew would be good about the trip: the warm sun, the beaches and mojitos, the chance to sleep and read books and not worry about our jobs.

The funny thing was that many of the things I feared came true, yet they didn't matter. Biking around the island *was* hard work, but the exercise felt good and we had the freedom to nap afterward. We got caught in the rain, mud splattering from our back wheels onto our bare legs, but we hosed off at a restaurant and carried on. We got lost trying to find our guesthouse on the way home from the beach, and so what? We had nowhere to be, and Culebra, with its colourful bunga-lows and sea-scented air, is a beautiful place to be lost in.

But the underlying issues that triggered the fight didn't go away just because we had a good time. And once we returned from Culebra, the stress of life cascaded back between us, more alienating than ever.

It was easy to avoid each other given our busy schedules: we'd leave for work at different times, have separate conversations while we ate dinner with a group of students in the cafeteria, and disappear into TV or our computers at night. We were more like roommates than husband and wife, friendly to each other but not intimate, not vulner-able. I don't blame Shawn for this. I understood what was going on at the time: he was protecting himself from my unhappiness, knowing he couldn't handle any more than the load he was already shouldering. If I had shared what was going on in my head, the sadness might have taken us both down.

When I think of how Shawn was then, I see him across the room on our threadbare futon, wary and detached, not wanting to set me off. We kept a physical space between us because touching meant my tears or hysteria could well up without warning and take hours to get under control. Without him to lean on, I had no choice but to take responsibility for looking after myself. I took long baths at night for the comfort of hot water on my skin; I went for massages and yoga classes. And I plotted about how to break the deadlock of silence be-tween us.

In this time of desperation, my husband gave me one costly and es-sential gift: he agreed to go to couples therapy with me. I had found a great therapist — Connie of the chintz couch — and was starving for a conversation about how to fix our life, but arranging the first visit was a delicate operation, like coaxing a skittish animal into a pen. Shawn is an intensely private person and had always hated when I shared details about our relationship with others. So the idea of going to talk to a stranger with the express intention of spilling the beans intimidated him. We walked into Connie's office ready for a polite tug-of-war: him guarded against revelation, me bursting with things to say. But I didn't want to spook him — I wanted him to come back. I needed a witness to our insulated world, some perspective on where I was asking for too much and where he wasn't giving enough.

And what was I so impatient to bring to light? I was unhappy because I couldn't write, and I wanted to quit my tech-writing job. Shawn, on the other hand, saw me constantly complaining about not writing but then not using the time I did have. He felt like quitting my job was too much to ask, that I needed to get it together before we could make that kind of financial sacrifice. Such a simple dilemma, and yet so very complicated to negotiate. I didn't see how you could put a price on your life's calling, and Shawn needed to know how we would pay our bills and save for a house.

There was no big drama in our therapy sessions, no shouting matches or name-calling. We were unfailingly kind and respectful to each other, which made Connie remark that the process would take longer because we weren't getting down to things. Yes, I was angry with Shawn for standing in the way of my writing ambitions, but I also knew that he was right: even if I had all day every day in my study, I wasn't healthy enough to use that time well.

I finally twigged to my depression a few months into couples therapy, and as much as we were scared by the diagnosis, we were also able to turn a corner together. Shawn saw that I was getting support from my doctor, from therapy and the medication, and he could risk moving closer to me. Our trip to Lac Brome reawakened our tenderness with each other and our shared dreams for travel and meaningful creative work. And with Connie's help, I realized that I had been projecting my own resistance onto Shawn, making him the bad guy who wouldn't let me write when in reality I was stopping *myself* from writing. My wise creative muse knew that the conditions of my life were beyond lousy, and I needed recovery and loving-kindness before the words could really flow.

If you asked Shawn today, he would tell you that having to articulate his feelings to someone who was evaluating our relationship was torturous. And he would also tell you it was worth the torture because the process did wonders for us. It gave us space to talk about what we didn't want to talk about because we were afraid of upsetting the precarious balance of our lives. Inside that safety, he was relieved to learn that things weren't as bad as he feared. The bedrock of our teenage love was still there to build on.

And he's very glad he doesn't have to sit on that chintz couch and explain himself anymore.

The effort of therapy seems doubly worthwhile now because we need our marriage to be strong enough to handle the demands of Operation Hejira. If it was hard for Shawn to contemplate *me* quitting my part-time job, imagine the risk involved in him quitting his own after thirteen years with the same company. Thankfully, I didn't have to do any convincing — he was ready to go and looking forward to the freedom of working for himself and trying something new. Still, sending that resignation letter felt to Shawn like jumping off a ledge: facing the future without the security and identity of having a job and having to explain his decision to coworkers and friends. I'm glad to have the chance to support him the way he has supported me with faith and earnings.

Between working and looking after the kids and selling our stuff, the days are just as long and full as when we were working at the university residence. The difference now is that we're carried along by joy, and we're pulling together instead of protecting ourselves from each other.

While I'm in Portland, Shawn juggles house showings and negotiations with our real estate agent. On Sunday morning, I take my laptop to the hotel balcony so we can have an early video conference call to decide how to handle the offer we've received. How lucky are we that the house sold in two days? So lucky, and also smart for buying the kind of place that would be in demand. I have the offer faxed to the front desk at the hotel and sign it before heading off to the Portland Museum of Art for that day's sessions.

On my walk in the chilly morning sunshine, I think about how the tables have turned — ten years ago, I could hardly bring myself to ask for a few hours to write on a weekend. I couldn't manage a week's solo trip to Ithaca for research. And now here I am, across the country for a weekend so close to our Operation Hejira launch date, and Shawn hasn't complained once. I have earned back his trust; he's seen how I take care of myself and he believes I can do whatever I need to do for my writing and coaching career. I remember the other complex and intense projects we've handled together, from our wedding to our residence job, and I know that we can rely on each other.

But we are pushing things to the edge now. Hejira is definitely the hardest and scariest thing we've ever done together. I can't wait until we're on the other side. When weariness or discouragement threatens, we paint each other a picture of life in Malaysia: relaxing by the pool, taking walks along the beach. Maybe we'll get to have that anniversary dinner after all.

Flow Exercise: Dismantling Roadblocks

So much of my relationship with Shawn was shaped by our young selves: him the popular golden boy and me the awkward brainy girl. For years after we started dating, I could hardly believe he had chosen me over all the prettier, more athletic, and less neurotic girls available. And my insecurity set up a pattern of swallowing my own desires and going along with what Shawn wanted (or what I guessed he wanted). Not all the time, but enough that it distorted my perception of the kind of wife I needed to be to keep our marriage happy.

By the time we'd been married six years, one version of that pattern looked something like this. 1) I made plans in my head for writing. 2) Shawn, unaware of these plans, asked me to do something with him. 3) I agreed and felt miserable, or turned him down and felt like a bitch.

I didn't realize, until our therapist Connie brought it to my attention, that when Shawn asked for my company, I was hearing, "Do my bidding! Your interests are always subordinate to mine. Prove you love me by giving up what's important to you!" Turns out that what he really meant was, "I adore spending time with you. Let's have fun together."

Who knew?

Think of a loved one who seems to be standing between you and what you want. Write down three things that this person does or says to keep you from your dream. For example, "I'm trying to write in the mornings, but my husband complains when the alarm wakes him up."

Then consider the meaning you ascribe to each thing. What subtext are you hearing? What motive do you attach to those words and actions? For example, "I hear that his comfort is more important than my work. He's trying to keep me in bed so he won't feel lazy."

Finally, turn each thing around. For example, "My husband rejoices when the alarm wakes him up." Is there any truth to that statement? Is he happy to know that you are committed to your writing, even if he can't express that at 5:30 a.m.? Or what about, "I complain when my alarm wakes me up"? Are you experiencing resistance to writing that you're blaming on your husband?

The next time your husband complains about the alarm, you can say to yourself, "I know he supports my work, even if he's too grouchy to tell me right now." Or you can say, "I know how he feels! I don't really want to get up either. But I will because my writing is important to me."

This exercise shows you that the roadblocks you think others are putting in your way are more complex than they first appear. And in exploring their complexity, you can find a different way forward, or even dismantle the roadblocks altogether.

If you want to take this practice further, try the Judge Your Neighbor worksheet, developed by Byron Katie as part of her process called The Work, to inquire into the truth of how other people are holding you back. Byron Katie's website and other resources are listed at the end of this book under Further Reading.

4 My Home Is Inside Me

"Home makes possible the possession of the world."
— Don McKay, "Baler Twine," *Vis à Vis*

We're down to our final week in the house on Nepean Street. I'm hoping that the days slow to a crawl because we need a time warp to get everything done. There are powers of attorney to pick up from the lawyer. A change of address to file with the post office. Friends to say good-bye to. And many belongings still to relocate.

Our campaign to empty the house has been escalating since the Great Glebe Garage Sale in May. We finally photographed and listed the rest of the big furniture items in the online classifieds. Some things move quickly: the teak bistro set from the balcony, a cream-coloured curio shelf, my green mountain bike. The IKEA pieces disappear too: BILLY bookcases and POANG chairs. I make a mental note to check the online classifieds before ever buying new again.

Juggling the listings, offers, negotiations, and visits is complicated but satisfying as bulky objects get converted into slim stacks of cash. I wonder what the neighbours must think? They've had a front-row seat to the goings-on as tables, chairs, and rugs are toted out of our house and loaded into other people's vehicles in a kind of slow Reverse-Moving Day.

It's strange to be dismantling, almost overnight, a household that took us fifteen years to build up. Under the busyness of the final week, when I stop to take a breath, there's a frisson of fear that we are foolish to let go of everything we've so carefully acquired and that we'll live to regret our decision. I wake one morning in a panic of remorse that I didn't take photos of the books on my shelves or some of the children's toys. I may not want to own those things anymore, but I still want to remember them. In my pyjamas, I go from room to room, snapping pictures of what's left and trying to quell the nausea in my stomach.

I remember the days before Shawn and I were married when I would visit his grimy apartment in Hamilton and huddle near the space heater to stay warm. All the furniture was pushed up against the walls: a single bed that sagged like a hammock and a tiny loveseat from the waiting room at my dad's dental office. The nicest thing Shawn owned was a metal file cabinet for his class notes and Student Senate paperwork. On our nighttime walks, we looked longingly into the yellow-lit windows around us, wishing that we had a proper house like you'd see in a magazine, like our childhood houses that we were homesick for. Living as a student felt so temporary, and *settling down* was exactly what we wanted — the grounded security of a beautiful dwelling to make our lives seem real.

Our wish started to come true after the wedding when we moved to Calgary with our pristine navy stoneware, crystal wine glasses, and toaster *sans* crumbs, plus a balance in the bank account to buy our very first couch: a gold-patterned futon with an oak frame. Our apartment felt just as temporary as Shawn's student place, but the futon gave us somewhere to sit and eat cereal from our stoneware bowls and some-where to sleep under our new cotton thermal blanket.

We sat on that futon so much that we had to replace the mattress and cover a few years later. By then we had moved to Ottawa and ac-quired framed artwork, a buffet table to hold our wine glasses, and an enormous writing desk for me. A visiting friend, twenty years older, once said to me, "You're so well furnished for your age!"

But the crowning piece was the walnut bedroom set from a fancy store in the ByWard Market — the sign that we were finally adults. We could afford it because of the extra money we made working at the university. No longer did our mattress and box spring sit on the floor. Now we had an honest-to-goodness headboard to lean against when we read in bed. Our bedside tables matched and had drawers for sleeping masks and coasters. Students don't have bedroom sets be-cause they are superfluous. Grown-ups have bedroom sets, and it means that their lives are solid and safe.

No one told me to fill my house with furniture. I was the one who ripped pages out of *House & Home* magazine, who read books on how to arrange rooms so they felt balanced and inviting, who salivated over the photos in Sarah Susanka's *The Not So Big House.* I wanted order and beauty around me — CDs organized in a cabinet alphabetically, lush houseplants in the window, accent walls painted yellow and or-ange — because I wanted order and beauty inside me. I wanted my emotions to be as tidy as my closets and my spirit to blossom with magical colours.

So I was happy to have nice things. But I was also troubled by what they cost me. I could never get away from the equation in my head that said Money = Writing Time. The $200 table lamp was a weekend writing retreat. A new bicycle? That could have been a short story. The bedroom set was a few chapters of my novel. Everywhere I looked I saw the words that I had sacrificed for material comforts.

Just before my depression diagnosis, the high tech company I worked for was bought by Adobe. We waited weeks to find out which employees would be laid off in the acquisition. Secretly, I hoped for a buy-out package, like a big fat writing grant that would finance a few months to work on my manuscript. And just as equally, I dreaded losing my job, the steady paycheque and stock options and health benefits. In May, as the school year was ending and I was waking up to the extent of my unhappiness, I found out that I was staying with Adobe: same pay, same part-time hours, same everything.

So of course we bought a stereo to celebrate.

Our old music set-up was the epitome of our student days: a broken-down ghetto blaster with crackly wiring and a finicky cassette deck. We'd put up with this atrocity for six years of marriage, and the time had come to upgrade. Music was a daily part of our lives and we wanted to give John Coltrane and U2 and Joni Mitchell the audio quality their art deserved. And when I say *we wanted*, I mean that Shawn *really wanted* and I convinced myself that I *wanted enough* to go along.

Shawn was so excited to get new speakers and components that we were browsing the audio store the very same night that I got the good-slash-disappointing news from Adobe.

And truly, the new equipment looked magnificent in our living room. Gorgeous floor speakers, a shiny receiver, state-of-the-art wiring without a crackle to be heard. I loved the stereo, and also my heart hurt when I listened to it. That purchase, more than any other, represented my feeling that I was always looking forward to the day when I would finally arrive as an adult and be able to start writing the way I wanted to. When the retirement accounts were maxed out, our advanced degrees were on the wall, and all of our crappy student possessions had been ditched for high-end replacements. When I'd finally earned a break.

With the arrival of the stereo and its several-thousand-dollar price tag, I despaired that my day would ever come. Here was yet another delay, taking me the long way around, further away from that enormous desk that sat neglected in my study. Yes, I had wonderful things in my life — a good job, a caring husband, lovely furnishings in our home — but they weren't enough if I couldn't write. I curled up on the futon in the dark, listening to a crystal clear version of "Both Sides Now" and crying.

In my twenties, I believed that I was trading my life for stuff. In a way, that was true. I knew writers and artists who had foregone the material comforts and advanced their careers more than their interior decorating. Shawn and I could have lived more cheaply and managed without my income.

But what's more true is that I stopped myself from writing. Of course I was terrified of losing my high tech job, because then the largest barrier between me and my manuscript would be removed, and I would have nothing to buffer me from the anxiety and possible failure that writing could bring. In retrospect, I was nowhere near ready to write full time. Thank goodness for my breakdown, which showed me the places in my life and psyche where I had plunged into the underbrush and lost my way.

Now, in my thirties, I believe I'm trading my stuff for freedom. I fantasize about the day when I only have a tiny pile of things to look after and I can go anywhere, do anything. No more scouring the stores for nifty organizers so I can pack my kitchen cupboards with more gadgets. No more afternoons spent rearranging dozens of picture books that the kids have scattered all over the room. No more gargantuan piles of paperwork waiting to be filed. I will be liberated.

As departure day nears, I remember the insubstantial, dislocated feeling I got when we moved to Calgary, and then back to Ottawa, and each time we changed apartments. The moment when everything I owned was on a truck and I saw just how little there was to my life. If I didn't have a home, who was I? Where was I? Did I even matter? I always felt vapoury until I could unpack and put down roots again. When we bought our condo on Nepean Street, I didn't want to move anywhere for a long time.

As the years in our condo piled up, though, the weight of that stuff shifted. The bookshelves, the buffet table, the comfy bed weren't grounding me anymore; they became a prison — an expensive prison with mortgage payments, heat and electricity and water bills, insurance and property tax bills, repair bills.

And with the arrival of our kids, it became clear that my life was not rooted in my house but in my family. Lia and Nico didn't care about having a fancy crib, matching throw pillows, or a full set of silverware. They just wanted to play, and their oblivion to decor was infectious. I stopped reading the magazines and shopping the furniture stores. One of the only home improvements we made after becoming parents was to put some removable vinyl decals on the walls: birds perched on tree branches in the kitchen and alphabet animals in the kids' room. Those made us happy.

I might be just as misguided now as I was in my twenties about the significance of stuff. My longing for a settled life, which has turned to distaste, may transform again as I raise kids and shed illusions and get wiser still.

But for the moment, I don't need the security of a house and furniture. My home is inside me.

I can let the bedroom set go for less than half what I paid for it to a French family with three little kids and a pick-up truck. Shawn can (reluctantly) let go of the stereo to an audiophile who knows the value of speakers manufactured in Canada. We will rent our beds from here on in. We will carry our music on a hard drive and listen to it through an elegant portable speaker.

Of course, we are keeping some important things. The countertop mixer I won in a Christmas giveaway, the heavy-duty blender that has whipped up many a smoothie, and a few place settings of our blue stoneware get packed in boxes to live with my sister Melody. Shawn's parents take a truckload of keepsakes to store in their basement, and we leave a last-minute stash with friends in Ottawa. But we will travel with what fits in the trunk of a taxi.

The Tuesday before we leave Ottawa, we decide that we can't wait for things to sell anymore. We have to start giving stuff away in earnest. The futon has seen far, far better days, and we had to flip the mattress to hide the rips in the cover. We have two decent mattress sets that no charity will take and a high chair that didn't sell.

So we make a creative decision. We are going to host a moving giveaway.

This could be the smartest or the craziest thing we do in our quest to get rid of everything. But we are tossing caution to the wind because we're running out of time.

I'm a long-time member of Full Circles Ottawa, an online network where you offer things to give away and then choose a recipient from the responses you get back. And likewise, if you see something you want, you can make a request and hope that you get picked. But I don't have time to list every coffee cup and throw rug separately, so we decide to do things *en masse*.

Late Tuesday night, I post a message to the Full Circles mailing list:

"We are moving overseas and have lots of odds and ends looking for new homes. Kitchen items, wall art, books, rugs, organizing containers, and other small furniture. Wednesday, July 6 from 7 to 9 p.m., anyone is welcome to come by our house and help themselves. Think of it as a Moving Sale with no price tags! Email me for address details."

The next morning I wake up with a knot in my stomach. What if the whole thing is a disaster? What if fights break out? Or someone cases our condo and comes back later to rob us? We're doing our best to take precautions, and I want to believe the best of people, but I don't want to be naïve either. Well, we don't have a choice now. Hauling everything to Goodwill would take hours and a truck we don't have. We need people to come and take things away for us.

By noon on Wednesday, we have about forty takers for the giveaway and I announce that the event is closed. Shawn and I work feverishly to haul stuff out of closets, drawers, and cupboards and arrange everything in the living room. The plan is to have people come in on the dot of 7 p.m. and hope that the small space and large crowd keep the proceedings civil.

In the afternoon before the sale, I get an email in reply to the online ad for our buffet table, the writer curtly requesting our address so he can come and look at the piece that afternoon. I speak to the man on the phone, but I don't have a good vibe from his manner — he's pushy and abrupt. Still, I want to sell the buffet if I can, so I tell him to come by.

When he arrives, he makes overtures to the buffet table but then immediately starts wandering through the rest of the living room, exclaiming over the crock pot and the toaster and starting to load dishes onto a tray. Every time I get antsy and start to open my mouth to say something, he goes back to the buffet table and admires it. By the time I realize that I should buck up and tell him it's not fair to help himself before the giveaway officially starts, he's got an armload of kitchenware and is heading down the stairs. He wants to come back for more, but I manage to say no.

Finally, he says he wants to talk to his wife about the buffet table, and can he come back when the giveaway is on tonight? "Sure, why not?" I say, trying to be egalitarian.

I really do wish I had kept my mouth shut.

I get another email from a woman working with a homeless shelter for native women. I invite her to come early and take her pick of our things before the rest of the crowd comes in, and she excitedly accepts my offer. I hear the doorbell ring promptly thirty minutes before the giveaway is set to start.

The woman is effusive with her thanks. We tour the living room and she exclaims over her finds. I even ask if she wants to take the loveseat with its black marker scribbles courtesy of Nico, and she says yes right away. By the time she's looked at everything, she has quite a pile, so I offer to set things aside for her, and she says she will return later with a moving van and an extra pair of hands.

As I escort her out the door, I see we've got a line-up: about twenty five people milling around our porch and parking lot, waiting for the giveaway to start. I open the door and get out of the way as the crowd surges into our living room.

Buffet Table Man is back, grabbing containers and piling in as much as he can carry. I see him snatch a wicker storage box just as another woman is reaching for it. He makes a trip to his car, and when he tries to come back in, I take a deep breath and tell him he's already taken his share, and I'd like him to leave. He starts arguing with me, mystified by how he's offended me, and I just keep repeating that I'd like him to leave until I lose my nerve and push Shawn forward to get rid of him. Thankfully, he's willing to take the discussion outside, and after a few minutes of protestation, he departs. I try not to think about what he's taken with him — I don't like to picture my beloved stuff with such a nasty owner.

That's the only encounter that leaves a sour taste in my mouth. The man's greediness seems so out of sync with the otherwise joyful, hopeful spirit of the giveaway. Everyone else is lovely and respectful, and they thank us on their way out. By the end of an hour, almost everything is gone. One couple lingers over my book collection, picking out the volumes on writing and creativity for an artists' group they run. A few college students decide to haul away the pink rug from the kids' room. At last, we close the door behind the last visitors. I am bushed with the stress and commotion and also relieved. We are nearly there.

Through the last year of planning for Operation Hejira, whenever I worried about how we would ever weed through all the things that filled our house, I went back to a mantra I got from the minimalist writer Ev Bogue: *You can always just rent a dumpster, throw everything into it, and walk away.*

In the end, that's what we do.

I call a junk removal service and a university student with a truck shows up on our last morning to take away everything that remains: a hill of garbage bags in the living room, stacks of paper for recycling in the study, and a pile of odds and ends for Goodwill. I could kiss the guy, Justin, who hauls load after load down our three flights of stairs and leaves everything swept and empty in exchange for a small cheque.

We walk through the place one last time, the rooms echoey and already losing the mark of our personalities, morphing from home back into a box of wood and drywall. We remember the beautiful things that happened here: a picnic on the kitchen floor the day we got the keys, waking up to the chirping of our pet finches, showing Lia her first glimpse of snow out the bedroom window, rocking Nico to sleep in the pink recliner from my own childhood bedroom. We thank our Nepean Street house for eight years of shelter.

Shawn packs the rental car with three suitcases in the trunk and auxiliary bags tucked in every other available nook and cranny. Lia and Nico struggle to shoulder their overflowing toddler-size backpacks. Time to hit the open road. We'll stop at my parents' place for lunch and then continue on to spend a week recovering with Shawn's family in Burlington and St. Catharines.

I try to get my bearings as we head out of Ottawa. We won't see this city again for a year. We're leaving our friends behind. And the only thing I've ingested since 5:00 a.m. is a cup of coffee. I'm so tired, I honestly don't know how I'm still conscious. The kids certainly aren't, slumped asleep against their car seats. I plug in the MP3 player and dial up Joni Mitchell's "Hejira." Her crooning tremolo fills the car — *I'm travelling in some vehicle. I'm sitting in some cafe. A defector from the petty wars that shell shock love away.* Shawn and I turn to each other, grinning like maniacs, and finally let the reality flood in.

Holy crap. We did it.

What have we done?

Flow Exercise: The Meaning of Stuff

One of the ways I comforted myself when I was unhappy was by buying yarn. Something about the rainbow colours, the squooshy skeins, the possibility of new sweaters and socks, made me feel rich and warm. I made regular visits to the local yarn store and also discovered the intoxicating ability to order *any yarn I wanted* over the Internet. The entire universe of hand-painted and novelty, silk and cotton, lace weight and bulky, discount and luxury, all lay at the command of my credit card.

One day, my profligate ways caught up with me. A double whammy, two lots of designer yarn in one week, earned me some very reproving looks from my husband. Most of my yarn purchases were posted against the Clothing line item in our household budget, and yarn for me meant no new pants for Shawn.

So I decided to enter into a Yarn Non-Buying Agreement until I had knit everything in my stash. I made a spreadsheet and counted how much yarn I owned: 328 skeins. Enough to keep me knitting for three years or more.

I was surprised to find how easy it was to quit buying yarn. The need it used to fill no longer existed, the need for beauty and comfort, and I had just held onto the practice out of habit.

You get to decide what your stuff means to you. And that meaning may change over time. In the beginning, yarn meant reconnecting to a childhood skill my grandmother taught me. It meant creating beautiful things, learning new techniques, and giving precious gifts. At some point, buying yarn morphed into mindless, fruitless consumption — acquiring more purely for storage. When my knitting slowed after the kids came along, my stash lost almost all of its meaning. And then, as we were preparing for Hejira, it became a hassle, something I had to photograph and list for sale, regretting the lost money and unrealized projects.

Choose a significant item or collection of stuff in your house and ask yourself these questions: What did this thing mean to me when I bought it? What did it tell me about myself? What need did it fill?

Reflect on the lifespan of that item. Does it still have the same meaning? Has your understanding of yourself changed in relationship to it? Is it helping or hindering your creative life?

Your answers will tell you what to do with that stuff.

PART 2: MICHIGAN

5 Amma's Labyrinth

"The labyrinth is thoroughly known. We have only to follow the thread of the hero path, and where we have thought to find an abomination, we will find a god."
— Joseph Campbell, *The Hero with a Thousand Faces*

Most people doing a round-the-world trip start somewhere exotic, but we have chosen to spend the summer in Grosse Pointe, a leafy suburb of Detroit, Michigan. My sister Melody lives there in a manse next to the church where her husband Ben is the pastor, and they have two girls about the same ages as Lia and Nico. I've always been tight with my slightly younger sister, from the vitamin-stealing and Lego-building days of our childhood to the night-wakings and tantrum-management of motherhood, but we've lived hundreds or thousands of kilometres apart ever since Shawn and I got married. Now, I am giddy at the thought of seeing Melody and her family every day for two months.

The kids are as excited as I am. They've been begging to see their cousins Isabelle and Charlotte, who share their love of sparkly costumes, trapeze bars, water fights, and popsicles. We knew Grosse Pointe would be an attractive destination for Nico and Lia, which would hopefully make it easier for them to leave Ottawa. So far the plan seems to have worked, since we haven't heard any complaints or homesickness for Nepean Street.

The arrangements for the summer came together like magic. The caretaker at Mel and Ben's church owns a sparsely furnished two-bedroom flat that he will rent to us at a good price. We can borrow whatever extra provisions we need from my sister — towels, clothes hangers, a television. The daycare that my nieces attend will also take our kids three days a week. Easy peasy lemon-squeezy.

An hour after crossing the border at Sarnia, we pull into the driveway of an old two-story brick house, and familiar faces come out to greet us. Melody and I could pass for twins except that she has blue eyes and I have brown — we share the same laugh and the same sway in our hips. My brother-in-law Ben, in rectangular glasses and black Converse shoes, is very stylish for a minister. Isabelle and Charlotte have blonde bobs, dainty fingers, and just as much energy as our rambunctious black-haired kids.

There's lots of commotion as we tumble out of the car and exchange hugs with the grown-ups while the four cousins go wild at the sight of each other. Charlotte and Isabelle drag us all over the house to show off their bedrooms, the book collection, and the basement playroom. I can picture many tea parties, acrobatic games, and craft supply explosions. This is a big part of what Hejira is all about: the freedom to connect with people we love in the places where they live.

After the melee of arrival, we head down the street to check out our flat. The single-floor apartment is almost empty — there's a double bed for Shawn and me, a dining table with chairs, and a recliner in the living room. Lia and Nico will sleep on foam mattresses with bedding borrowed from their cousins. We've kept the basics from our kitchen to use over the summer: dishes and pots and Shawn's indispensable coffee maker. Not terribly cozy, but it's clean and air-conditioned, which will be a boon in the scorching July heat. And did I mention, two blocks away from my sister's house?

We eat dinner back at the manse — fajitas and Spanish rice — and the kids can barely sit still to eat a few mouthfuls before they're off and running again. After the dishes are done, Melody gives me a package — a custom necklace that I ordered and had delivered to her house, featuring an entry cut from a vintage dictionary. The word framed under glass is *irresistible*. I slip the necklace over my head and enjoy its weight and tickle on my skin.

The word *irresistible* came to me at the World Domination Summit in June, on a small card given out by a business coach named Mark Silver. Each card had a Sufi name for God, and mine was Ya Allah, Ya Jabbar, The Irresistible. "What hit you could not have missed you, and what missed you could not have hit you," it read, and the words took hold of me like hands gripping my shoulders. In the midst of enormous change, I wanted to believe that I couldn't stray from my desire lines if I tried, that every person and event was crossing my path for a reason. That God was coming with us on Operation Hejira.

I wrote *irresistible* on my forearm during a workshop at the Summit. Some women noticed it over lunch and teased me that I really *was* irresistible, which made me blush. I certainly wanted to be that magnetic to my coaching clients and readers, to new friends and old. After years of being quiet and close about my inner world, I wanted to present myself in the spotlight so people would fall in love with my work.

And it dawned on me that *irresistible creativity* was another way of talking about flow, that delicious immersion in life and art-making described by psychologist Mihaly Csikszentmihalyi, where time disappears and everything falls into place at the right moment. If resistance is a synonym for procrastination, avoidance, and writer's block, then flow is the opposite of all of these, marked by movement and a joyful faith in the process. Flow was what I'd been searching for in the dry days of depression, and now I feel swept along in its divine torrent.

With one of God's names hanging around my neck, I look forward to the summer's wonderful ride.

I have another name for God, one that came to me the summer after my breakdown.

My therapist Janice gave me a flyer for a women's retreat on the divine feminine, and instantly I wanted to go. During my depression, God had seemed to disappear, and I knew that my healing wouldn't be complete until I had reconnected with the One I believed to be the source of all love and creativity.

I'd also been reading a book called *The Dance of the Dissident Daughter* by Sue Monk Kidd, who grew up in a conservative Baptist church and had a mystical feminist awakening that introduced her to the spirituality of the Goddess. The story is structured around the important revelations that guided her on the journey, from a dream of giving birth to herself, to seeing a painting in a museum, to visiting the caves of Crete. I nodded along with many of the difficulties she had with how women were treated in the church and in spiritual narratives. Still, despite my attraction, I found it disturbing to have my image of God challenged by the introduction of the Goddess.

The retreat was led by a holistic psychotherapist and spiritual teacher named Madeline Dietrich — a large, motherly woman with a deep voice and compassionate eyes. Arriving at the retreat centre, a renovated log farmhouse on one hundred acres in rural Ontario, I felt very out of my element. Many of the other women seemed to know each other, and I was secretly pleased when everyone else bunked together and I got a room to myself. I was the youngest attendee by a decade or so.

On the first night, we gathered in a circle in the main hall, and at the centre was an altar on a white embroidered cloth set with candles and surrounded by cards. There was also a stick and a metal bowl holding a mallet. I couldn't get comfortable — I was even self-conscious about the position I was sitting in. Cross-legged? On my heels? Back straight? I ended up hugging my knees. I was sure I was doing it wrong.

We lit candles invoking the four directions: East for new beginnings, South for fullness of life, West for the harvest, and North for emptiness. I was too nervous to step forward and light one myself, but if I had, it would have been the North. I felt empty and wanted to be silent so that I could be filled again. I really wanted God to appear and speak to me, to show me who to pray to and what name to use.

Over the next few days, Madeline led us in exercises to help us look at how our childhood and our parents shaped our view of God. My parents became Christians when I was very young, and I was raised to think of God as a powerful invisible father and of Jesus as my older brother. God delighted me with the sense that life was full of secret messages and unseen forces and satisfied my child's desire for someone mysterious and larger than myself who kept watch over everyone.

I lapped up Bible stories and morality tales, learning how to stay safe in an unpredictable world: tell the truth, be kind to others, don't get angry, give generously. "Obeying" seemed to come more easily to me than to my sister Melody, who would often get into fights with my parents for not doing her chores or practicing piano. With my compliance I could win perks and praise from Mom and Dad and stick it to my sister at the same time — the quiet rebel still in operation.

But as I approached adolescence, my eagerness to please God and my parents with good behaviour ran up against my growing appetite for forbidden pleasures. I got messages from preachers and summer camp and books on abstinence that, because I was sinful from birth, my desires were not to be trusted. My very self was suspect and needed to be denied at every turn so that I could follow God's will. If I wanted something, no doubt it was the opposite of what God wanted for me. When I was young, I wanted candy and books about witches and magic. But when I was older, I wanted sex (in movies, in books, and in real life), which was much more dangerous.

I did my best to keep up appearances. My parents didn't want me to date until I was sixteen, and I was two months' shy of my birthday when Shawn and I had our first kiss. All through high school I went through cycles of ecstasy and agony, letting my libido run for a bit and then guiltily reining it in. I was determined to be a virgin when I got married, more to avoid shame or condemnation than because I really believed that two young adults in a long-term relationship shouldn't have sex. But I was forever warped by all the internal gymnastics I went through to believe that *Sex is a wonderful gift from God! Unless you're single, in which case it's dirty and sinful, and so are you for wanting it.* Now God seemed more like a frowning father turned overprotective and distrustful.

Many of us at the women's retreat shared that we hadn't felt good enough for God and that we were tired of trying to earn His approval. I also talked about how God seemed unpredictable, that we could call Him but He might not come, and there would be no reason for His not coming. I feared that God would not show up for me at the retreat.

One of the women at the retreat was a labyrinth facilitator, and she taught us about the significance of this ancient symbol and practice. Unlike a maze, a labyrinth has only one path to the centre, its spiral form evoking the feminine journey deep inside, often covering the same ground but at different levels. The path inward is called *purgation*, a time of letting go. The sojourn in the centre is called *illumination*, a time of epiphany. The return outward is called *union*, when the new insights gained are expanded and enfolded into the whole. Everyone walks at her own pace, occasionally stepping aside to let someone pass. Because of the winding nature of the labyrinth, it's hard to tell whether others are behind or ahead on the path, or even whether they are walking in the same direction, but there is a sense of companionship all the same.

That evening, we gathered to walk a labyrinth that had been laid out for us in the *Petite Chartes* pattern on a high point of the acreage. We wore long pants and jackets to deal with the mosquitos. We brought flashlights and torches to light when we reached the hill. I carried an open eye drawn with crayon in my jeans pocket. I was hoping that I would find a new name for God in the labyrinth, one that spoke to me of the feminine but also connected with the God of my past. We called in the spirits, and I invited the Dove of the Holy Ghost. I was thinking she would end up being my feminine image of God.

At the entrance of the labyrinth, I dipped my hand into the basin of water and put it to my forehead in a gesture of baptism. Then I started to walk slowly, and at each turn of the path I let go of a feeling or belief that was keeping me from seeing God: doubt, fear of rejection, anger, confusion, loneliness. As I approached the centre, I began to feel what I thought was a powerful energy. I had to push my way in, and my legs were shaking. I stood in the heart of the labyrinth, trembling, and wondered whether I was just making myself tremble. Then I thought, perhaps I'm trembling because I'm trying to keep the energy out, and I need to let it in. So I took a deep breath, said a silent yes, and stopped trembling.

I knelt down on the ground and began praying quietly. It came into my mind that I might call God *Mama*. But that felt too human, too common. I wanted a name that was singular and reverent. Then I remembered that Jesus called God *Abba* in Aramaic, meaning Father. Could I maybe call God *Amma*? I said the word aloud a few times, and as the syllables passed my lips I began to weep, realizing how much I needed and wanted a Goddess to hold me and comfort me as a mother would.

By the pure intensity of my response to this name, I knew that I had found what I was looking for. Amma and I began to talk to each other as I left the centre of the labyrinth, and my head was filled with all the new ways to understand our relationship now that I could see Her as female. She told me She had given birth to me, and I stopped to curl up and be birthed by Her again. She said that She wanted to fill me with good things, and I stopped again to open my arms and mouth to the sky. She told me that I am Her truth, Her Ali filled with truth. When I came out of the labyrinth, I washed my eyes three times in the basin of water, once each for the Maiden, Mother, and Crone.

I have kept Amma mostly to myself in the years since. Even though my church teaches that God is neither male nor female, many people still find the Goddess image strange or uncomfortable. Shawn listened to my story of the labyrinth but didn't really get the significance of a divine mother who cradled me to her breast. So I talked to Amma in my head, substituted female pronouns for male under my breath, and bought an icon of Mary and the child Jesus to keep on my buffet table.

The labyrinth has become an important metaphor for me in designing a creative life that encourages flow. I love how you cannot get lost in a labyrinth. There are many twists and turns, leaps forward and doublings back, but you are always moving closer to the centre. Once you enter, you can give yourself over to the path — progress is inevitable as long as you keep walking.

Labyrinth is now my word for structures built into daily life that channel my energy in the direction I want to go. Taking a writing class, selling my car, installing Internet blocking software on my computer — all of these are systems that take intention and effort to put in place and that then shape my time and my actions automatically. In a writing class, I get deadlines and encouragement that help me produce work. Without a car, I get lots of exercise and time for thinking because I walk and bike everywhere. The software stops me from frittering away my work time.

Operation Hejira itself is a labyrinth that promises certain conditions: material simplicity; the stimulation of new people and places; more time with my husband and kids; a mindfulness and cherishing of each moment; days away from work for travel and visiting; a retreat into solitude that clears space for me to write. I trust that Hejira will carry me along and safeguard the life I want to experience.

At the end of my women's retreat, Madeline had us ask God a question. I wrote to Amma, "Will I always find You in the labyrinth?" Then she had us reverse it so that Amma was asking me, "Will I always find *you* in the labyrinth?" And I laughed at the reminder that I am not only the one seeking, but am also the one sought.

Flow Exercise: Listening to Love

Talking with Amma helps me stay in flow. I notice that I have the hardest time writing when I'm feeling down and full of doubt, when I'm beating up on myself for not being good or fast or disciplined enough. Amma offers me a source of unconditional love and faith that I am perfect just as I am. Her voice acts like a gush of meltwater to wash away the gunk inside. Her words have this clear, bracing quality that carries me along to a new place.

You can get a similar effect from listening to anyone who loves you: your partner, a friend, a coach, or an aspect of yourself. You can even tune in to the spirit of what you're trying to create — your book or story or painting. Love reminds you that you're doing your best, that you have something valuable to offer, and that you're not alone. When you remember those truths, you can prioritize your work and access your imagination more easily.

With a pen and notebook or on a computer, write down where you're at, how you feel, some of the thoughts running through your head. Write down what you want and why you can't seem to get it. Notice especially where you feel bogged down, where your joy and progress are halted by some belief standing in your way.

I'm so behind! Everyone is doing bigger, better things than me, and I have no idea how I will catch up. I really feel like I've missed the boat.

Now pose a question or simply invite God to share something with you. If you don't believe in God, you can imagine this response coming from any source of love: a benevolent mentor or your own wise, best self. You shouldn't have to strain to hear — just sit quietly and breathe until the words appear in your head.

Darling, you haven't missed the boat. You are the boat.

This is a good ritual to practice whenever you find yourself stuck. If you're trying to force things to happen all by yourself, you're not in flow. Remind yourself that you are in relationship, whether with God, your work, or another part of your self, and that there's an easier way available, and your energy will start to move again.

6 Practicing Motherhood

During our first week in Grosse Pointe, we get ourselves outfitted. Lia and Nico have orientation at God's Kids, the church daycare — Nico is very excited to go to "school" with the girls and use his new froggie lunch bag. Our landlord gives us a Grosse Pointe park pass that lets us into the community pool and splash pad just for residents. Melody introduces us to Trader Joe and his delicacies, such as chocolate with caramel and black sea salt and a beverage known as Arnold Palmer (a mixture of iced tea and lemonade).

Melody and I get out our calendars and make plans for the summer. On Tuesdays and Fridays, Shawn and I will cook dinner for everyone at their house. On Thursdays, Mel and I will take the kids for an outing: the zoo, the Henry Ford museum, Greenfield Village. Mel and I will have lunch, just the two of us, once a week. We're negotiating a novel arrangement, a new labyrinth — never before have our lives entwined so closely. I don't want to impose on Mel and Ben too much or take over their schedule just because we've set up camp down the street. But I do want to take advantage of this rare chance to spend ordinary time with them.

I make Mel promise that she'll tell me what they need and if there are any problems. She and Ben have more structure for their kids than we do: quiet time in the afternoons, pictogram lists of routines for morning and evening, regular bedtimes. They pay attention to Charlotte and Isabelle's moods and make sure they don't get too much stimulation. I learn a lot from watching my sister. When Isabelle jumps impulsively on the trapeze and knocks Nico down, Melody doesn't bark at her from across the room; she goes over, looks her in the eye, and quietly reminds her of the rules.

I can see all four of us adults trying to cope with the pressure of today's parenting culture. The books and blog articles tell us to praise effort, not accomplishment. Give choices instead of orders. Empathize and set consistent limits. Make time for child-led play. When the techniques don't work on my very emotional and persistent daughter, I blame myself for not doing things properly, not having enough patience or presence. I hear myself saying the same things my mother did: *What were you thinking? Get back here! I'm not going to tell you again.* Using my child's name as remonstrance instead of endearment. I can see when Lia and Nico can't contain their exuberance and curiosity, I know when I'm asking too much of them, but my frustration just spills out in response.

How funny that Amma, God as mother, is the divine image that speaks to me most, when my relationship with motherhood has often been fraught. After spending my teenage years helping raise my little brother and sister, I was less than eager to have babies myself. Getting out of the house for university was a relief, and even after Shawn and I married, we both agreed that graduate school came before kids. I looked forward to five or ten years of having my husband all to myself before any children arrived to distract us.

When I finished my creative writing degree, we made the long hot drive from Calgary back to Ontario, this time going through the American plains states: North Dakota, Minnesota, Wisconsin. The sun was so strong that I hung a towel in the window to stay out of its rays. I rested my bare feet against the Chevette's dashboard, and we talked lazily about the future. And somewhere in the badlands, Shawn said, "What if we didn't have children?"

The idea had never occurred to me. Children were such a given in our Christian communities that the thought of being married and childless by choice was bizarre, almost perverse. But I still felt detached from the subject — Shawn had three years of grad school ahead of him and I needed to work to support us, so we weren't planning on becoming parents any time soon. I let myself wonder, what would life look like without kids? Could our days still be full and happy? Would we regret the decision later on? Would others judge us? Was it selfish or selfless? What did God want us to do?

I thought about the various married women I knew who had chosen not to have kids. My thesis supervisor, Aritha, was devoted to writing and teaching her students. So was Joyce Carol Oates, a prolific writer I was obsessed with. I had talked with our minister in Calgary, Jean, about the decision she made with her husband to focus on her service to the church rather than split herself between vocation and family. I respected these women, and they seemed content with their choices and vibrant in their careers.

When we arrived in Ottawa, I started to read books about intentional childlessness and found I had a lot of sympathy with those who took this path. I knew exactly how much time, money, and energy it cost to raise kids and how a disproportionate amount of that burden fell on women. I had read *The Feminine Mystique* in high school, and even though decades had passed since Betty Friedan wrote about the mysterious illness and malaise afflicting 1960s suburban housewives, I thought that her warnings about women failing to find fulfillment in marriage and motherhood alone still rang true today. And after I got a job as a junior technical writer, I discovered first-hand how draining it was to work full time, do the cooking, cleaning, and groceries, play squash, visit with friends, and still try to write. I couldn't imagine adding children to the mix and staying sane.

I was twelve when I first started practicing motherhood. The doctor had said there was only a ten per cent chance that my mother would get pregnant after my father's vasectomy reversal, so my family began praying for a miracle. We got our answer on Christmas morning when I opened the last card left on the tree, the last gift in a room of shiny treats and strewn paper, in which my parents told us that a baby was coming next August. Melody and I squealed and hugged each other at the good news, like we had been promised a real live doll to look after.

We debated names for months and finally chose Joanna Dawn because she was God's gift and our family's new beginning. When the baby arrived, we crowed over her curly red hair and dark eyes that mellowed into amber. Mel and I dressed her in a new outfit every time she spit up and fought over whose turn it was to bathe her. We paraded her through the neighbourhood in her stroller and rocked her to sleep singing Brahms' lullaby.

Then my mother got breast infections that never seemed to go away. She was run down from the long birth and the night feedings, hosting company and homeschooling Melody and me. And after weeks of medical appointments and prescriptions, the breast infections turned out not to be infections at all but fibromyalgia, an ache in her muscles and joints that felt like a constant flu. "A few months' vacation in Florida would fix you right up," the doctor told my mother, and I don't think she knew whether to laugh or cry.

The following spring, when Joanna was seven months old, we moved to a new house, a back-split with a bigger kitchen, more bedrooms, and bright windows. At the time, I was oblivious to how much work this move involved, but now that I've done it myself a few times,

I can't imagine how my mom managed with a baby and a chronic illness. I was in my own little world, packing my crossword books and craft supplies, pestering my dad about painting the mirror frame on the back of my new bedroom door. My mom's mother, Marjorie, was recently retired from her job at an insurance company, and she came to help, scouring and shining the old house until an ungodly hour on the night of the move. I imagine that my mother thought things would be better once we unpacked and Joanna started sleeping through the night. Maybe she even enjoyed thoughts of renovating the kitchen and putting in a big soaker tub downstairs. Maybe she hoped that the fibromyalgia would disappear all by itself once things settled down.

That was the last visit we had from my grandma before they discovered inoperable cancer all through her liver and bowels. She must have already been in pain when she was cleaning our house, vacuuming the beige carpet in my basement bedroom, scrubbing the oven with steel wool, and taking the streaks off the shower stall. She had ignored her symptoms for so long that there was no hope of treatment. My mother shuttled back and forth between our house in Kingston and her childhood home in Windsor, a long seven-hour car trip, with a baby in tow.

Suddenly motherhood wasn't something to play at anymore — it was a serious necessity. Now I was in charge of homeschooling when my mom was gone. Melody and I sat in the dining room and solved math problems, typed research reports, and answered questions about literature readings, all ready for my father to check when he got home from work at his dental office. Mel and I lost our neighbourhood friends when we moved, so we only had each other for company. We had outgrown our Lego and dollhouses, but we played Payday and watched *Degrassi High* and knotted friendship bracelets together.

I took care of the house and the cooking too. I made tuna broccoli casserole, but I could never get the white sauce as thick and creamy as my mother's. I cleaned the bathrooms every week according to a particular routine my mother showed me — cleanser in the toilet bowl to soak first, then mirrors, sinks, counters, and tub swabbed, and finally the floors. I ironed my dad's shirts for the office, working the tip of the iron around each and every button to get the wrinkles out. I would have made Mrs. Cleaver proud.

I looked after my dad too. He needed someone to talk to after the hectic pace of seeing patients, so we did the dishes together while we rehashed our days. We listened to Saturday morning radio while we ran errands. I helped him choose music for church services and sang harmony to his tenor. He took me to parties and concerts when my mom couldn't go.

I tried to take care of my grandmother from a distance. I prayed for her every night, and I sent her a framed verse hand-written with my calligraphy pen. "Christian, keep on trusting when the wind blows ill. Learn to keep on trusting, come whatever will. Christ the risen Saviour lives and loves you still. Doubt and fear are futile, trust His sovereign will."

And of course, I mothered my mom. When she was home, I played inspiring songs for her on the piano: "It Is Well with My Soul" and Amy Grant's "In a Little While We'll be With the Father." I brought water for her pills and kept Joanna quiet when she needed to sleep. I wrung out the dishcloth and hung it to dry on the faucet just the way she liked. I changed the sheets on her bed and made tight, neat hospital corners. When I did these things, she would smile a little, hug me and say thank you in this tired voice that broke my heart.

Six months after they found my grandmother's cancer, she was gone. And so was my mother, in a way — she disappeared into pain and grief and unconsciousness. In my memory, she is in bed, her beautiful bed with the teak frame and thick duvet, sleeping under the influence of antidepressants and Gravol. Of course she got up: she made our lunches when Melody and I went back to school, she cleaned up Joanna's toys, and she cut my father's curly black hair. But I could look into her eyes and see she wasn't really there.

A year after my grandmother died, my parents sat us down to give us important news. This time I wasn't a starry-eyed preteen but a hardened tenth-grader, worn out from long bus rides, homework, housework, and babysitting.

"Don't tell me you're pregnant!" I blurted out to my mother, unable to hide the exasperation in my voice.

But she *was* pregnant: she wanted another child, one last chance for a boy. She was thirty-nine, which seemed to me an ancient age at which to have another baby, and everything was harder this time around — she gained more weight, got more tired, and had a seemingly endless labour three weeks after her due date. But at the end of all that, miraculously, we had our boy, Benjamin.

I helped as much as I could between English essays and volleyball, yearbook committee, youth choir, and a new boyfriend, all while riding the school bus for two-and-a-half hours a day. I sat with Mom while she breastfed, I read books to three-year-old Joanna and took her to the park, I changed the sheets on Ben's crib when he flooded his diaper, I folded tiny sleepers and undershirts, I made more tuna casserole for dinner, I helped tidy the house the night before the cleaning lady came.

No wonder I wasn't eager to become a mother. I'd already been one.

Shawn and I might have settled slowly and happily into a childfree life if he hadn't gone to Holland for his *beppe*'s funeral two years after our move to Ottawa. While he was there, he stayed with his cousins, the Kloostermans. Anne and his wife Tiny had two children, Wiebren (a boy of ten) and Adeline (a girl of eight). In between family gatherings,

Shawn and his cousins had long chats comparing their respective childhoods. Anne and his family also took some time to sightsee and vacation with Shawn — visiting a Frisian pole-vaulting competition and taking the ferry to a North Sea island. The children were charming, and Shawn had a fine time teasing and playing with them. He could see that their family life was something special; there was a closeness, respect, and delight in each other's company that was captivating.

When I picked Shawn up from the airport after his trip, he had some news for me. Spending the week with Wiebren, Adeline, and their parents had awakened a longing in him to become a father. Although we had seemed set on a life without children, his time in Holland opened a crack of doubt that he couldn't ignore. He wasn't sure whether that longing was a momentary phase, a factor of the emotional events, or whether it was something larger and more permanent. For my part, I was taken aback by the reversal and not ready to unmake the decision so easily. I resolved to wait and see whether his desire grew or faded.

The university residence job gave us a chance to practice pseudo-parenting for the students we supervised, and dealing with their challenges and upsets, trying to shepherd them into maturity, had a peculiar joy to it. We would visit their dorm rooms, eat with them in the cafeteria, and plan funny games for our residence meetings. We hosted Kraft Dinner evenings and scavenger hunts. In between the paperwork and midnight phone calls from security, we loved the company of these amiable, searching young people.

But when my stress and unhappiness came to a head in 2002, and I realized I had fallen into the very pit that had claimed my mother, parenthood seemed a very precarious proposition.

"I don't know whether I can have children if I'm going to be like this," I said to Shawn on that trip to Lac Brome. He didn't reply, but I learned later that my words made him deeply sad. His yearning to be a father had only strengthened, and because I loved him, I took that yearning seriously. Still, the last thing in the world that I wanted was a pregnancy.

I used to scan the columns of alumni news in my university newsletter and roll my eyes every time I read a birth announcement. Where were the notices of women's graduate degrees and job appointments and publications? Was this all my classmates aspired to, making babies? My mother had earned her BA in nursing but never worked; in fact, she was pregnant with me when she got her diploma. It looked to me like she had subsumed her life to raising children, keeping our house, and helping out at church. Where were her dreams and desires? What did she do that was purely for herself? Even her hobbies involved sewing clothes and making things for the house. (This contemptuous attitude would soon give me good fodder for therapy.)

Once, I missed a few birth control pills and was gripped by a sudden fear that a child would be forced on me when I wasn't ready. Perhaps not coincidentally, I was also scheduled to go on a writing retreat that very day. During the whole drive to the retreat centre in the Gatineau hills, I clutched the steering wheel with cold fingers and raged. Why, with all that God had asked me to do as a wife, daughter, writer, and volunteer, would He now make me pregnant? Was He trying to break my spirit? Had I misunderstood what He wanted me to do with my life? I dreaded everything about having a baby — I didn't want the physical changes, I didn't want to occupy my mind and time with making decisions about birthing options, I didn't want to give up my job at the residence. Most of all, I didn't want to abandon the book I was writing.

Still wearing my coat, I sat on the couch in the chilly retreat centre and pulled an orange crocheted afghan over my lap. I couldn't concentrate on the manuscript I had planned to work on, so I wrote about what was happening: how I had cramps, how I kept crying and everything hurt. How every thought was painful because my whole life could change. I'd never been so scared of not writing as I was at that moment.

A few days later, a test at the clinic confirmed that I was not, in fact, pregnant. I alternated between feeling jubilant and foolish. But if nothing else, my reaction solidified my intention not to have children biologically.

Shawn's longing to become a dad wasn't going away, though, and adoption was still a possibility. So a central theme of my therapy sessions — I was now seeing Madeline from the women's retreat — was this question of what had to change so I could trust myself to stay happy and healthy as a mother. I knew I didn't want to put my kids through what I'd been through.

Depression and fibromyalgia had made my mother so unpredictable. Sometimes she'd catch me by surprise with her affection for some little thing I'd done like taking out the recycling or setting the table. Other times I'd go all out, cleaning out the junk drawer or baking cranberry loaf, and I'd get almost no reaction. It was a bit like living with an alcoholic — never knowing what mood I'd catch her in, whether she'd be well enough to come to my piano recital. This capriciousness made her approval strangely more desirable. And somehow I decided that the best kind of love had to be earned with good behaviour.

Discussing my mother in therapy felt like so much of a cliché that I had to resist an exasperated sigh when Madeline brought it up. Yes, yes, my people-pleasing behaviour comes from trying to secure my mother's blessing, can we move on to something more interesting? Let's talk about why I'm not writing, even though I want to! Let's talk about my horrible, demanding job!

But Madeline kept bringing us back to this place and asking questions that made me cry. She wanted to know how I felt about my mother having two more children when I was a teenager. And I told her how angry I was at what had happened to our family, to my high school years, because of the choices my parents made to have more kids. And at the same time, I was so glad that Joanna and Ben were born. "I care about them so much," I sobbed, "I'm so glad they're in the world." I didn't know what to make of this contradiction.

I told Madeline about my contempt for pregnant women, triggered by the birth announcements in the alumni news and my mother's aborted nursing career. Madeline sat up straighter when she heard me describe this disdain for mothers. "There's something powerful here," she said. "It's important to know where you spend your energy hating something because that energy is not going into creating."

And a question leaped into my mind like a tiger with fangs bared. Did I hate my own mother?

My throat choked on the answer, but my heart knew it was true. God help me, I did. I hated my mother. The tears were coming in torrents as my chest heaved to get breath between sobs, leaving me horrified at the truth and relief of admitting this out loud to another person.

I hated my mother for being weak, for not standing up to people. For saying yes even when she couldn't handle it. I hated her for being sick and unavailable when I needed her. I hated the way she gave herself to the church or people outside the family and left nothing for us. The way she would yell at us and then pick up the ringing phone and change her voice instantly to polite calm. I hated her for not getting help for herself, for not getting medication or therapy quickly enough. I felt like she had failed herself and all of us in the bargain, and I hated that too.

But how could I bear hating my own mother? That hatred had to be turned somewhere safer, somewhere private. And so, I became my mother so I could hate myself — overcommitted, self-annihilating, and depressed. Now I lived with a vitriolic internal voice that berated me for being weak and sick and anxious, for failing to say no, for neglecting my writing. No wonder I became wickedly unhappy. I didn't see how I could be a mother and a writer too, without paying my mother's terrible price. I hated that impasse. I hated having to choose between myself and those I loved.

"Remember that you have much better supports available to you than your mother did," Madeline said gently.

And this made me cry more because life was so unfair and because I felt guilty for having more than my mother, who was such a wonderful person, whom I loved so much.

The summer that Madeline paced me through these revelations, I was writing another short story, this one about a pregnant nursing student who takes an introductory fiction course with a famous author. The idea came when I realized that my mother had been attending the University of Windsor at the same time that Joyce Carol Oates was teaching there, and I imagined what it would have been like for these two very different people to meet.

In therapy and on the page, I wrestled with these questions: How do we decide what work to do, and is some work better than others? Why are some people prolifically creative and others not, and how do we make peace with the difference? What is the purpose of literature, and how does one appreciate it? Are there ways to get past the barriers of class, education, and vocation so that we can truly connect?

All of which could be summed up very simply: *Who am I? And do I have a right to be me?*

Madeline said that I was struggling with identity issues, a phrase that struck me as ridiculously obscurative, but which had to stand in as shorthand for "I'm trying to live my mother's life over to get it right, and I feel guilty for having things she didn't, and I'm uncomfortable with my own calling as a writer because I don't have a good role model to show me how to be a writer and a mother at the same time, and something about all that is blocking my creative energy." Quite the morass.

In the story I was writing, "Understanding Fiction," the nursing student, Nan, is hiding her pregnancy from the school and is still detached from the baby herself. She is fascinated by the woman teaching her English elective, an author who has written eleven books at the age of thirty three. When Nan reads the Flannery O'Connor short story "A Good Man Is Hard to Find," she has a strong personal reaction to the family being massacred by a serial killer and realizes that she doesn't want to work in a hospital for the rest of her life.

In writing this story, I was trying to understand and forgive my mother for choosing homemaking instead of a career, for being so different than the ambitious and childless writer. I wanted to believe that there was a way for us to connect across the chasm, or at least a longing to do so, because we were mother and daughter.

When I finished that story, I knew that it was the best story I had ever written, and I knew that if we adopted, I wanted to find a way to write without abandoning my kids and a way to parent without abandoning myself.

I am a writer. I have a right to write.

Flow Exercise: Who Are You?

Many people have a hard time saying, "I am a writer" or "I am an artist." They think that they can only claim that identity when they have the real-world credentials to prove it: an academic degree, an agent's representation, a published book, a royalty cheque, a full-time career.

Some tell us that our creative identities are determined by our actions. "Writers write," they say, with the unspoken reprimand that if you are not writing, you're not a writer. This maxim is meant to be motivating, but I read it as another way of policing art, making people prove that they're walking the walk before they can gain entry to the writer's club and exercise its privileges.

I believe that our creative identities are grounded in our desires. I was a writer before I ever set down a sentence because as a child I discovered that I wanted to thrill myself with stories I created. At age five, I lived for the afternoons when Melody and I built the Phoenix spaceship out of couch cushions and fought over who got to be Princess from G-Force. At age eight, we woke up early to play Lego before school, each day carrying on the serial narrative with mini-figures named after characters from Anne of Green Gables and the Chronicles of Narnia. At age eleven, I waited all day to go to bed so I could spin my infatuation with a boy into elaborate daydreams, feeling the shape of rising tension and climax in my belly as I constructed coincidences to bring us together and obstacles to keep us apart.

As a kid, my artistic desires morphed easily into actions. As I grew up, though, I learned to separate the two, to deny and downplay and dismiss these desires because they seemed frivolous. I would have abandoned literature altogether if it hadn't been for my freshman poetry and drama class in college. Reading Ibsen and Herbert and Arnold revived my longing to tell my own stories and inspired me to change my major from chemistry to English.

Who are you? Is there a creative identity that you've hesitated to claim for yourself because you thought you had to be knighted or certified or in some way externally validated? Or have you harboured a secret identity since childhood but stopped yourself from making choices or changes that would allow you to live it out?

Today, tell one other person, "I am a _____!" and let your own voice and conviction remind you that it's true. And tell them what one way you want to turn that desire into action.

7 About a Girl

"Every child is a born adventurer and every traveler a born-again child."

— Pico Iyer, *The Lady and the Monk: Four Seasons in Kyoto*

How do you undo the momentous decision not to have children, after all the research and reflection, after you've made peace with never experiencing pregnancy, birth, and breastfeeding, after you've come to terms with always being the aunt and never the mother, never the most important woman in a child's life?

Here in Grosse Pointe, with the very real sun-browned bodies of my children in my arms, their squeals and whines and chatter in my ears, all of my internal wrangling seems very abstract and far away, like the mapping and planning you do before a trip, when your destinations are just flat photographs and mental pictures full of gaps. But without the wrangling, I never would have reached this land of motherhood.

My reversal happened slowly and respectfully, the way a labyrinth winds every which way to take you back where you started. I didn't want kids until all of my doubts were resolved, and Shawn didn't want to blackmail me — *have kids or else I'll leave you.* We started talking with Connie, our couples therapist, to move forward together. I needed to hear that Shawn accepted and was committed to me despite the limits on my mental and physical health — which is funny to think about now, since it turned out my health wasn't limited, I just needed things like freedom, pleasure, rest, and writing time in order to flourish.

I sorted through the potential jealousy of seeing my husband attached to another female (Shawn was intent on having a daughter, and since we were considering adoption from China, that seemed very likely). Connie showed me that my hyper-focus on the sacrifices required from me as a mother blinded me to what I would also receive from my kids.

In the end, I had two epiphanies that illuminated my desire lines. Shawn and I watched the movie *About a Boy*, and at first I was nodding along with the bachelor played by Hugh Grant, who insists that, contrary to what John Donne might say, he *is* an island, he's bloody Ibiza. Part of me prized and craved that level of independence — when you're alone, no one can hurt or disappoint you. And I cringed at the boy Marcus' predicament when his mother descended into sloppy depression. No way was I doing that to my kids.

But the boy's need and the raw awkward beauty of his spirit crossed the distance between him and the bachelor, and by the end of the movie, Hugh Grant acknowledged that even islands are connected underneath. I bawled during the final scene, this gathering of an unconventional family of people who cared for each other, and I finally admitted to myself that yes, I did want backup. I wanted more love in my life. I wanted a richer fabric of connections around me. I wanted kids.

The other piece fell into place as I was walking home on Sparks Street one night, the heels of my knee boots clipping the paving stones, the stars clean and sharp overhead. Amma and I were chatting in my head, and suddenly I saw that by calling me to be a mother, God was inviting me to become more like Herself, nurturing and creative, all while preserving my identity as a woman and a writer. I stopped in my tracks and gasped. For so long I had looked at mother-hood through a lens of martyrdom and ruin, and now I could see it as an honour, a path of growth. I finished the walk home grinning, clasping my gloved hands together in the deliciousness of feeling cho-sen. I wanted to be more like Amma.

After one of our last sessions with Connie, Shawn and I came out of her office building and got into the car to drive home. But when I read the license plate of the car in front of me, my jaw dropped. AKYD, it said. Get it? A kid. "It's a sign!" I said to Shawn, and he laughed and kissed me.

So, we started moving ahead with adoption. I let myself do the fun stuff, like buying a quilt for the baby's room and knitting cute little clothes. We talked about names and figured out where she would sleep. We signed up with an adoption agency and a social worker, and I actually liked talking about ourselves and managing all the paper-work. I had been waiting to quit my job until after the baby arrived so I would still qualify for parental leave, but in a pivotal conversation with Madeline I realized that I didn't need to wait — I could get started on building a freelance career, and Shawn could take all nine months of leave we had allotted from the government. I loved how becoming a mother was already helping me take better care of myself.

My "identity issues" didn't disappear just because I'd made a deci-sion, though. As the time grew closer for us to be matched with a baby, my confrontation with the shift into motherhood grew more intense. One weekend, my parents came for a visit, and we were working on getting the house ready for when the baby arrived — moving furniture and cleaning. Shawn and Dad left to take our huge console sewing machine to Melody's parents-in-law and pick up a carpet steamer.

I was already out of sorts, having my parents there while the house was a mess, feeling the stress of telling them what chores to do and accepting their help. Mom and I kept tidying up and getting things off the carpet so it would be ready to clean. And all through this activity, I had a strong sense that this place, my life, the adoption, none of it was real. The house seemed like a cardboard construct, the set of a play. There was nothing to it: the carpet, the bookshelves, the boxes of wine were all fake. My mom and I talked about the baby and put my childhood books onto the new bookshelves, but I had this feeling that the baby was never coming, we were just pretending to get ready. When Shawn returned with the steam cleaner, I had the impression that we were not really married, just acting out our lines, going through the motions of living together.

And then I looked at myself in the mirror and saw a shell and thought, "I'm not a real person."

Do I deserve to take up space on the planet? If I'm not my house, or my marriage, or my belongings, who am I?

And again I clung to my response: *I am a writer. I have a right to write.*

Could I claim my right to remain myself as I moved into parenthood? What if writing wasn't something that tore me away from my children? What if writing made me a good mother, a better mother? What if these two identities, writer and mother, didn't have to be clawing me over for their share? What if I wrote as a mother and mothered as a writer? Could I just be one whole person instead of a fragmented collection of competing identities?

I didn't have all the answers, but I knew that they lay in honouring my desires, not quashing them. I decided that part of my preparation, one of the things in my baby trousseau would be a new draft of a novel I'd started a few years ago. A novel about a sick woman with a teenage daughter and a new baby. I would trace the nascent desires of my characters and show myself that writing could be done in homage to my children, not in spite of them.

Shawn and I wanted to adopt. That's the simplest and most truthful way I can explain how we decided to create our family. From the earliest days of our marriage, when we talked about the distant possibility of having kids, we talked about adoption. According to the lingo, Shawn and I are *preferential adopters* — we took that route not because of infertility, but because adoption was our first choice.

We wanted to connect to another race and culture; we wanted travel to be part of the fabric of our family life; we wanted a Chinese daughter and son; we wanted Shawn to be more involved in parenting from Day One. In some ways, I also think being a writer inclined me toward adoption because of the drama, the novelty, and the uncertainty.

The other way to explain our decision to adopt is to talk about the desires we didn't have — being related to our children by blood wasn't a necessity for us, and I wasn't attached to giving birth to my kids. This absence of desire is something of a mystery to us, especially considering how important biological ties are to many parents and the lengths they'll go to in order to have a pregnancy or conceive genetic offspring through other means. We seem to be missing that compulsion, and its absence opened a space to pursue our longing to adopt.

The years-long adoption process gave us a lot of time to think about everything. We read up on attachment theory, the needs of kids who are parented interracially, and the emotional difficulties that adoption poses for everyone involved. At times, I felt tied in knots by all the ethical considerations — the possibilities of coercion, trafficking, and even kidnapping. For a while, I felt guilty for taking a child away from her birth family *and* from another infertile family. For so long, motherhood had been the domain of others — by this time, my sister Melody had her first child, Isabelle, and how many hours had I spent keeping other women company while they breastfed, babysitting other people's kids, buying presents for my nieces and nephews? I had to alter my view of myself and claim my right to be a mother too.

A cynic might say that I had a subconscious desire to avoid pregnancy given the contempt I had had for women in that state. A few people have asked whether I adopted because I was afraid of giving birth, or because something was not right in my marriage, or because I wanted to keep my figure and avoid the demands of caring for a newborn. All I can say is that, for me, adoption felt like moving toward something I yearned for with all my heart, not like running away from something. I wanted Lia Na-Fei and Nico Han-Kun, even before I knew who they were.

After I did all that inner work to come to terms with my mother's role in my life, we had slowly found our way back to closeness again. I remember long, deep conversations as we walked along the Ottawa River, sewed the bedskirt she made onto our guest bed, went on girls' weekends with Melody and Joanna. I made presents for her, hugged her, and held her hand. Sometimes I felt like we'd come full circle back to the infatuation of mother and infant.

Going through depression myself had given me more compassion for my mother, and I wanted to honour the strength she showed in the face of great difficulty and loss. The novel I was working on asked me to get inside her head and feel what it would be like to have a baby later in life, lose your mother to cancer, and develop a chronic illness. No doubt I was off the mark in many ways, but trying to see things from her viewpoint helped me love her more.

I asked my mother to come to China with us when we adopted Lia. I might have been independent in other ways, but I really wanted my mom with me when I met my daughter — to help out, yes, but also to witness, to represent the lineage of mothers I was joining. Allowing myself to want my mother in China, want her there very badly, was a big risk for me because it opened me up to reliving the disappointment of my childhood when she missed my big events.

And it was touch-and-go whether she could actually come on the trip given her health. Mom's fibromyalgia was always there in the background, flaring when she was under stress and not getting enough rest. And her depression came and went in parallel cycles. Mom had never travelled outside of Canada and the US, so she was worried about food and being in a strange environment. But somehow that year, even during her usual blue winter period, she stayed well physically and mentally, and I'll admit to jumping up and down when we booked an airline ticket with the name BRENDA GRESIK on it.

The moment came when we were in a crowded, noisy hotel conference room in Nanchang, China, and above all the children's voices we could hear one baby shrieking her heart out, and we knew that was Na Fei, the ten-month-old girl we were chosen for. Shawn took her into his arms, a hot, tiny bundle in her padded suit, sweat soaking her hair, and he jostled and I coaxed while my mother turned on the video camera to record our coming together. Except that she kept forgetting to hold up the camera, letting it slide down to film our legs and the wall, because she couldn't stay detached from what was going on. When we looked back at the footage that night, we were chagrined, but now it seems entirely fitting. A moment that chaotic and pivotal shouldn't be captured perfectly, but in fragments and snatches. Now my mother is in the video too, in the way the visual image cuts away but the audio continues as though the sight of the three of us was too intimate to stay with.

For the next two weeks, the world revolved around Na Fei. Shawn was the closest, holding her on his body in the baby carrier or his strong arm. I orbited next, preparing bottles of formula and dishes of clumpy rice cereal, bringing up breakfast from the buffet so Shawn could stay sequestered with Na Fei in the hotel room. And my mother cared for all of us, fetching bottles of water and bananas, giving advice on burping and bowel movements, writing down the events of the day for her blog, the Granny Report.

Through all of this, I had a wretched cold, like a vise around my throat and cement in my head. Our second night with Na Fei, we decided that Shawn would stay with her in our room while I slept in my mom's room. Part of me felt guilty for getting an uninterrupted rest while Shawn got up with Na Fei when she cried — what kind of mother leaves her baby on their second night together? The kind of mother, I suppose, who makes sure her own needs are met as well as her child's. That quiet night in my mom's pristine hotel room, I got to be the daughter again, with someone fussing over getting me medication and tissues, making tea and conversation, squeezing my hand in hers.

Most new parents feel unprepared and overwhelmed in their first weeks with a new baby — I know Shawn was certainly hit hard by the double-whammy of love and responsibility that Lia laid on him. I, on the other hand, had a profound sense of familiarity and relief. Dressing Lia in her little outfits, washing out her cloth diapers in the toilet, feeding her bottles and pureed spinach took me right back to the sweetness that often flavoured my days caring for Joanna and Ben.

Not long after we arrived home, I found myself the lone conscious person in the house. Shawn had passed out on the couch, still getting over jet lag, and Lia was a champion sleeper, napping twice a day and sleeping most of the night, despite the time change. I remember doing a little reading, writing a blog post for our family website, feeling bored and lonely, and realizing with utter wonder that *my life wasn't over*. Here I was with a baby under my roof and I still had time for myself. I think I had believed, on some level, that there would be no Alison left once I became a mother. I looked into the huge mirrored closet door and thought, *I'm real. I'm here. I made it.*

Flow Exercise: Infusion

When we are in the middle of depression, illness, or burnout, or just emerging from these states, it's hard to truly gauge our ability to do creative work. We apply an arithmetic of scarcity that says, *Anything I add to my life will subtract from me* — from my time and energy, from my store of goodwill, from the identities I'm trying to nurture. If I take on something new, whether it's a job, a child, a course of study, a move, or a trip, there will be fewer resources available to me, and my capacity will diminish.

What we forget when we're making these calculations is that when we are doing creative work in service of our desires, there is a two-way exchange. The effort and positivity we put out comes back to us multiplied. We are happier, healthier, and stronger when we're doing what we want and love to do.

One of the ways I taught myself this new arithmetic of abundance was by doing Julia Cameron's *The Artist's Way* in the months after we arrived home with Lia. I wrote morning pages by hand in a pink striped notebook, I went on artist's dates, and I let myself dream and remember my imaginative, inspired self. And I learned that a little meaning went a long way to keeping me centred and filled up.

I also learned that caring for Lia didn't take nearly the toll on me that I imagined it would. When I was thinking about parenting in the abstract, anticipating the sleep deprivation, the expense, the huge demands a child would make, it made me very tired. But what I hadn't factored in was the particular person of my daughter. I gladly changed her diapers, fed her, and did her laundry because I loved her and enjoyed being with her. I had gotten so caught up in what I would have to do for Lia that I forgot about what she would do for me.

Set aside the idea of life as a pie to be divvied up, or even as Dr. Stephen Covey's fabled jar full of rocks, sand, and gravel. Instead, take a clear glass or mug and fill it with boiling water. Then drop in a teabag. Watch as the colour of the tea leaves spreads through the water. Let it steep for a good while until it's nice and dark. Then drink and enjoy.

The creative work you desire is like that teabag. Its flavour infuses and transforms what is already there, turning it from a ho-hum glass of water into a fragrant, sacred brew. Nothing is lost, and everything is gained.

8 Operation Hejira

Thursdays in Grosse Pointe are my day with the kids. Today, Melody and I take the frolicsome foursome on an outing to the Hands-on Museum, which requires a drive out to Ann Arbor and a packed picnic to eat in the museum lunchroom.

We take our time with each game and exhibit at the museum: building a house out of big foam blocks, touching animal skeletons, whispering into a parabola that sends our voices across the room. There's a platform where you can stand and lift a ring that forms a bubble cocoon all around you, and a full-size ambulance, and machines to test your strength and reflexes. The kids call out with excitement at each new discovery, and Mel and I grin at each other and join in like big kids ourselves.

In the afternoon, we decide to split up, and Melody takes the two older kids to the upper floors while I stay in the preschool room with Charlotte and Nico, where they mess about amiably. They put on vinyl aprons to play at the water table, load balls into a spiralling metal track, and share driving duties in the miniature fire truck. I savour the chance to watch them co-operate and build their friendship — and to sit down in one place for while!

On the way home, I press the day against my heart, squeezing out every drop of joy like juice from an empty grapefruit half. Add the fun of exploring a new activity centre to my sister's companionship and the cousins' exuberant play together, and I know that this, *this*, is exactly what I wanted from Operation Hejira. Thank goodness for the inspiration, which came way back before the kids arrived.

About the time that we submitted our first adoption application to China in September 2005, placements began to slow down. Based on timelines up to that point, we had expected to be matched with a child within six months, but by Christmas it was clear that we'd be waiting a lot longer.

As a treat for ourselves, we booked a trip to Florida in March for Shawn's birthday. His parents had towed their fifth-wheel trailer to a park near Tampa, and we joined them to play shuffleboard, lounge in the hot tub, and watch manatees at the wildlife reserve. One morning as we were walking the paths around the golf course, we ran into two couples — one young, one old — out for a stroll with a new baby. We chatted for a bit (everyone seems to know everyone in these parks) and the younger couple told us that they had taken some simultaneous parental leave so they could stay in Florida for a month. The grand-parents were loving the visit, and the parents were relishing the warm weather and company. Everyone looked smiley and blissed-out, even the baby.

And I felt like I'd just been seized in the bear hug of an idea —

We could travel. With kids. For months.

Later in the week, Shawn and I drove out to St. Petersburg and stumbled on the narrow finger of Passe-a-Grille Beach, only a few streets wide, a swathe of sand down one side and boat docks on the other. We ogled the Don CeSar hotel, known as the Pink Palace, a grand Jazz Era resort that stood at the entrance to the tiny peninsula. We were enthralled by the little vacation homes with their candy colours, second-floor balconies, and white picket fences. Shawn had forgotten his bathing suit, so we found a thrift shop and bought one for him. Then we spread our towels on the shore and started spinning out dreams for the future.

After our baby arrived and Shawn took time off work, we would book a little spot here in Passe-a-Grille with a view of the ocean. Every day we'd bring our darling to the beach, set up our umbrella, and watch her wiggle her toes in the sand. While she napped, we would sit on our balcony and drink *Cuba Libres*. I'd visit the Saturday morning market, and we'd gorge on fresh strawberries and whipped cream. Our suitcases would spill out adorable baby rompers, flip-flops, and a red bikini for me. The fantasy seemed outrageous and yet achingly possible.

At a certain point, we got so fired up with planning that we started wandering the streets looking at For Rent signs, stopping in corner inns and asking about rates and efficiency kitchens. We held hands and pictured ourselves with a squishy baby in a sling, out for a morning jaunt with nowhere to be, nothing to do. Boutiques, fishing piers, and outdoor art markets would be our daily scenery.

And just before we climbed back into our baking rental car, pleasantly worn out with imaginings and a little sunburned, Shawn looked into my eyes for a long minute and then said, "We're going to do this."

"Yes. We are," I said.

That was the day Operation Hejira was conceived.

When it came down to it, we didn't carry out our Passe-a-Grille plan with Lia the way we had envisioned it. We had enough on our hands with a three-week trip to China, and we needed to keep things simple and close to home while Lia recovered from the shock of leaving her caregivers and familiar surroundings and started to attach to us. But by then the idea of travelling with kids had expanded from a month on a Florida beach to a long-term lifestyle — we were finding stories of people who left houses and possessions behind and wandered through Europe, South East Asia, Africa, and South America on a permanent world tour, many of them with children.

We knew we had a long way to go before we could join them: deciding what to do with our house, figuring out the money piece, researching destinations. And most importantly, we wanted to adopt a second child and needed to stay in Ottawa for a few more years to do that. Shawn and I both agreed that Lia should have a sibling who shared her ethnicity and adoption experience (more backup, of course, à la *About a Boy*).

And I'd been hit with a yearning for a little boy. We were playing Ultimate Frisbee one night with friends, including a Vietnamese guy named Long, who was kind, funny, and athletic. Watching Long run around the field, teasing his teammates and making great plays, I thought, "That's what my son could be like." And I felt it in my stomach, something like infatuation, a warm, sugary fluttering. I wanted a boy. We started the process to adopt a second child as soon as we were legally allowed to — it felt like there was no time to waste.

Lia proved to be a good traveller. We took her to Georgia when she was fourteen months old to visit Shawn's sister Denise and her family. Lia was excited by the bustle of the airplane trip and comfortable sleeping in strange rooms in her travel crib. She quickly won over her cousins and had them chasing her around the house while she screamed with delight.

Over the next few years, Lia became a veteran of road trips and family vacations. Okay, there was the night at Shawn's parents' place when she didn't want to go to bed and stood in her crib wailing every time I thought I had rocked her to sleep. And there were times on the highway when she behaved as though the car seat were a red-hot torture device. Heck, that was life with a toddler.

But we wouldn't know whether we could travel long-term as a family until we met kid number two. We had to know his needs and his personality before we could commit to making Operation Hejira come true.

The summer after Lia turned two, we got a referral from our adoption agency for a little boy with a round face and chubby cheeks. I was smitten at once, and the six months that passed while we waited for all the approvals from China and Ontario felt like an eternity. It's the strangest thing to have a child on the other side of the world whom you know almost nothing about and can do nothing for except pray and send care packages. My desire to hold him in my arms grew every day until it threatened to bury me.

Han Kun had cleft lip and palate, so he would need various surgeries and therapy in his first few years with us to close the triangle-shaped gap below his nose and help him learn to speak clearly. We would have to stay close to home for treatment for a while, but perhaps, maybe, we could get away for a few months while Shawn was on parental leave. Time would tell.

Shawn's mother Boukje came on this trip to China, as did Lia, who was almost three. Even though it was harder to travel with a kid who was entering the prime of her tantrum years, we just couldn't leave her out of such an important family event. We wanted her to see China again, to remember the sounds of car horns and Mandarin, the pungent scent of the street air, and the taste of steamed egg from when she was a baby. We bought her a pink rolling suitcase and prepared a stash of books and toys, wrapped in gift paper and ready to bring out at a moment's notice when she needed a distraction.

That February, we flew to Shanghai to meet our guide, Lily, and make our way to Nanjing, the capital of Han Kun's province. The first nights in our hotel were marked by the smell of rice crackers that Lia munched all through the hours when jet lag kept her awake. Lily took us to the top of the Pearl Tower, showed us the grounds of a Buddhist temple, and took our photos in the Zhouzhang water village. All the while, we were feeling odd about sightseeing when we were really there to meet our son. But how could we go to Shanghai and not visit the Bund?

In Nanjing, Lily got us the most wonderful hotel suite in all our travels before or since: two spacious bedrooms joined by an equally large sitting room and kitchen; two full bathrooms; desks, tables, and couches everywhere. Lia slept on a loveseat pushed up against the wall to form a little nook. And there was a crib ready and waiting for our boy, still a baby at fifteen months old.

On the appointed day, Lia put on her Big Sis T-shirt, and we went to the civil affairs office and watched out the window for Han Kun. This time, the room was silent and almost empty since we weren't travelling in a group of other adoptive families. Soon Han Kun arrived in the arms of his caregivers, apprehensive but alert, clutching a plum tomato in one hand and an onion cracker still in its wrapper in the other. He did cry when I held him, but quietly, and it didn't take much to calm him. His lip had been repaired the previous year, so now instead of a gap he had a reddish scar. I could have stared at him forever.

Once the papers had been signed and photos taken, we returned to the hotel. Shawn, Lia, and Boukje went out to get some food, and I stayed back with Han Kun. We sat together on the couch for a long time, him on my lap, his body in its puffy blue suit pressed against me. The only time he protested was when I pulled him off my chest, so I held him close and relished him, the way he melted into me and the tangy smell of his hair.

For dinner we went to a crowded restaurant nearby. I was ready to leave if Han Kun got overwhelmed by the stimulation, but after we arrived, he lifted his head and looked around. I held him on my lap, and he got very interested in the food, accepting mouthfuls of rice, vegetables, and pork from my chopsticks. He watched Lia's antics with a smile on his face and twisted around to see the bright twinkle lights in the window.

That night in our enormous bedroom where the two kids slept, I booted up my computer and sat down to do some editing for a client. Yes, I could have told him I was on vacation and I'd look at his document when I got home. But somehow, working from my hotel room in Nanjing felt like a momentous act. I was declaring to the universe, *I want this life. I want to travel and care for my kids and write and earn a living, all from the same room. I want everything to come together.*

It was only a guess, but even on that first day, I felt that Han Kun would be able to handle the kind of life we were planning. He didn't seem traumatized or neglected. He was showing curiosity and even delight in the new people and surroundings. We would still do everything we did with Lia to foster attachment — only Shawn or I would hold, feed, or change him for the first few months, and one of us would be home with him for the first year. But above the heads of our two black-haired children, my eyes found those of my husband.

We're going to do this.

While bureaucrats processed the paperwork needed to bring Han Kun back to Canada, Lily took us around Nanjing. She and I had many hours to talk in the van on the way to various attractions — the Nanjing Massacre Museum, Purple Mountain, the mausoleum of Sun Yat Sen — and we opened up to each other. Lily is an enthusiastic Chinese woman with rosy cheeks and unflagging energy, and I couldn't resist telling her our hope that we could come back to China in the fall. When I explained how we wanted to live in Beijing for a few months while Shawn was on parental leave, she practically knocked me over with a hug.

"I can help you!" she said. "I can find you an apartment. And Lia can go to kindergarten. You will love it here!"

Lily's excitement and promises of assistance just fanned the flames of my desire to take a little sabbatical overseas. Beijing was a far cry from Passe-a-Grille Beach, but the big cosmopolitan city, with ancient and modern side by side, suited us just fine. In fact, as the site of these momentous early weeks with our kids, it was beginning to feel like a second home.

We said a tearful good-bye to Lily in the Beijing airport and promised that we would see her again soon. I don't know whether she believed us, but I knew we would do our utmost to make it happen.

In the months after we arrived back in Ottawa with two kids under three, writing saved me.

This time around, I was staying home first, and Shawn went back to work. Lia was in daycare three days a week, and Nico was with me constantly when he wasn't sleeping. I had fallen for him hard, so the days were sweet: carrying him on my body in the sling; feeding him a bottle while gazing into his eyes; teaching him to walk and learning the games his caregivers had played with him, like bumping foreheads and nodding thank-you. I spent hours rocking him to sleep, wedging him in my arms and swaying back and forth or pedalling my foot while we sat in the pink recliner. But much of the time I felt like a stick of rock candy that was being sucked at and worn down with love, and I needed some way to replenish myself.

As a matter of survival, I went to bed shortly after Nico fell asleep at night. This felt like a quietly rebellious act — ignoring the dishes and phone calls that needed to be made, even the lure of television or conversation with Shawn, and sinking directly into blissful unconsciousness. And as I caught up on rest and shifted my circadian rhythms, a window of solitude opened up in the mornings before anyone else in the house stirred. I would wake up, often before my alarm at 5:00 a.m., alert and eager for a little time by myself. Then I would curl up downstairs on the couch with my laptop and do another kind of dreaming, building back up the self that had been eroded by the exigencies of the day.

I set aside the novel I was writing based on my mother. The story had wriggled out of my hands for various reasons, and I had no idea when I would be able to pin it down again. So I turned back to the book about the boy who was bullied with a new angle; I was no longer writing literary fiction for adults, but a children's book — a middle grade novel for nine- to twelve-year-olds.

In hindsight, it's silly that it took me so long to realize that many of the stories I had to tell were for children. The majority of my characters were kids or teenagers. The one piece I did for my story collection *Brick and Mortar* that came the most easily, tumbling out in a few days, was about a four-year-old boy. I was still an avid reader of middle grade and young adult fiction, turning to the children's section of the library when I wanted comfort, re-reading old friends like E. Nesbit and Elizabeth Enright or discovering new authors like Sara Zarr and Garth Nix.

When I pulled up the old files that I had set aside during my depression, I found a new spark of life in the story now that it was being told by a ten-year-old for ten-year-olds. Before I plunged into the writing, I decided to plan out the story and characters more thoroughly, like mapping the route before setting out on a journey. My outline was only a one-dimensional guide to the complex topography, but at least I knew where I was headed and roughly how many words it would take to get there.

During the mindless moments of my day — pushing a stroller, rocking Nico, making applesauce — I called up the story of this boy, Jerome, and pored over it for new tributaries, bits of detail that I could add to my map. When things got hard — like the time it became clear that Lia was giving up her afternoon naps, or during and after Nico's palate surgery when he couldn't feed himself for weeks — I comforted myself with the prospect of those quiet morning hours when I didn't have to cater to anyone except the people in my head.

This was the kind of existence I had wanted to avoid during the years when I aspired to childlessness — being at the beck and call of two unreasonable beings whose need for me seemed bottomless. Now that I was here, it was just as difficult as I had imagined, and more so, and yet I was happy because I knew it would pass, and I had this novel like a flashlight, a narrow beam that promised I would make it out of the weeds, my artist's heart drawing me forward.

And there was one spectacular development. Way back in October while we were still waiting to adopt Nico, I had applied for a writing grant to finish the draft of my children's book. One morning in March, I left an oatmeal-smeared Nico in his highchair while I scooted downstairs to check the mailbox and found an envelope from the Canada Council for the Arts with the results of my grant application. I slid the letter out with a pounding heart and unfolded it just enough to read the salient words: *pleased, successful, best wishes.*

A fizzing eruption of joy in my chest — my writing was good, I would be paid to finish my book, we would have money to support us while Shawn was on leave. I kissed Nico's sticky cheek, bounded over to the phone, and punched in Shawn's number at the office with shaking fingers.

"Hey," he said. "What's up?"

"We're going to Beijing!" I said. "I just got a grant and we're going to Beijing."

Beijing was our trial run for Operation Hejira. How would it feel to be away from family and friends for three months? Would we miss our house and our routine? How would the kids handle the change, and could we manage them on our own in a foreign country? Would we have fun or feel lost and homesick?

I had a few fuzzy cell phone conversations with Lily about making arrangements to get visas and find an apartment. She assured us we could get a two-bedroom for $500 a month, but as the date approached for us to fly out, we still didn't have a firm place to stay. We were moving forward in complete faith that Lily would come through for us as she had before, going above and beyond to help us with paperwork snafus and special outings. If she said she'd find us an apartment, I believed she would.

I updated the packing list from our adoption trip with a few additions: travel crib for Nico, potty seat for Lia, folding double stroller. Shawn registered for parental leave benefits through his employment insurance. We found housesitters — our friend Andrew and his Chinese wife Sula who had met in Yangshuo when he dropped in to her café and stayed to help out and fell in love. Andrew offered to drive us to the airport in their minivan, given that we had more than a trunk's worth of luggage, and while we were piling bags in the back seat on the morning of our flight to Beijing, he said, "Aren't you nervous?"

The question caught me off guard, coming from someone who had done more than his share of international travel, who supported himself through various entrepreneurial ventures, including the best hot dog cart in the city of Ottawa, who just a few years before had sold his own house and furniture to be with Sula and their child-on-the-way in Yangshuo. I did a quick body scan, looking for the vibration of nerves, maybe light-headedness or fear-induced nausea, but I came up empty. Instead, there was the rock-solid satisfaction that, after years of being the quiet rebel, I was declaring to myself and everyone else who I really was: an explorer with a pen in one hand and a toddler by the other. And pogo-ing on that foundation, a wild excitement promised to carry me right over the ocean, airplane or no.

Good thing too, because our first week in Beijing was no picnic. Lily showed us one (tiny, grimy) apartment that my unreasonable optimism convinced me we could live in, but the owners got cold feet on renting to foreigners. We bounced from one hotel room to another while Lily searched for something else. We suffered through interminable nights of jet lag, multiple showings of *My Neighbor Totoro*, and Lia's deteriorating commitment to potty training (you've got to admire a kid's stubbornness when she struggles and shrieks, "I don't have to go pee!" just before letting loose).

And then, Lily did her magic and delivered: a clean two-bedroom apartment with sunny bay windows near a subway stop for $500 a month. The owner was another adoption trip guide who also had a new baby and was going to visit her family — Lily convinced her to stay away a bit longer and got her train tickets when none were available. We arrived and set down our bags gratefully, and Lily took us to the police station to register as foreign residents and helped us stock up at the local grocery store.

In the absence of all our commitments back in Ottawa, we soon settled into a cozy routine. On weekdays, Shawn took the kids out by himself to explore, manhandling the double stroller over narrow sidewalks and high curbs, carrying it up and down the subway stairs because the elevators always seemed to be out of service. I had a technical writing contract plus a novel to write, so I stayed behind to work amid the din of drills and jackhammers from the constant construction and renovation in our building and beyond. On weekends, we went together to the enormous Beijing parks and wandered the paths for hours. You could find everything from kiddie rides and flower displays to line dancing and flocks of brides getting photographed at Ritan or Chaoyang Park, two of our favourites. We enjoyed the break from our usual schedule and felt rich with time to play and relax.

Without an oven or a pantry full of specialty ingredients, cooking became very simple: stir-fry or pasta. I felt so liberated from the complexities of my old recipes and menu planning. We also visited a small neighbourhood barbecue restaurant every week, always ordering our pork skewers *bú là de* (not spicy), getting plain rice and dumplings for the kids (Lia was in a phase where she only seemed to eat white food), and trying new dishes like lotus root and corn fritters. Even with beer and orange juice, the bill only came to seventy yuan (about $10).

Through another adoptive family in the city, we found an *ayi* who would come to babysit the kids and clean our apartment twice a week. That meant Shawn and I could go out for meals of hotpot, shop for clothes at the fashion market, and have uninterrupted conversations before coming home to floors scrubbed clean of the Beijing dirt that filtered in relentlessly. Lily also got Lia enrolled in a preschool class, so she spent her mornings in a pack of other Chinese kids, shouting songs and rhymes in Mandarin and being doted on by her teachers.

I staked out early mornings as my time to work on the bullying novel, just as I had when I was home with both kids in the spring. If I got my writing done first, in a quiet apartment with a clear mind, then I was content to do contract work for the rest of the day. My goal was to add 333 words to the draft in each session, filling the spaces in the outline I had created, discovering new developments for my character Jerome. I hadn't enjoyed writing fiction this much in a long time, maybe ever; the story was a pleasure to spend time with, and I felt confident in my ability to make it good. No surprise that I was able to finish the draft that year.

Towards the end of our three months in Beijing, Shawn showed me online photos of a resort in Fiji and another on the southern Chinese island of Hainan. "Don't you wish we could keep going?" he said. "Fly down somewhere warm instead of going back to Canada?"

"Yes, I do," I said. I'd hardly given a thought to our house on Nepean Street, and I had been talking to friends and family even more than usual. The only thing I really missed was the library — I was making do with the books I'd brought with me, and a few that I'd chosen for their length had turned out to be duds. If only there were some way to get any English book I wanted in an instant!

But back to Canada we went. Our trial run had been a smashing success, and we returned ready to do everything necessary to travel long-term — at least two years, maybe as many as five. We figured we needed about a year to prepare. When we got home and I felt overwhelmed by the volume of stuff in our house after living in a simple apartment, I created a spreadsheet and listed out each room and what needed to be done — rip our CD collection, sell my big *Oxford English Dictionary*, sort through the mountains of paper in the study.

I clicked the button to save the spreadsheet file and realized it needed a name. What would capture the sense of adventure, of pilgrimage and art and the unknown, the thrill and melancholy that we had felt in Beijing?

Road trip, I thought. Joni Mitchell. I placed my fingers on the keys and typed. Operation Hejira, here we come.

Flow Exercise: A Dream to Catch Meaning

Why do we invent dreams for ourselves to chase? Why did I decide that I wanted to be a writer? Why did Shawn and I set our hearts on parenting adopted children? What was Operation Hejira for?

Eric Maisel talks about *meaning containers* as structures that hold the meaning we create each day. We do little things — writing for half an hour, filling out a form, saving a spreadsheet — and our dreams collect these actions and give them shape and purpose. Without a container, our minutes and hours might seem to dribble away, wasted, but when we have something larger to catch them, they add up to something grand and purposeful.

A bigger story holds all the little scenes together and helps them make sense. When I have a dream at hand, I can find all kinds of things to fill it with: a quote from a book, a song on the radio, a snippet of someone's biography. The world pulses with signs and symbols, fragments laid out for me to discover. Meaning containers can be a powerful stay against depression. Dreams are not just for future pleasure, but to give weight and value to our present.

I love how so many of my dreams are sparked by other people's stories. Friends who adopted from China years before us. The new parents we ran into on the golf course in Florida. *The 4-Hour Workweek*. A blogger sending her kids to preschool in Penang. Something I see clicks together with my own latent desires and suddenly there's a dream bucket at my feet, waiting for me to pick it up and begin filling it.

When a dream fails, does the bucket tip and spill? I know it feels like that sometimes, like our meaning is lost when we have to give up on a beloved goal or activity. But a more hopeful way to see it is that our bucket has sprung a leak, and we can pour our meaning into a new, more solid container. What we did and learned can now serve a new dream.

What dream are you carrying to hold your meaning? Create an actual container for this dream: a notebook, a treasure box, or a Pinterest board. In the next few days, notice when you do or find something — an idea, a picture, a quotation, a book or blog, a task for you to do — that feels extra meaningful because it's serving this project. Add these things to your meaning container and notice how they build your faith and joy in your dream.

9 Loved and Lost

"The ship is safest when it's in port, but that's not what ships were built for."

— Paulo Coelho, *The Pilgrimage*

These two months in Grosse Pointe have zoomed by, despite my efforts to slow them down by paying acute attention to each moment. Melody and I have ticked off nearly every item on the list we made at the beginning of the summer: visit the Eastern farmer's market, go to the zoo, spend a day at Greenfield Village. During all the meals and driving and trips to the playground, Mel and I have gorged ourselves on conversation, and the roots that connect us — our shared childhood, our love of books and music, our common motherhood — have thickened and tightened, pulling us together like two trees planted side by side. The intimacy is almost painful since we know that we will be separated soon.

Shawn and I have spent our working days in the church basement where it's cool and the Wi-Fi is strong, and we've accomplished a lot.

He wrote a research proposal for his old company, finalized matters from the house sale, and set up our international bank accounts. I've been coaching clients, editing technical papers, and digitally scanning the last of our important documents.

I have also started writing another book — as though I don't have enough going on. I had planned to do a weekly newsletter about our first year of Operation Hejira, a real-time chronicle of events. Then, in June, I met up with a book-designer friend, Michelle, and she had a vision for something deeper and more crafted. A beautiful book that would take people along on the journey with me. A book in which to pour the story of my recovery from depression and the design of my art-committed life. Part memoir, part travelogue, part personal development. After many discussions with Michelle and Shawn about the project's potential, I've produced an outline and drafted a first chapter that holds real promise. I love the idea of combining my writing and publishing ambitions with my coaching work and our family travel. Looks like the middle grade novel I wrote in Beijing will have to wait a little longer for its next revision.

A week before we are to leave Grosse Pointe, my brother Ben arrives for a visit and brings me a package from my mom — the journal that we've been writing in and passing back and forth for the past fifteen years. The book has a brown cardboard cover with a black cloth spine and hammered metal inset, and we've filled the pages with photographs and alternating sections of our handwriting. I came up with the idea of keeping in touch this way just before Shawn and I moved to Calgary; the journal seemed more special and permanent than email, an object to tie us together. My dad and I have a journal too. We've written in the books less since the kids came along, but every so often, at significant moments, we add an entry about what we mean to each other.

That night, I take the journal to bed with me, our too-small double bed with sheets askew that sits on the floor without a frame. Shawn lounges next to me, engrossed in *A Game of Thrones*. I take a moment to re-read some of the earlier journal entries: Mom's account of my birth; a snapshot of me as a toddler hiding in the kitchen cupboard; the story of our first camping trip together when I was in my twenties; the letter I wrote pleading for her to get treatment for her depression.

I page to her newest entry and read about how she loved our visit together in Grosse Pointe a few weeks ago, how her heart sank when she had first learned of our plans for Operation Hejira but that she has come realize that we are following our dream and that she's happy for the experiences we'll have as a family. She's looking forward to Skype chats and photos and stories about our adventures. Then I come to the final section.

"I've left the hardest part for last," it says. My neck prickles.

As I read the next two pages, the phrase "rebuking in love" comes back to me. My mom means to be helpful, to set me back on the right path. I've been on the receiving end of her admonishment before. When I was a kid, she told me I shouldn't be reading books about magic and romance novels or listening to rock music, even Christian rock. When I was a young adult, she and my dad questioned my decision to live in Toronto after I graduated university instead of moving back home because of the cost and the difficulty of finding work. I always used to be careful not to do things my parents disapproved of (at least, not openly) to avoid this awful feeling of shame and intrusion. And they've mostly been supportive, although sometimes disappointed, since I got married and started going my own way.

Now my mother is concerned that my priorities are all mixed up. "I feel you are putting your work ahead of God and your family," she writes. She's unhappy with how I handled her weekly visits in the spring, when she would drive an hour from Westport to spend the day at our house. "When I used to come to Ottawa on Tuesdays, I thought we would spend time together, but you wanted me to cook and babysit while you left to write." She also thinks my children are hard to look after because I'm not doing my job as a parent.

In an instant, I go from pleasant fatigue to agitation, and my tears are pure animal hurt. *She still doesn't understand me,* I'm thinking. *She doesn't get how God and work and family are so bound up together that I couldn't separate them to put one ahead of another.* Maybe she doesn't know how much my writing and coaching mean to me — even the contract work that pays our bills. And somehow she doesn't see that Operation Hejira is about spending *more* time with my family.

I let Shawn read the pages and start defending myself in quiet, urgent tones. "She isn't distinguishing between her feelings and her opinions," I say. Of course she has every right to tell me that she is hurt and disappointed about not spending time with me on the Tuesdays she came to see us. But to say that I'm putting my work ahead of God and my family feels like a leap too far. I can't believe she wrote these things in our special journal. How can I possibly leave them there for my kids to read someday? I'll have to cut the pages out and decide what to do with them later.

What stings most is the shard of truth buried in her disapproval. I do want to get away from my children sometimes. Their loud voices, their demands, the frenzied play and uncontrollable emotions. When I'm in the grip of a creative project, like this memoir I'm writing, I find it hard to be completely present with them — my mind is elsewhere, working out conundrums and imagining new scenes. But I know that about myself, and I try to accommodate for it. That's why I've worked part time while they've been young, that's why I'm taking them travelling so we can go on adventures together.

Shawn is angry. He wants to email my parents right away and tell them how much Mom's words have wounded me, but I won't let him. I need time to sort out my feelings and decide how to respond. I don't want to get mired in emotional drama, especially not if my mom is in a manic phase of her bipolar disorder. And the fact that that she is not displaying her usual sensitivity tells me that is a very likely scenario.

But I do not turn my mother's criticisms on myself as I once might have when I was depressed, when anyone's disapproval became fuel for my own self-hatred. Instead, I feel a kind of force field protecting me, made up of the truths I know about myself: that I am loving and responsible and doing my best to take care of myself as well as my family and clients.

I go to sleep wrung out with little-girl sadness at having fallen from my mother's good graces, but proud that I haven't broken in the tumble.

I don't remember exactly when my mother first slipped into mania. Sometime after we adopted Lia, Mom came out of a depression and kept feeling better and better, and of course we were all happy that she was doing so well. But she just kept rising, like a runaway balloon at the fair. I noticed that she was making a lot of new friends and coming up with schemes for helping people, having epiphanies about what had gone wrong in her life. She was spending more money and commenting a lot on Facebook. When we got together, she talked nonstop about herself and couldn't sit still.

I didn't know what to do with this new mother. Yes, I was glad that she wasn't depressed, but I found her a little overwhelming. I had come to terms with a mother who was withdrawn and unavailable, and I had the sympathy to sit with that mother and love her. I cherished the times when she was present and steady, when we met each other as equals and could have intimate conversations. But this pinball of a mother, who shot from one idea to another and hardly noticed whether I was following along behind? Who blurted out whatever came into her mind, all of her judgmental opinions and private diffi-culties? She was a stranger.

While my mother was manic, I had my feelings hurt and asked her to back off on more than one occasion. To be fair, her behaviour was mild compared to some of the stories I've read about people with bi-polar disorder who gambled away life savings, became sexually pro-miscuous, or drove family members off with vicious outbursts. In fact, Mom's personality would have been within the realm of normal for a generous and gregarious extrovert, but it was not normal for the mother I'd known my whole life.

I think my memories of this time are fuzzy because, with a new baby in the house, I had to detach from my mother to focus on my own life and family. I didn't have the time or energy to track her ups and downs or try to take care of her. I do remember one visit when Mom was particularly wired. She chattered at me in the kitchen while we prepared coffee and snacks — she had so many anecdotes to share that she kept interrupting herself and doubling back. All I could do was nod and try to keep up. I had a feeling that I could have vanished under her nose and she wouldn't miss a beat. When we went back to the living room, she couldn't slow down enough to focus on the kids.

Mom decided that she needed a carrying bag for her new laptop, and she insisted that we go to Mountain Equipment Co-op that day to buy one. My dad and I took her, and it reminded me of herding a puppy, just trying to keep her contained. She told the sales clerk all kinds of extraneous information, paced back and forth between vari-ous options, and mostly ignored our suggestions. When we got home, she rushed ahead of us into the house and Dad and I came behind, exchanging a look that parents might give each other when they are overwhelmed by their impulsive children.

When the visit ended and Mom swirled out the door, I was re-lieved to be rid of her whirlwind energy. I missed the version of her that was calm and thoughtful, who listened compassionately and responded with measured wisdom. I felt like I had worked so hard to become friends with that mother, to forgive, trust, and appreciate her.

Then my mother crashed. Hard.

In a few weeks, she went from chatting up strangers on the street to hiding in her bedroom. She deleted her Facebook account. She stopped taking phone calls. And finally her doctor identified the extremes of bipolar disorder. I was relieved to learn that the manic version of my mother was not going to be permanent.

Mom cycled through high and low several times. I thought she would get on lithium and that would even things out, but the medication side of things was complicated: there were antipsychotics, antidepressants, mood stabilizers, and combinations thereof, and everything had awful side effects like grogginess, weight gain, and stomach pain. I had a hard time keeping track of what she was on — I didn't like to ask because it was none of my business, and it seemed that every few weeks she was switching up her regimen.

Mom seemed to like being manic, and maybe that was part of the reason she wasn't stabilizing. She said she enjoyed the way her brain sparked with ideas, everything seemed meaningful, and she could stay up for hours working on projects and reading her Bible. Every time the mania reemerged, she told us that she could manage, that she could keep herself from spiralling out of control.

But with each episode, she only fell deeper into depression afterward. During our last Christmas together before Operation Hejira, she had the worst episode she'd ever experienced. She didn't want to be with family for the holidays, but my siblings and I organized all the food and accommodations, and she came with Dad at the last minute. She could hardly speak or be in the same room with us. The grandchildren were mostly oblivious to her distress, but it triggered my memories of looking after little Ben and Joanna when Mom was incapacitated, trying to shield them from her sadness.

In January and February, I felt helpless to do anything for her — I just waited out the cycle, hoped she would come back, talked to my dad to get updates. What a relief when she recovered around March! She was still quiet and shaky, but we could have a conversation. As we moved toward summer, she was more and more herself again, and we had a sweet visit in June when I went alone to Westport to take my parents out for lunch for their birthdays.

And now, with this entry in our journal, it looks like Mom has tipped the other way again, towards mania. Damn.

The days slip away, and it's time to leave our makeshift flat for good. Farewell, little closet under the stairs. Farewell, front porch. Farewell, kitchen with spotty Wi-Fi. Farewell, Grosse Pointe, with your beautiful parks and libraries and Saturday morning markets. This time next week, we'll be on an airplane to Hong Kong and the hard-core travel portion of Operation Hejira will begin in earnest.

On our way out of town, we stop at Melody and Ben's place one more time to return the sheets and towels we borrowed and have a bite of lunch. Melody is out with the girls, so Ben makes us grilled cheese and pickles. Lia and Nico have one last play with the toys they're leaving here.

Then we hear the metallic creak and bang of the screen door opening and snapping shut.

Melody has dropped back in to pick up a forgotten something. She left Isabelle and Charlotte in the van so the kids don't have to go through good-bye again. I can hear her rustling and murmuring in the hallway, and I hold my breath, wondering whether she'll come into the dining room or just slip out again.

She comes.

I can hardly look at her face, with its mix of love and pain. We hug each other one last time, press kisses against cheeks, and then she's gone.

I've left a little surprise for her, though. A shoebox labelled "Sister Detox Program" is filled with presents and mementoes for her to unwrap one day at a time: a picture book called *Tell Me Some More* that we used to read as kids, a necklace that matches the one I've worn all summer, except that it has the word *labyrinth* framed in its pendant. And I've promised to email her every day for a month as we wean ourselves off daily contact with each other.

We drive away from Grosse Pointe with Nico sobbing in the back seat, "I want to go home!"

"Which home do you mean?" I say, noting to myself the oddness of having to ask this question. I may know that my home is inside me, but children have their own definitions.

"With, with, with Isabelle and Charlotte! And God's Kids and my froggie lunch box!" he says. He cries for a long time.

We are all learning the cost of Operation Hejira, the sadness when we leave a place and people we adore. We can never re-create that little era of summer in Michigan, not even if we come back. Is it better to have loved and lost? For me, yes. For the kids, I don't know. How many times can they get attached to something and have it taken away without suffering permanent damage? Will they learn to weather endings better because they are followed by new adventures? Perhaps, for all of us, the colours of this season are brighter and sharper because of the ups and downs.

I think of my mother hours away at her house in Westport. We've exchanged a few emails — I told her that I was hurt by what she wrote, but I'm not ready to talk about it yet. I've torn out the last few pages of the journal and tucked them into a pocket of my purse. I'm sure there's a way to work things out, that our relationship is important to both of us, but right now I can't see my way through the tangle of wounds and misreadings. A part of me is glad to be leaving so I don't have to face her. Another part thinks, *What a shame, what a shame for things to turn sour just when it's time for me to go.*

Flow Exercise: Hold Onto Yourself

The night I read my mother's journal, a phrase kept coming back to me: "Hold onto yourself." It comes from the work of David Schnarch, a marriage and sex therapist who teaches that an important task in relationships is to learn to *differentiate*, to maintain a sense of who you are and what you want even in the face of conflict. When you are able to soothe yourself and keep your self intact, you open the door to change and growth for you and your loved one.

This approach helped me a lot when Shawn and I were going through our various marital crises. The more I succumbed to the temptation to abandon myself to make Shawn happy, the more distance I had to put between us in order to keep from losing myself altogether (hence the parallel lives we ended up leading at Carleton). The lack of intimacy created more frustration and conflict. My Christian upbringing told me that I needed sacrificial love and empathy for Shawn to bridge the gap, but first I needed to define and hold my own boundaries so I would have an intact self to cross the gap with.

So "hold onto yourself" reminded me to wrap my arms around my edges and send love to all the wonderful and flawed parts of me instead of criticizing and rejecting myself for disappointing my mom.

Why is it important for artists to hold onto ourselves? Because that is where the art comes from — our ideas, desires, obsessions, and peculiarities. Our mistakes and patterns and enthusiasms. If we get too warped and compromised, we lose access to our source of truth and beauty, and that's when depression steals in.

David Schnarch doesn't call his approach *the crucible* for nothing. Holding onto yourself is damn uncomfortable. But it's also necessary for transformation.

Think about the last time you had a conflict with someone you're close to. Do you remember an impulse to disfigure yourself in order to make the conflict go away? Did you make yourself focus on empathy with the other person's feelings instead of owning your own? Did you try to get him or her to understand and affirm you? Or were you able to powerfully and gracefully state what you wanted and needed? (I often struggle with the graceful part because I'm so unpractised at being powerful. But I know it's possible.)

Now, create some art inspired by the conflict. Can you see that the inspiration and charge in what you make comes from your uniqueness? From the reactions that are sparked when your self encounters the other?

PART 3: MALAYSIA

10 Sick in Paradise

The day we fly to Hong Kong, I come down with a cold. Not surprising given all the germs that float around in airplanes and the depressed state of my immune system after late-night packing and emotional good-byes. The flight itself is fifteen hours, and then we take a train and a taxi to our matchbox apartment, and then we go back out in an effort to stay awake until after dinnertime. We are staying on a street populated by dried fish and seafood vendors, and Lia holds her nose and whines as we head toward the ferry terminal. I can hardly put one foot in front of the other, so it is lovely to sit on the ferry across Kowloon Bay and enjoy the breeze. After walking for ages, we find a pizza restaurant, and Nico falls asleep on his plate. Somehow we make it to the tram and arrive back at our place to collapse in bed around 8 p.m., by which point we have pulled the equivalent of an all-nighter.

I wake up at 1 a.m. with a woolly throat and clogged nose. Morning light is still hours away, but the kids' bodies are telling them to rise and shine, so I send them into the tiny living room to play with the toys in their backpacks. After an hour or so, they start fighting and hitting each other, so Shawn takes Lia into one bedroom, I take Nico into the other, and we try to get some more shut-eye. Nico is squirmy for a while but finally conks out and snoozes through until 9 a.m. What a difference from our previous trips to China! The last time we were here, the kids would wake at 1 a.m. and never go back to sleep.

On our first full day in Hong Kong, we need to be outside walking in the sunshine, so we decide to ride the funicular train up to the Peak and take in the view. The kids dance around the baking observation deck overlooking the slope of skyscrapers and sparkling water beyond. They write love letters to Isabelle and Charlotte and leave them fluttering there with hundreds of others. I struggle to breathe the hot, heavy air with lead-lined lungs, and the sun feels like it's beaming through a magnifying glass.

That evening, I catch my parents on video chat and show them our little apartment through the webcam — the minuscule kitchen and bathroom, the bedrooms that only have room for beds, nothing wider than a hallway but all the space we need to get over jetlag. I tell them about our trip, little things like how Nico walked into the Hong Kong airport and said, "Chinese! All my Chinese friends! They looked after me when my nose was broken."

My dad goes to work, and I'm a little nervous to be left alone talking to my mom. I can hear the overenthusiasm of mania in her voice. She commandeers the conversation now that he's gone, and I brace myself while she goes to find her notebook to read me a quotation from Charles Stanley.

"It just blew me away when I read this last night," she says. "'What the Lord plans for another person's life and how that other person lives out God's plan is the business only of the Lord and that person. We are to encourage and help others, but we are not the policeman of their plan and purpose.'"

My eyes are welling up, and it's not just the cold making my nose tickle.

"Ali, I'm sorry for trying to be the policeman. I hope you will forgive me. I think you and I are very different personalities, and we need to give each other grace for that. I can't be you, and you can't be me, and God doesn't want us to be."

I try to take a deep breath, but my congested lungs won't let me. "Thank you, Mom," I say. "That's very healing for me to hear."

She keeps going, reading more quotations, talking about how God has been speaking to her through her children, through the books she reads, through nature and animals. She makes me laugh by saying she's taking off her policeman's uniform and putting on a cheerleader's outfit with short skirt and pompoms. This is still not the mother I know, but I admit she's kind of fun. At the end, we hug our respective computers and say I love yous. I'm so relieved that she realized on her own what was wrong with her journal entry so I don't have to explain it.

I crawl into bed next to Nico snoring on his back and fall gratefully to sleep.

From Hong Kong, we are making our way to the island of Penang, where we will stay for seven months. Each morning for the next week, I wake up wretchedly sick and think, *I just need to make it through today, and tomorrow will be better.* I want to feel elated and gleeful the way I did when I got married and when I met Lia and Nico for the first time — *My dream is coming true! I'm living overseas with my family!* And I have moments of delight: riding a roller coaster high over the ocean at an amusement park in Hong Kong; eating an elegant breakfast buffet in view of a waterfall at the Sheraton in Singapore; watching Shawn and the kids swim in the hotel pool in Kuala Lumpur. There are quiet times when Shawn and I exchange a look that says, *Can you believe we're actually doing this?*

But mostly I'm hanging on, waiting for my body to get better so I can enjoy myself. My head and torso feel like they're encased in bubble-wrap. I develop a wracking cough, and my ears are completely plugged. Swallowing is excruciating. I'm starting to wonder what this cold means. Why do I feel like death right now when I'm starting a new life? And what can I do to make the suffering go away?

In Kuala Lumpur, I figure I've developed pneumonia because of the chest pain, so I go to the hotel lobby and ask the concierge to send me to a doctor in a taxi. The driver asks all kinds of questions about how I'm feeling while he zooms around looking for an open clinic on a Sunday morning — he declares that I need to drink more water. Soon we find a place, and an older Indian woman in a white coat ushers me into her office. More questions (in response to which I emphasize how long and severe the cold has been) and a listen to my chest with a stethoscope, and she prescribes antibiotics, antihistamine, cough syrup, and throat lozenges, all of which she dispenses from the clinic pharmacy. The whole visit, including my bag of medicine, costs forty ringgit (about $13). I'm really hoping that this does the trick because I am so over being sick.

We take the train from Kuala Lumpur to Butterworth, and I stare out the window, trying to absorb the reality that we are here in a tropical country surrounded by palm trees and temples. Lia gets bored with her toys so I download *The Penderwicks* onto my Kindle (in the middle of the Malaysian countryside!) and read to her, but I keep having to rest my scratchy throat.

Once in Butterworth, we hump our luggage over to the ferry terminal and ride the brightly painted boat to the island of Penang. At last we'll have a resting place — no more travel for a while. With the kids at this age, we're not interested in constantly wrangling suitcases and changing rooms every few nights. Instead, the plan has always been to set up house, get to know Penang, and do short trips nearby, more like an expat's lifestyle than a tourist's.

We wait at the ferry terminal to be picked up by a family we've never met. Tracy and Colin Burns are Australians, and we've been reading their blog, Our Travel Lifestyle, ever since they starting wandering South East Asia with their two kids, who are close to Lia and Nico's age. Their posts about life in Penang were what convinced us to make this our home base overseas — the low cost of living, great food, and access to Mandarin education for the kids.

When I emailed Tracy to ask a few questions about schools, she offered to host us at their house while we got settled. I'm nervous about meeting them, feeling like a poser trying to join this tribe of vagabond families that Colin and Tracy are part of. While we wait, Shawn goes to find himself a drink and comes back with a plastic bag hanging from a string and bulging with hot brown coffee that he drinks through a straw. The oddness of coffee in a bag cheers me up.

A dark blue minivan pulls up and a cheery Colin jumps out to help us stuff our bags into the vehicle. Tracy is a little tired — she's just arrived from Bangkok with her kids, Noah and Hayley — but there's still a twinkle in her eye. I sit way in the back and listen to six-year-old Noah chatter about Angry Birds video games and the trampoline in their yard. We drive through the congested streets of George Town, past malls built directly across from village huts, and finally along a winding seaside road that leads to the resort area of Batu Ferringhi. I'm surprised at how far Colin and Tracy's house is from the main city.

Looking out the car window, I'm remembering what that woman said at the garage sale in May, "Penang is my favourite place in the world." I can't quite see it yet. Maybe because I can't breathe, my head hurts, and I want to crawl into bed (the antibiotics aren't helping, so it must not be pneumonia). Again I wish that I could feel elated at the sight of colonial buildings, lush greenery, yellow beaches, and luxury condo towers, but I console myself that I can look forward to falling in love with the place gradually.

Colin and Tracy have a large two-story stucco house on a quiet street up the hillside. I can't believe they only pay $300 a month for four bedrooms and two bathrooms. They've made Penang their home base for now, but they still do extended trips in South East Asia and are planning a few months in Europe over the winter. Lia and Nico are in heaven with the masses of games and Lego in the play area and two other high-strung kids to run around with. We have a hard time herding them all off the trampoline so we can go to dinner at the hawker market.

I've been looking forward to eating out in Penang because I'm very excited about not having to cook so much. The hawker market at Long Beach is a big tin-roofed space filled with tables and chairs, surrounded by small carts advertising every kind of food: Chinese, Indian, Malaysian, and Western. The noise and the choices are a little overwhelming, so I'm glad that Tracy is there to help me navigate — she takes me around to the satay stand and the pizza stall, explaining that you order and give them your table number, and they bring the food when it's ready and you pay then. Shawn and Colin tuck into a few beers but I decline; alcohol will only make me sleepier. Instead, there's fresh watermelon juice and lots of bottled water. Nico munches his way through a fistful of chicken satay sticks, and Lia declares the pizza delicious.

The next morning I'm amazed to wake and find that everyone has slept past eight o'clock. We are close to the equator here, and the sun rises late. For breakfast, we head down to the main road for our first taste of *roti* — Indian fried bread with curry sauce on the side. I can't figure out the menu, as there are no English translations listed, but Colin explains that *roti telur* is made with egg inside and *roti pisang* has banana, both of which turn out to be chewy and delicious (the kids skip the curry sauce, of course). I order a hot sweet pulled tea that's comforting on my throat.

Tracy has arranged to show us a few apartments and take us around the schools today. She's a fount of information about where to buy groceries and where to take the kids to get out of the heat (the mall cinema shows cheap movies and one hotel has an indoor playground). I feel the effort of making conversation when I'm so dang sick, interrupting myself to cough and blow my nose every few minutes, but house-hunting is a good distraction. We see places in a few developments, making sure to check out the pool facilities, which to me are just as important as the living space! The apartments we tour through are nice enough, but Tracy thinks we can do better. She suggests that we see what's available at Miami Green, the complex they lived in when they first arrived in Penang. She tells me which websites to check, and I scour them for listings when we get home.

The schools we see are more promising. Public education in Malaysia doesn't start until age seven, so there are lots of private establishments offering lessons and daycare for younger children. One place we visit has a Montessori-based program for Nico with some seatwork and pencil practice, and a more academic program for Lia, with English, Mandarin, Bahasa Malaysia, math, science, and morals. The head teacher is an elegant Chinese woman, really lovely, and Colin and Tracy sent their kids to the same school last year, so we have a good recommendation from them. The cost for the two kids will be about $200 per month, and the program is from 8 a.m. to 1 p.m. every weekday. I arrange for a trial day the following Monday and cross my fingers that all goes well.

The next day, Tracy drives me to Miami Green, and I can't stop gasping with glee while she shows me around the network of pools — a wading pool! A bubbling soaker tub! A lap pool! A water slide! — as well as the weight room, the sauna, the squash courts. I can just picture myself lounging in the shade with a book while Lia and Nico splash and frolic in the wading pool. Yes ma'am, we've found our spot. Now we just need to choose which condo unit we'll call home. I see a bare-bones two-bedroom that looks onto the pool deck and a more comfortable three-bedroom next to the tennis courts, both less than half our mortgage payment back in Ottawa. Shawn and I will have to talk it over.

Colin and Tracy think that we need a treat after all this running around, so they take us and some friends to a beach-side barbecue restaurant for dinner. We settle into wicker chairs under a shady grass umbrella and the children take off to dig sand and chase waves. I decide to get crazy and order a whole coconut to drink. The sun sets over the ocean while I eat fresh *naan* bread and grilled lamb, listen to the lively conversation around the table, and sigh with something close to contentment.

"Tonight is payback for a year's worth of hard work," I say, and everyone beams.

Shawn and I debate which apartment to rent, the cheaper one by the pool or the pricier one higher up. I argue that we had a modest apartment in Beijing that suited us just fine. "I don't want to have the best place right away," I say. "Let's save some good stuff for the next time we rent."

One of the other dinner guests says that she would go for the more frugal option too — that is, until she hears that the other one has a gorgeous sea view. "How much more does it cost? Oh, that's totally worth the money. I'd put my writing desk in front of the window."

And of course, that settles the matter. We're getting the nicer place. Haven't I learned yet to go straight toward what I want instead of taking the long way around?

The agent has our new apartment cleaned and ready for us to move in the next day, despite the fact that it's a national holiday. He unlocks the metal lattice door to the entrance and the kids surge in to run through the rooms and explore every cabinet and alcove. I make a mental note of "Things in our Penang Apartment that I've Always Wanted": a view of the ocean, a gas range, crown mouldings, separate bedrooms for the kids, a pool, a front-loading washing machine. Oh, and the smell of incense wafting up from the shrine behind the parking garage.

What a joy to unpack our suitcases, knowing that we'll be staying put for months. Settling in Penang gives us the best of both worlds: the comfort of routine and our own space plus the excitement of a new city. We make several trips to Tesco and get provisioned with sheets and comforters, a laundry basket and drying rack, clothes hangers, and coffee mugs. Everything has a place in the custom-built closets and under-bed drawers, which provide triple the storage that we need. Lia spends an hour arranging the contents of her backpack on the dressing table in her room — hair elastics, jewellery, combs, pencils, and figurines, all in neat rows.

The next week, we start introducing the kids to their new school: a few hours on Monday, a day off because they're sick and cranky on Tuesday. Nico is unhappy when we drop him off on Wednesday, saying that he hates his friends and he's scared. He cries a few tears, but I have a feeling he'll be okay once he gets into things even though Lia is in a different class with the older children. I really want to get them settled so I can get back to work in the mornings.

Shawn and I head to the mall to print photos, copy birth certificates, and withdraw money for their school applications. Every little thing is so hard to do in a new place; for three days we haven't known where to get passport photos taken or printed, and when we finally find the spot, I feel triumphant. I have a strange fondness for that progression from bewilderment to discovery, which is a good thing because I bet it will happen a lot while we're here.

Nico is in a cheerful mood when we pick him up. I ask him how school was and he says, "Not good," but he doesn't sound like he means it. Lia comes out of her class with an air of mature self-possession and shows us her morning's work: three pages of the neatest printing I've seen from her and a sheet of math problems, well beyond what she was asked to do in her Canadian kindergarten. She's excited to start wearing her school uniform tomorrow, a dress with a lime-green pleated skirt.

I wish that moving into our apartment meant the end of my cold (I've been suffering for two weeks, isn't that long enough?), but instead, afternoon sinus headaches begin. My cough continues, deep and rattly, leaving me breathless with stomach muscles aching. At last, in desperation, I email to ask for help from my friend Bridget, a counsellor I met through my online network. I can't believe that this cold, which by now has turned into bronchitis, could possibly be a random thing. I'm sure there's something deeper happening, that my body is expressing something going on in my spirit and psyche.

Surprise, surprise, Bridget thinks that the crux of the issue is with my mom. Damn. I had hoped that our conversation in Hong Kong was enough to resolve things between us, but Bridget believes there's more to address. The clue is in my lungs, she says, which are the place in our bodies that carry grief and anger.

It's not hard for me to tap into those emotions again. Anger at the choices my mother is making around treating her illness, at her lack of understanding of who I am. Grief at losing her to the crazy highs and scary lows, at leaving her behind in Canada.

"By flying halfway around the world, do you feel like you're abandoning your mom?" Bridget asks.

This question makes me pause and sigh. "Yes, a part of me does. But I have to. I can't stay for her."

"Do you feel guilty over that?"

"Yes," I say softly. I have tried to ignore that guilt, but it's there. My mom's sadness about not spending Tuesdays with me in Ottawa brought it up all over again.

"Do you wonder what you did to deserve this situation? Like, 'What is wrong with me that I got a mother like this?'"

"No," I say right away. "I think, what did my mother ever do to deserve this? And what right do I have to have a better life than she does?"

Ah, there it is. The same pain of having more than my mother that came up in my work with Madeline. I may be willing to leave my mom physically, but it's not so easy to leave emotionally. I still want to look after her, even when I know I can't.

Bridget tells me to picture my connection with my mom as a cord coming out of my back. "We're going to release that cord so you can heal. Are you ready to let your mom stand on her own two feet?"

"Yes," I say, "I know I can't help her. But I'm still worried about her."

"I'd like you to understand that not only is she going to be okay, but she's okay right now," Bridget says. "The choices she makes may not be the ones you would make, but underneath she has a deeper, wiser layer."

I think about how my mom has been ill for decades, how she's been seeking healing all this time, trying so many things, going through cycles of hope and despair. I feel a key turn in my heart that floods me with compassion for her.

"You know what?" I say to Bridget. "I've judged my mom for not being able to get well, for enjoying the mania and not seeing the damage it does."

"Right. And it's important to remember that we only make choices that hurt people when we're really stuck."

"I bet she's drawn to being manic because it doesn't feel like being stuck, it feels powerful and illuminating." I have a flash of gladness that my mother has experienced momentum after being bogged down for so long. Realizing that I've judged her in the same way I felt judged by her somehow releases me from holding a grudge. And I can feel that unhealthy cord between us let go.

Bridget and I also talk about my throat, how the broken-glass feeling there means I'm pushing things down, keeping my truth locked up. I think about my memoir and how writing that book will bring out all the things in my heart, the stories of the last ten years that are hard to express. Bridget encourages me to tell my truth in lower-stakes ways too: in my journal, with Shawn and my friends. She calls me out for not wanting to burden other people or poison them with my negative feelings.

"You need to break this idea that you're alone in this world and you have to take care of yourself and be completely self-sustaining," she says. "Think of how you feel when your kids are scared and upset, you're that loving, swaddling mom. You give them the conviction and understanding that you're there to keep them safe. You have people in your life who are that for you, even if you're afraid of imposing on them. Recognize that you have those people. Then you'll feel better."

I think of how Colin and Tracy opened their home and helped us so generously, how Shawn has been patient and close while I've been sick, how Melody has sent me precious emails, and I know she's right.

I'm exhausted after two hours on the phone with Bridget. "You're doing such brave and great work," she says. "Now get a good night's sleep." The sun is just coming up on her in North America, and midnight approaches here in Penang. I love how we're connected over such vast distances, how the world is a place where there's space for people waking and sleeping, suffering and healing, raging and loving. Space for my mother and me to be who we are.

Before I go to bed, I pull a sheaf of folded pages out of my purse — my mother's words that I tore from our journal. I take them to the gas range, click the flame alive, and dip a paper corner into the fire. I turn and turn the pages until they have burned to nothing but an edge between my fingers. *I'm not carrying that anymore*, I think.

Flow Exercise: The Mother Wound

I know I am not alone in my struggles to make peace with my mother and all she represents.

In her article "Why It's Crucial for Women to Heal the Mother Wound," writer and teacher Bethany Webster describes the mother wound as "the pain of being a woman passed down through generations of women in patriarchal cultures. ... The mother wound includes the pain of comparison (not feeling good enough), shame (consistent background sense that there is something wrong with you), attenuation (feeling you must remain small in order to be loved), and a persistent sense of guilt for wanting more than you currently have."

This is the wound Madeline knew I needed to heal, even when I couldn't recognize it as the reason that I sabotaged my writing life and fell into depression. I was caught in what Webster calls the "double bind" between my mother and myself — "The daughter may unconsciously sense that her full empowerment may trigger the mother's sadness or rage at having to give up parts of herself in her own life. Her compassion for her mother, a desire to please her, and a fear of conflict may cause her to convince herself that it's safer to shrink and remain small."

I believe this is why I encountered Amma when I did, because I needed a mother God who understood my pain but wouldn't pass on her own. Amma could hold my whole self without feeling rejected or threatened.

The wound flared again when I became a mother to Lia. I still feared that having a child meant the obliteration of my self. I soothed the wound by continuing to write and look after my needs for rest and help while I cared for my new baby.

And this is the wound that required more attention in Penang. Stepping into a new adventure that took me even further from my mother and her path triggered pain for both of us.

Webster writes that, "The truth is that no child can save her mother. No sacrifice a daughter makes will ever be enough to compensate for the high price her mother may have had to pay or for the losses she has accrued over the years simply by being a woman and mother in this culture." I couldn't help my mother by staying home. But I could release my own guilt and grief so it didn't come between us.

Unsurprisingly, my encounters with the mother wound are often accompanied by physical illness — the bronchitis in Penang, the months-long series of colds that started in Beijing when we adopted Lia, and the depression itself. Even though I railed against being sick at the time, I'm grateful that my body showed me I needed to slow down, pay attention, process my emotions, and take care of myself.

I suspect that the mother wound is particularly problematic for artists, writers, and other creatives — those who are especially driven to self-expression and who are more empathetic and sensitive to others. I believe the wound manifests in resistance to doing our work and in choices we make that restrict our time and energy in the studio. As Webster says, "The mother wound is ultimately not about your mother. It's about embracing yourself and your gifts without shame."

Here's an exercise that Madeline taught me. It can stir up some powerful emotions, so it's best to do it with a therapist, a coach, or a good friend who can support you through the experience. Make sure that you are centered and steady before you begin by saying a prayer, breathing deeply, or simply grounding in love.

Sit in front of a mirror and look at yourself. Take time to rest your gaze on each part of your face. Notice what you love about yourself and what is hard to love.

Now find your mother in your face. What emotions come up for you? Let them wash through you — feel them to the depths.

When I did this exercise, I was so filled with shame that I could do nothing but cry. I couldn't find any part of myself that I loved. When I looked for my mother, I saw her in my tears. Her pain and my pain came together. And I found that I could love my eyes, slick and shining, because they told the truth.

Like me, you may find yourself walking the labyrinth of your life and circling around to the same places again and again. Each time, you grow further, reach deeper, gain more wisdom.

If the idea of the mother wound resonates with you, let yourself investigate your next step along the labyrinth's path to healing.

11 Rich and Lucky

"Pleasure is a brain wave right now. Happiness is a good story of your life."

— Deirdre McCloskey

Lying in bed on my thirty-eighth birthday, listening to Shawn and the kids make breakfast for me, I am hit with full-force sadness at the loss of my old life.

Back in Ottawa, our birthday tradition was to get fresh scones and Devon cream from a nearby bakery and make lattes with our milk frother. I'd get a tray delivered to my bedroom, where I sat cozy on my pillow-top mattress under the silk quilt we bought in Beijing. I can taste the cold clotted cream on my lips, imagine slurping the sweet latte and ending up with a foamy moustache that makes the kids laugh.

We had such a comfortable life with such nice things. Why did I give it all away in exchange for this lumpy pillow, these cheap synthetic sheets that are bleeding orange dye onto my pyjamas, this sad approximation of a breakfast with its chicken sausage and unfrothed coffee?

What kind of birthday is this? None of my friends are here to take me out for a drink. My parents can't visit to go for walks and order in Chinese food. I'm still bloody sick, and I hate the haircut I got in Grosse Pointe, and I'm tired of my own Pollyanna optimism that says everything is okay. Maybe this whole trip has been a wild goose chase after an idea of freedom that is just another form of deprivation. Maybe I've made a horrible mistake.

Nico starts crying about going to school the moment I try to get him dressed in his uniform. He sobs during the car ride and clings to me like a parasite when we walk into the building. "I hate my friends. I like *you*, Mommy. I love *you*!" he says desperately. I go through our little routine — put your water bottle in the basket, say hello to the turtle — but when I try to leave, he screams and grabs my leg. I kneel to give him a hug and he cries louder, clutching my clothes, and then vomits all over both of us.

The teacher gives me a box of tissues, and I clean up as best I can, then pick Nico up and get the heck out, ducking my head in shock and embarrassment. "We'll try again tomorrow!" I call to the teacher over my shoulder.

If we'd been in Ottawa, he would have skipped happily into the school daycare room with his sister. He already knew all the caregivers' names and couldn't wait to get his hands on the toys he'd seen Lia playing with all year when we picked her up. Instead, he has to get used to a strange new place in a different country.

We drive home in subdued silence. My heart aches for putting my son through this distress, and at the same time, I am anxious to get him settled in school so I can get back to work. I do have to admire the way he gets what he needs, though.

The afternoon is better. That's when we go swimming.

Oh swimming. Swimming has always been the holy grail of Hejira, from the sparkle of Passe-a-Grille Beach to the splash pads of Grosse Pointe and now the pool complex of our Penang condo. Swimming when Ottawa is frosted in snow. Swimming without grimy change rooms and taking the bus home with wet hair. Swimming every day. Decadent, sensual swimming.

I have a new red bikini, and Lia and Nico have several suits each so they can wear one while another is drying. I don't have to tell the kids twice to get changed, and they run around collecting flutter boards and goggles and floaties. We slip on our flip-flops, sling towels over our shoulders, and take the elevator down. We walk past one pool (the cold pool, so called because it doesn't get much sun) and climb the stairs to reach the big pool on top of the parking garage.

It's funny that *beach* and *pool* are our shorthand ways of identifying the good life because they mean warmth and recreation and luxury. Maybe we'll take it for granted in a few months, but today I feel very rich and lucky to have this pool. I don't have to test the waters — I plunge right into the blue. Nico is nervous about coming down the steps, so I pull him into my arms and sweep him around in circles while he shrieks and clings to me. What feels so good as a little boy with his fingers clasped around my neck, buoyed up by the benevolent water around us?

Shawn is that awesome dad who plays games with the kids, picking Lia up and tossing her into the water, doing dolphin dives while Nico rides on his back, pretending to be a sea monster grabbing at their toes. I watch them and grin and grin. This is what families were made for, isn't it? After a little while, I dry off and settle on a chaise while the kids putter in the wading pool. No shivering, no blue toes, just basking like a lizard in the heat. Shawn does laps, his broad shoulders and muscled arms sliding through the water.

We have nowhere to be except here. There is no checking the clock, no rushing off to another activity. Dinner will be a roast chicken from Tesco, jasmine rice in the rice cooker, and broccoli steamed on the cooktop. The dishes will be done in five minutes. Then we will put the kids to bed and watch the sun set over the ocean.

Okay, so maybe not a horrible mistake after all.

When we moved into our apartment, I asked the agent whether he could recommend someone to clean for us. He gave me Mariana's name and phone number and told me that we would need to have her come at least twice a week. Any less and it wouldn't be worth it for her. "Not a problem!" I said.

Mariana and I chat on the phone and arrange for her to come that Tuesday. She is familiar with our place because she cleaned it for the agent before we moved in. She tells me her rate per hour, and considering that it's about one quarter what I would pay a housecleaner in Ottawa, I'm happy to agree.

On Tuesday afternoon, I hear Mariana's cheery voice calling from the open doorway. She looks Malaysian although I learn later that she moved here from Indonesia. Her russet-brown hair is tied up in a ponytail, and she has a wide, bright smile. I like her instantly — sweetness radiates from her face. We walk through the apartment to go over what I'd like her to do: make the beds, clean the bathrooms, mop the tile floor.

Shawn has taken the kids swimming to get them out of the way while Mariana cleans, but she notices the toys and asks about them. "I have a son too!" she tells me. "He is 6 years old. Maybe I can bring him with me sometime."

"Of course," I say, "Lia and Nico love to play with other kids. Does he like to swim? Maybe we can take him to the pool."

"Yes, he would love that!" she says.

For the next two hours, I sit at the kitchen table and write while Mariana makes everything sparkle. She works briskly, straightening the bedding, scouring the shower, and cleaning the fingerprints off our glass coffee table. She even arranges Nico's books neatly on his headboard. We chat a little after she finishes; she saw our copy of *The Jesus Storybook Bible* and tells me that she is also a Christian, and we smile to have this in common.

"See you on Friday!" Mariana says as she leaves.

Yes, you will! I think gleefully.

We persist with school, and by Thursday Nico has turned the corner. From vomiting all over me at the beginning of the week to waving happily at the door when I leave, he's done his trademark quick adaptation. What a relief.

The moment I've been waiting for comes when we're at the pool again for our afternoon swim on Sunday — my ears pop, and all of a sudden I can hear the roar of ambient sound: bird calls, splashing water, the kids' shouts. The pressure in my head eases, and I can feel my sinuses starting to drain. Hooray! The ordeal is over.

I look around and spill over with joy at finally being well. The sky is peacock blue, and the warmth in the air is like a constant caress on my skin. At last I can get down to work.

Despite my short-lived birthday doubts, moving to Penang has reminded me that joy for this life is not just a feeling — I *am* rich and lucky. I am privileged to have the money, health, and freedom to fly to a country where my Canadian dollars buy so much more than they do back home.

Growing up as the daughter of a dentist, I learned early on that our family was rich and lucky. My parents took pains to explain to Melody and me that we had more money than others because they didn't want us to be braggy about what we had. They also taught us the importance of being generous — my parents gave ten per cent of their income to the church and made many other donations and gifts on top of that, often anonymously. So these were my earliest lessons about money: be grateful, give even more than you think you can afford, remember that being rich doesn't make you better than anyone else. Try to imagine what it's like not to be rich, and treat people the way you would want to be treated.

I also knew I was lucky to live in Canada, a safe, prosperous country where there were no wars or droughts or epidemics, where we had good schools and free hospitals. I was lucky to be book-smart, never worrying about a report card, basking in the teachers' praise.

And lying in bed at night at seven years old, contemplating the vastness of the universe, the miracle of creation and humanity, I felt lucky just to be alive and conscious, like I had won a cosmic lottery. I could have been a tree or a salamander or a virus, but instead I was a person who could think and learn and create.

In grad school, I started taking a hard look at my racial and heterosexual privilege. Being white and straight made life pretty easy — I could marry whom I wanted, I lived with people who looked like me, I had never been bullied for my skin colour or sexual orientation. It seemed that the only privilege I didn't have was male privilege, but although I understood the disadvantages of being a woman theoretically, I would have had a hard time claiming undue suffering because of it.

The lessons my parents taught me about money transferred to these other privileges: be grateful, use what you have to help others, remember that you're not better than anyone else. Treat people the way you would want to be treated.

I was never more acutely aware of my privilege than when we went through the process of adopting a girl born in China. The more I read stories from birth parents and adoptees, the more I realized what a power imbalance occurs in the act of adoption because of race, wealth, and social standing. I even heard adoption compared to colonialism and kidnapping. I saw my share of adoptive parents acting entitled and ignorant of their children's identity and losses, of birth families' rights. I saw my complicity in participating in an adoptive system that contributed to less privileged people being taken advantage of through financial incentives, moral grandstanding, and political influence.

My guilt and dismay at the injustices of adoption, especially international interracial adoption, had me seriously considering calling the whole thing off. Our application had already gone to China, but we could still pull out.

Then I returned to my parents' lesson: use what you have to help others. On a micro scale, if we withdrew from the adoption process, it wouldn't stop children from being adopted. But if we went ahead, we'd be more invested in making changes to the system. And we could do our best to give our children what they needed — love, belonging, honesty, connection to their birth country, nurturing of their gifts — as well as an unflinching look at all the dimensions of adoption.

If this sounds like a justification of doing what we wanted to do anyway, I'll freely admit that. But I came to see that living with my discomfort about the problematic aspects of adoption was part of my job as a mother. I needed to acknowledge my ambivalence without letting it stop me from enjoying my kids. And I needed to work for change on whatever scale I could by writing and speaking with people, developing relationships, and supporting other advocates.

Here's the tricky part, though. If I make an uneasy peace with being rich and lucky by using what I have to help others, how do I answer for putting so much of my time and resources into writing? Shouldn't I be doing something of more practical benefit, like my father's profession in health care, or more social good, like environmental activism? Because even though I've soothed my conscience with the idea that I can enjoy the benefits of my privilege as long as I'm helping, I secretly fear that I'm copping out, not doing enough.

I know I'm not the only creative person who has questioned the usefulness of his or her work. Some years ago, I read John Daniel's *Rogue River Journal*, in which he muses on the difference between his father's career as a labour organizer and his own vocation as a writer:

> "I like to think that in the long haul writing helps make a better world, or at least that it's essential to any good world, but that's a pretty hard claim to defend. It sounds suspiciously like a rationalization for doing what I want to do anyway, make satisfying wholeness out of language and get some attention for it. God knows I'm not in it for the money, but still, serving Beauty or Imagination may just be a dressed-up way of serving myself."

This worry about writing being frivolous and self-indulgent has often kept me away from my desk, trying to finish my more legitimate, paid, helpful work first. Part of me believed that if I treated writing like a second-class pursuit, less important than my job, family, and community, I could let myself have it without guilt. But too many years of that turned into depression, eroding my ability to work at all. Now I know that to be any good to the world, I have to write — it's the anchor of my health, energy, and positive outlook. It's like an inoculation against bitterness and despondency, effective even in moderate doses — the difference between life and death. Knowing that helps me claim my right to write.

The author Justine Musk has written incisively about the difference between pleasing and serving, which I think applies here. In her article "Service Is an Act of Leadership," she says:

"Pleasing is obligatory. Pleasers often feel they have to be everything to everybody. Pleasing can be its own kind of addiction: people will do it even when they're resentful, or tired, or on the verge of burnout. They're looking outside themselves to fill a hollowness within, which is always a losing battle. Service is freely chosen. Servers know you can't serve everybody, and don't try. They know who their people are and trust that others can find service elsewhere (from more capable and appropriate individuals). They also know their own value, and where the needs of the world intersect with what they offer."

So here I have to qualify my parents' lesson with a phrase from Frederick Buechner: use your "deep gladness" to help others. This is the irony, that when I was pleasing and giving people what they were asking for, I was really just trying to meet my own needs, as Musk says, "for approval, validation, control." But now, when I serve as a writer or mother or coach, I can give from a more generous place, "get outside of [myself] and address the needs of someone else (even if they themselves are not aware of them)."

My suffering and struggling doesn't help anyone else. Me giving up writing for something that looks more noble doesn't help anyone else. I can trust that those whose needs I can't meet will get them met elsewhere. The world is a big, bountiful, diverse place.

These thoughts run through my head when Mariana comes back on Friday. That echo of, "Who am I to sit here and write while she cleans my house?"

It's all well and good to talk about "deep gladness" to rich, healthy, free people, but what about those who are hustling to pay rent, who can't leave the house because of chronic pain, who are trapped in hopeless or dangerous situations? Is it demeaning or narcissistic of me to spend so much attention on doing what I love when others don't have that option?

Maybe. But again, me being miserable doesn't help. The vision I have of wholeness and health, choice and design, flow and joy, isn't something I want to keep to myself — I want it for everyone. Mariana and I might be at different places in the journey, but by God I hope we're both headed in the same direction.

So Mariana and I, we do our best to serve each other. We talk as friends. I take her son swimming while she works when she doesn't have childcare. She teaches me to cook spicy chicken stew. I pay her when she can't clean because she's sick or we're out of town. She takes us out for dinner to a seafood restaurant near her apartment. She and her son come to Lia's birthday party.

In short, I try to be generous while comfortably taking up the space I've been given, and I hope she does the same. And I am grateful that we crossed paths.

Flow Exercise: Claiming Your Artistic License

I imagine most creative types have had people in their lives discouraging them from the arts because it doesn't pay well, isn't respectable or important enough, isn't the highest use of their talents. Some of us get subtle hints, others get outright disapproval, even threats of banishment. I devoured books like *My Name Is Asher Lev*, *The Diviners*, and *Lives of Girls and Women* for stories of how budding writers and artists dealt with this kind of opposition from the parents and spouses they loved.

And I think it's common for us to turn these questions on ourselves in moments of difficulty, failure, or rejection, when a partner complains that we're not spending enough time with them, when we're scrambling to pay the bills, when a child sobs and clings to our leg when we try to shut the door. "Is this work really worth the cost? Does it matter enough to justify the sacrifices?"

When these doubts plague me, I remember two scenes in the lives of writers I admire. One is the picture of poet Donald Hall in his book *The Best Day The Worst Day*, faithfully writing in the chair next to his partner Jane Kenyon's hospital bed as she fought leukemia. He claimed his right to work even in these dire circumstances, this forbidding place. Jane also wrote poetry as much as she could when her health permitted. They wrote in the face of death because writing meant life for them.

The second scene is of Alice Munro babysitting her grandchildren so that her daughter Sheila could work on her memoir *Lives of Mothers and Daughters: Growing Up With Alice Munro*. Yes, the future Nobel Prize winner felt that her daughter's work was important enough to merit babysitting. No doubt she enjoyed the hours with her grandchildren and remembered her own years as a homemaker, stealing time for her stories. Sheila, in turn, allowed herself to take up that space, to accept that gift.

This is service. To the work, to the self, and to the world. This is life.

I'd like you to claim your artistic license. Could you let Alice Munro babysit for you? Could you write next to your partner's sickbed? Your right to write, to make art, to create, isn't granted by some external body — you bestow it on yourself. And that right comes from who you are: your gifts and talents, your desires, your personality, your personal history and culture, your need for meaning. You have the right to create simply because you are a creator.

Write or fashion an artistic license for yourself, whatever that looks like. The only requirement I ask is that you make this license valid for the rest of your life.

12 Recovering Workaholic

By mid-October, I am hard at work. Although many round-the-world trips are sabbaticals for the people travelling, ours is not. Shawn and I need to make money to continue funding our life, and I want to keep writing and coaching regardless because I love doing so. We have a cushion of savings that was padded with our house sale, but we don't want to touch that. Our airline tickets for the year were purchased with a combination of cash and Aeroplan points, which made them affordable. The cost of living in Penang is quite manageable compared to Ottawa: our monthly rent is about $700, school for the kids is $200, the rental car is $450, and we can easily get a week's worth of groceries for $75. So we don't need to rake in our full-time North American salaries, but we do need steady cash.

Although I plan to work less overall during Operation Hejira, there will necessarily be times when I'm working more. I've just had six weeks off, from the time we left Grosse Pointe until I recovered from my illness, so now I need to double down. I check in with a client in Ottawa to see whether she wants me for the same three-month contract I did for her last year. She emails to say yes, and I throw my arms in the air and bounce around on the bed! This is a big contract, as in *good-bye money worries* big.

I've also got coaching work to do: working with clients, writing blog posts and newsletters, doing social media, guest posts, and interviews to promote my business. The Internet is a wonderful thing for learning how to develop your services and market yourself, but there's also constant opportunity for comparing, and you can always find a dozen people who seem to be doing what you do, only faster and better. That contributes to a feeling that no matter how much I do, it's never enough. Sometimes I do all the right things but I don't get the results I want, and that's discouraging.

Between coaching and my contract work, I soon find myself glued to the computer from early morning until late at night. Because of the twelve-hour time difference between here and North America, calls with friends and clients often happen before 7 a.m. or after 9 p.m. Shawn looks after the kids every afternoon so I can put in more hours. Some days, I don't even leave the apartment.

I'm trying to remember when I started working long and hard. Not when I was young, certainly. Homeschooling felt like a three-year vacation, always lots of time to play music, read, knit, and do crafts because school work only took a few hours in the morning, and there weren't any awkward social scenes to negotiate (except for swimming lessons at the neighbourhood pool). There weren't really any hoops to jump through either — the only people around to impress were my parents and my sister.

But when I started Grade 9, all of that changed. Now I had a full load of classes with official grades that would eventually go on my transcript and affect my university admissions. I had new teachers and classmates that I wanted to dazzle with my brilliance since they weren't going to be won over by my charm or appearance. I quickly got recruited for extra-curricular activities — the yearbook teacher found out I had a typewriter and knew how to use it, and he had me type out the meaning of every student's name for the photo pages. A few friends persuaded me to join the volleyball team, which meant overnight sleepovers if we had evening practices or games. On top of all this, I caught a 7:15 a.m. bus in the morning and wasn't home until about 5 p.m. at night. Evenings were for housework and homework, and I started staying up later and later.

By my senior year, I had crammed in as much as humanly possible: I played Anne of Green Gables in the school play, I had the vocal lead in our youth choir production, I was yearbook editor and sat on student council, and I was fast-tracking by taking all the classes required to graduate in four years instead of five. No one was forcing me to do these things, so I must have developed a hunger for the pressure, the hectic pace, the validation of being in demand.

I do remember, in Grade 12, my friend David horsing around to celebrate the end of exams and dousing me in a water fight. Instead of joining in the fun, I just froze there with my face in my hands and started to cry and cry. I remember being shocked at how tightly wound I was and how it could come out like this in a surprising burst of tension and tears. Poor David felt awful and tried to comfort me while I sobbed that it wasn't his fault, I was just too stressed out.

And so the pattern began. Every few years I would move and get a blank slate: Hamilton for university, Toronto for a year of work before our wedding, Calgary for grad school, and then Ottawa. Each time, life would feel spacious for a few weeks or months until I started adding activities, committees, projects, friends. I was lousy at saying the little daily no, so the only thing that got me out was the big final no. *Sorry, I'm moving across the country. Sorry, I'm quitting. Sorry, I'm having kids and you'll have to find someone else to do that volunteer job.*

Workaholism seems to be the most socially acceptable addiction around. My gateway drug was the agenda notebook they gave out in high school, where I recorded all of my class assignments with little hand-drawn boxes to mark off with fat Xs. Then, before I knew it, I was at the office at 11:30 p.m. on a Saturday night before a product release, my eyes itching with cathode-ray fatigue, my brain running at half-speed as I tried to fix errors in documents without adding new ones. My left shoulder lit on fire every time I sat down to the keyboard. Between church and cohousing, I spent my entire Sunday in services, rehearsals, and meetings, wired on performance anxiety.

And no matter how hard I worked, I still thought I was lazy because I wasn't writing. I had a room of my own, mornings off, and no kids, so what was my problem? Never mind that I was trying to do complex, demanding work in the artistic equivalent of the salt mines. My spirit was weary, my imagination parched, and my intuition blinded. And the problem was not working hard, or being busy, or wearing many hats. People write books under all kinds of challenging circumstances. The problem was working hard on the wrong things, being busy with the wrong stuff, and wearing other people's hats.

I went through withdrawal symptoms for months after I quit my software job. From hyper-productivity, I crashed hard and struggled to do even an hour or two of work a day. The dread of making a phone call would wipe out my entire morning. Preparing a speech for a writing conference felt like water torture. During this time, I was grateful for Neil Fiore's book *The Now Habit: A Strategic Program for Overcoming Procrastination and Enjoying Guilt-Free Play*, which was so gentle and affirming in its approach. I started keeping an Unschedule, in which I blocked off times of guilt-free play and wrote in work periods after the fact — the very opposite of my high school agenda.

My love-hate relationship with work played a big role in my becoming a creativity coach. I was reading everything I could find about the writer's process — Dorothea Brande, Brenda Ueland, Anne

Lamott — looking for the secret to flow. I started working with a writing coach myself because I wanted so badly not just to finish a book but also to develop a sustainable writing practice. Cynthia Morris started me with the basics, creating a list of my twelve core values, including Truth & Beauty, Story, Persistence, Joy, Curiosity, and Community. Then we spent nine months experimenting with all kinds of tricks and techniques for supporting flow: cleaning and decluttering my studio, writing in different places and different times, examining my self-defeating thoughts in the light of day, writing love letters to my current manuscript. By the end of our work together, I was writing at least an hour every morning and had finished a full draft of my novel about the woman with chronic illness. I felt transformed.

Training as a creativity coach solidified the lessons I learned with Cynthia. As I read and studied the work of Eric Maisel and coached practice clients, the principles of a thriving creative life became part of the way I lived and breathed. When it came to my addiction to overwork, I saw that the combination of perfectionism and trying to prove my worth to the world was overriding my natural limits. I needed to reframe work as something I did for myself as much as others — a way of caring for myself, a source of meaning and joy, not just of money and approval.

I also recognized that working myself into the ground meant ignoring my body's needs for sleep, food, exercise, and non-thinking time. Living in my mind felt so much more important, a way to pretend that I almost wasn't human — just a brain in a jar. And of course, it was my body that called me back from the brink every time, through physical and mental pain and illness, insisting that I take things easier and stop stuffing my emotions into its hidden places. When my knee wouldn't stop aching, when eczema broke out on the middle finger of my left hand, when I had bouts of dizziness, I had to pay attention and get help.

This is where my ideas around designing an art-committed life emerged; I couldn't pretend any longer that my creative work lived in a vacuum, separate from my body and career and family. Everything affected everything else, and I wanted my life to support my writing rather than competing with it. It wasn't just a matter of being more disciplined and trying harder — I needed healthy conditions in which to create.

Becoming a parent was another evolution in this lesson. Nothing slows you down and removes your dependence on accomplishment and the life of the mind than spending all day with a baby. Gradually I came to enjoy the rhythms — walking for hours, playtime on the floor, constant snack breaks, the quiet of afternoon naps. Everything took longer and had to be done over and over again, and I learned to find meaning in my moments of connection with Lia and Nico rather than in climbing the ladder and ticking off boxes.

In the months leading up to Operation Hejira, I was once again in hyper-productive mode, but it felt very different this time around. I had little resistance or fear around writing, promoting my business, or preparing for our trip, just lots of enthusiasm and energy. I did wonder whether I was going to crash, but I seemed to be getting as much back from my work as I gave, maybe more. Instead of feeling bored and drained at the end of the day, I was pleasantly tired and full of joy.

But eight weeks into our time in Penang, I see how easily I slip back into old habits.

Despite being in the perfect place for chillaxing — warm climate, clear schedule, interesting city to explore, kids in school half time — I can still override the conditions and work too much because of the pressures of needing to make money and build my business and because the grooves of workaholism are inside me, not just in the hectic North American environment I left behind. The constant summer weather means that I'm not naturally prompted to go into hibernation mode come October. It's like having the ceiling lifted on my time and energy, but instead of wisely distributing those benefits, I concentrate them all in one area (work) and neglect other areas like play and exercise and family connection.

In November, I get many reminders that life is off-kilter. I haven't worked on my memoir in two months, not since I finished the prologue on the flight to Hong Kong. We've hardly done any sightseeing in Penang. The kids often beg me to spend time with them, and I keep putting them off, handing them over to Shawn. I'm feeling a lot of anxiety about the timelines I've set for various business projects. I'm not in flow. I realize the engine I needed to launch Operation Hejira is still revving, and I need to turn down the throttle intentionally.

Once I read the signs, I realize that there's no way I'm going to waste our time in Penang chained to my computer. Shawn and I talk over our options and decide that it's time for a proper getaway.

He starts researching the Thai islands just north of us, and when he learns that some Canadian friends are planning to visit Koh Lipe with their two teenage boys, that settles it.

Koh Lipe is the tropical island on the travel brochure. The little patch of palm and sand in sapphire-blue ocean that you can only reach by speedboat ferry. So tiny it doesn't even have cars. To get there, we throw swimsuits and snorkels into our bag, drive to the terminal in George Town, take a ferry to the nearby Malaysian island of Langkawi, and then a taxi and a speedboat to Koh Lipe, all in the course of half a day. I find it ludicrous that this idyllic tropical island is just a weekend trip away from our everyday life in Penang. For tourists coming from North America, a visit to Koh Lipe would be a long-planned and elaborate trip; for us, it is almost an afterthought — "Oh, I suppose we could go to this little paradise for a few days."

We arrive at Pattaya Beach, where chalky sand glitters emerald under the shallow water, broken up by dark green patches of coral. There is no landing pier, so a longboat comes to meet us and transfer passengers and baggage to shore. The kids are excited to jump into the water when the boat hits the beach, and the white sand feels like talc squishing between our toes. This is definitely one of our more pleasant border crossings!

We clutch our luggage and the kids as a motorbike with sidecar transports us along the concrete laneways to our resort. We splurged on an ocean-front cabin (well, splurged — it cost $95 per night) because when will we get to stay on a gorgeous Thai island again? Lia and Nico are thrilled with the square little swimming pool abutting the beach, but I can't wait to get into the ocean. I haven't been snorkelling since we went to Puerto Rico seven years ago, and I want to explore the coral and fish life right outside our door. I tempt the kids into the shallows to try my mask and snorkel, but Lia sees something moving under the water and boots it back to shore.

My chance comes the next day, after our friends arrive. Their two boys play with Lia and Nico in the pool while Shawn and I head off into the surf. We swim toward an islet just offshore, and as I float over the coral and watch clownfish dart out of anemone and parrotfish nibbling the reef, it strikes me that snorkelling is a kind of meditation. I hardly have to move, borne up by the sea and nudged by the current. My breath naturally becomes yogic *pranayama* as I take in air long and slow through my snorkel.

I think of nothing while the underwater beauty draws me forward. It's only when I raise my head to get my bearings that I feel the need to make an effort, to get somewhere. And the minute I dip back down again, I'm at peace.

This is the quality of flow I want to bring to my writing. When I think about my travel memoir, which Michelle and I have named *Pilgrimage of Desire,* I feel tired and adrift, like I can't get my feet under me. The upset with my mom and weeks of being sick took the wind out of my sails. There's new pressure on me to make money since Shawn's contract work has slowed down. And I have my own workaholism to contend with. I can't even begin to get my head around how

I will write about what happened with my mom in the summer, even though I know it's an essential part of the story.

I can see the book a ways off, but I don't know if I have the stamina to reach it. What seemed like an exciting sprint a few months ago is now a long-distance swim. I'm thinking about turning around to let the onshore breeze carry me back to a quieter easier life, with more glasses of white wine and *massaman* curry and less salt water in my nose, fewer buffeting waves and menacing rocks.

But as the warm water surrounds me, I realize that's the old way of looking at work — as an exhausting struggle fuelled by willpower, an epic battle against resistance. I remind myself that flow is all about surrender, the open hand, using resistance as a friendly guide to show me what I need to release.

I need to drop my head below the surface of my writing, stop trying to get somewhere and just be drawn along by the words. A few minutes of breaststroke tires me right out, but I can snorkel for hours. And when I'm rested and confident, I'll be able to dive deep enough to unearth the shipwrecks and treasure that are waiting for me.

Flow Exercise: The Irresistible Current

In 2005, when I was in the iron grip of workaholism at my software job, I read Steven Pressfield's book *The War of Art: Break Through the Blocks and Win Your Inner Creative Battles*, and I thought it was the answer to my problems. I'd been struggling to get a book done for years, flogging myself as a lazy undisciplined procrastinator who didn't have what it took to be a writer.

And here came Steven Pressfield with this demonic portrait of Resistance with a capital R, which had all this time been hell-bent on stopping me from writing. He compared Resistance to predators like the Alien, the Terminator, or the shark in *Jaws* — powerful, unreasonable, and destructive, focused solely on preventing creation from happening.

I wanted to believe that there was a force outside of me opposing my every creative impulse, because then I could stop fighting myself and start fighting this universal enemy. Even if it meant buying into a lifetime battle.

I found it reassuring to learn that a bestselling author and screenwriter was constantly combating this terrible malevolent force because it meant there was nothing wrong with me. I was ready to turn pro and redouble my efforts in a life-and-death match against Resistance. Beat my chest and rattle my sabre! Never take my eye off the adversary!

But to my surprise, Resistance grew stronger the more I fought. I was even more tired and discouraged. War was not a happy place to live. I needed a new metaphor, and I eventually found it in the irresistible current of flow.

"What makes a river so restful to people is that it doesn't have any doubt. It is sure to get where it is going, and it doesn't want to go anywhere else," writes Hal Boyle.

I needed to stop trying to push the boulders out of the stream and just slip effortlessly around and over them. Sometimes that meant finding the path of least resistance — probing around a project until I located the easiest way in. Other times it meant switching channels when I reached a dead end. Always it meant being willing to go forward in uncertainty, risking imperfection and failure. I was still putting effort into my writing, but instead of that effort meeting an immovable object, it was just speeding me along, like a kayaker paddling through whitewater.

Now I believe that when I take care of myself and design my life to support my art, I couldn't escape the flow if I tried. I get drenched in inspiration. Words pour out of my fingers like rainwater from a spout. I get up early, stay up late, whatever I need to do in any circumstance, because I love my work like crazy. And it loves me back. My books *want* to be written.

I would like you to lay down your arms and wave a white flag to end the war of art. Find some running water — in the woods, the park, the bathroom. Surrender your hands, your feet, your whole body to the current. Feel its insistent power, the way it chases itself headlong, plunging along in thrall to gravity. Name each of your rocks of resistance: "I'm afraid of wearing myself out. I don't know what project to choose. What if someone gets angry with me?" Then let resistance be engulfed in the flow.

13 Hybrid Mom

In the weeks after our trip to Koh Lipe, I'm trying to ease up on my hours at the computer, but it's hard to counter the momentum of work. I'm scrambling to finish my contract job and website updates before the Christmas holidays, when we plan to spend a few days in Kuala Lumpur. It's one thing to have an epiphany while floating in the ocean, but it's another thing to create that feeling of peace and flow in real life.

At one point I get stuck in the bathroom when the deadbolt breaks. Shawn and I hammer at the metal frame from both sides but it's no use — we have to call a locksmith. Shawn slides my Kindle under the door and takes the kids out for dinner while I enjoy several hours of empty alone time, free from my to-do list and the relentless pressure to make headway. I'm almost sorry when the locksmith arrives on his motorbike and releases me from my hermit's cell.

I never thought I'd be a working mom. When we were preparing to adopt Lia, I disliked my paid work so much that I assumed I would use motherhood as an excuse to give it up, at least until she and her future siblings were in school. Why shell out for daycare to do a job I didn't want to do?

At least, that was what I thought before I experienced the realities of seven days a week, twenty-four hours a day with a toddler who was more headstrong than an untrained Rottweiler! Yet another reminder that, when it comes to building a life with kids, you can never assume anything. The ground is constantly shifting.

After his six months of parental leave with Lia, Shawn went back to work full time in August, and although I would miss his company and the tag-team parenting while I worked from home, I was excited to set up a fun fall program for Lia and me. On Tuesdays, we went to Chinatown for swimming lessons and ate pork buns on the walk home. Wednesdays, we had story time at the library. Thursdays were for playgroup at the Chinese Alliance church. Other days we did grocery shopping, went to the park, and walked by the river. I was relaxed, and we were having a blast.

But by November, Lia was approaching eighteen months old and headed for a perfect storm of toddler misery: a bad cold, the time change, teething, wintery weather, and a surge of separation anxiety. Our once docile girl now spent her days screaming and crying, making irrational demands ("Give me a bottle! But you can't put me down to make it!"), clinging, biting, scratching, hair-pulling, waking frequently at night, and saying no constantly. Two days out of three, Shawn came home to both of us in tears and the house a disaster.

Once I was up with Lia in the middle of the night because of her teething, and I got so tired from pacing the room with her in my sling that I tried sitting down on the floor. She started crying immediately. I stood up. She stopped. I sat down again. More crying.

"Are you fucking kidding me?" I said. "I'm not even allowed to sit down?"

And that's what full-time parenting felt like — that I wasn't allowed to do seemingly harmless things to make it easier on me. If I took Lia for long walks in the stroller, she'd fall asleep, and then I'd miss being at home for the precious naptime, or else she'd wake up when I tried to transfer her from stroller to crib. If I left her in the high chair with a snack while I went to washroom, I'd come back to screaming and food thrown all over the kitchen. If I let her watch kids' videos so I could take a shower or make a phone call, she'd throw a tantrum when I turned the TV off.

On one hand, I knew this process of separation and asserting her selfhood was an important developmental stage for Lia, and I appreciated the chance to grow a stronger, unconditional love for her that embraced the light and dark, the easy and challenging days. But at the same time, I was spent. No, more than that, I was in deficit. I was overdrawn on energy and good temper.

One night, I went to yoga class with a few other mom friends, and one of them told me about her childcare arrangement: her son spent three days a week in a small homecare at a cost of $45 a day. I swear the clouds above were parted by angel's trumpets when I heard this — it sounded heavenly. "I want that!" shouted the part of me that needed some quiet and solitude before I went nutty. Working would feel like a vacation compared to the physical and emotional challenges of looking after an eighteen-month-old.

So I started searching the Internet, and in a miracle of perfect timing, I found a spot in a newly opened homecare ten minutes' walk from our house, run by a wonderful woman who had worked as a certified ECE caregiver in larger daycares. Grace was willing to take Lia three days a week. Lia got new toys, new friends, and a stable attachment with a caregiver, and I got respite from the demands of motherhood. She started in January, just a few months shy of her second birthday.

I remember a moment on Lia's first day. To get Lia acclimatized, she and I only stayed for an hour with Grace and the other kids. We all went for a slow snowy walk around the block, and I could feel the anxiety roiling in my chest: would Lia be okay? What if she felt sad and lonely? What if she had a tantrum? Was I being derelict in my duty if I wasn't there for her all the time?

Lia was toddling happily ahead of me, holding onto the stroller while Grace pushed. I took a deep breath and decided that I wouldn't worry until there was something to worry about. With Grace, Lia was safe and loved, just like she was with me. She made no fuss when we dropped her off in the mornings. She had other kids to play with and fun activities to do. Letting her go to grow up a little more was part of my job as a parent.

From then on, Shawn and I did a better job of creating a hybrid life that combined good proportions of work, family, and leisure. When Nico arrived, we each took six months of parental leave, and we kept Lia at Grace's house three days a week so Nico would get some one-on-one time with us. When we got home from Beijing, Shawn went down to four days a week at his job so he could spend an extra day with the kids. That change in schedule made him really happy. We'd been focused on saving money before the kids came, but now we reconciled ourselves to having less income during these fleeting early years with them.

My writing is also work that takes me away from my family. The fact that it's not paid work makes it harder to prioritize, but I keep trying. I've been doing regular overnight writing retreats since Lia was little, booking a room at a hotel or retreat centre and writing for two or three days.

Before we left Ottawa, I got into the habit of actually leaving the house in the early mornings to write at a local food court, because if I was in the house, one or both of the kids might wake up and insist on my attention. Many mornings, I returned home to full-blown crying or got a call from Shawn asking me to come back early. I know it won't hurt them to miss me sometimes — they learn that they're okay when I'm gone and that I always come back. It's distressing to me, but it's the price I pay to be a working mother, to have a whole life.

And of course, my decision to work isn't a one-time choice — we are constantly recalibrating as the kids get older and our careers ebb and flow. The freedom and flexibility of remote freelance work is wonderful, but it also places the responsibility on me to get the mix right, to manage my workload and step away from my desk to be present with my family.

I do worry about working too much: that secret fear my mother exposed in her journal entry. I know my personality — introverted, independent, with a focus bordering on obsession — makes me prone to treating the kids as an obstacle to solitude. I get a jolt of shameful panic when I realize I haven't thought about them when we're apart. I imagine bitter regret when they're grown up that I didn't spend enough time with them. I worry that, because of their early life, not always having care and attention when they needed it, that I'm retriggering them by working. I wonder whether they'll complain to their therapists about my absence and preoccupation.

And then I go back to work.

I can't get around the holidays, though — not that I would want to. This year, Christmas is very low key for us. Normally we would be negotiating visits with our two families, setting up a pine tree in our living room, and wrapping a closet full of presents. Instead, we spend a few days in Kuala Lumpur for a big-city vacation, and Santa pays a visit to our room at the guesthouse.

As with any trip with kids, there are highs and lows. We spend a day wandering through the twenty one acre bird park, admiring pea-

cocks and cranes, Asian fairy bluebirds and rainbow-feathered ma-
caws. We watch the Muppet movie at a glittery air-conditioned mall,
and we go to church at St. Andrew's Presbyterian. I love the strange-
ness of walking to a Christmas service in the hot sun, sitting in a
mostly-Chinese congregation and singing "Mary's Boy Child" and
"Feliz Navidad," eating spicy curries and watermelon in the community hall afterward.

We also have a disastrous Christmas dinner at a fancy Italian restaurant — Lia and Nico are too hyper to behave, and Shawn and I
both lose our tempers. At the Petrosains Museum the next day, we
enjoy the dinosaurs and petroleum exhibits, but the kids are pretty
wild and over stimulated. Nico barges in wherever he can, shoving
kids out of the way and running off on his own. At one point, he
slams my hand in a display by accident when I try to stop him from
spinning the panel.

We go to Kuala Lumpur City Centre next door so the kids can let
off some steam at the park. They are flushed and sweaty from tearing
around. I take Lia to the toilet four times and joke with Shawn about
getting extra pay for doing bathroom duty.

After the kids are in bed that night, I ask Shawn why we're not
having a good time. He says, "It's more like, we're not having a bad
time." Most of our day is spent herding the kids around, telling them
not to do things, shushing them in the guesthouse. Our goodwill gets
all used up, and it's hard to appreciate their energetic selves. Once
they're asleep, Shawn and I retreat into our books and computers for
comfort, so we're not really talking or connecting much. I think we'll
have good memories of this trip, it's just that parenting is still a lot of
hard work at this stage.

Christmas in Malaysia is just a minor holiday, though, with only
one day off on December 25. Chinese New Year is a much bigger
event, and school is closed for an entire week in January to celebrate
the Year of the Dragon. When I first realize this, I'm a little panicked.

We just had our Kuala Lumpur vacation, and now I'm losing another week of work? But I've made a resolution to take things slower in 2012 — my word of the year is Chillax — so I decide to really give myself over to the time off. I have no video calls booked because the time was marked as busy in my online calendar, and I start to get excited about a week away from the computer.

Lia is always asking me to play with her, and I'm often inclined to say no — playing doesn't come naturally to me. I get bored or impatient with make-believe games like hair salon, which Lia would play every day if she could. But this week I'm saying yes. She squeals and runs off to collect supplies: hairbrush and elastics, nail polish and clippers. Then she commands me to begin. I am the stylist, and she is my client, "Miss Miranda." I seat her on the stool and begin preparing her for the wedding she's about to attend.

The relationship between Lia and me is sometimes prickly. Her desires are many and deep. I can never give her enough of everything she asks for, whether it's candy, screen time, or attention. We are similar in many ways, starting with our incredible tenacity (one might call it stubbornness). We both have intense feelings, although she expresses hers loudly while I tend to suppress mine. We share a quick intelligence and love of reading — it's a delight to watch how she's picking up Mandarin at age five. She's very verbal and never misses a chance to argue, holding strongly to her sense of fairness. All this means that I love and understand her but don't always jibe with her.

My fingers massage Lia's fine black hair as I pretend to give her a shampoo. I ask about the colour and style of dress she'll be wearing, and she sits very still while I paint blue polish onto her fingers and toes. At the end of her visit, Miss Miranda pays me $10 and flounces off to attend the wedding, very pleased with her adornments.

When Lia was four, we saw a psychologist to help us deal with her tantrums, which were extreme and almost daily. One of the practices the psychologist recommended was *special time*, where we would spend twenty minutes doing whatever Lia wanted to do. This power thrilled her to no end, and the hair salon game was a frequent choice. We did special time faithfully for a while, but when Nico stopped napping in the afternoons, it became hard to fit it into the day. I'm glad for things like holidays and travel that make special time more common.

Nico still loves to cuddle and coo, touching foreheads and gazing soulfully into my eyes. He's an exuberant kid, always dancing, laughing, and making silly faces. He's also very thoughtful, often giving in to Lia when she's upset about something and making conversation with strangers when we're out. "I like your outfit!" he said to an astonished woman at church the other day.

Even though the kids have been in the pool almost every day, Nico is still not swimming on his own or even comfortable getting his head wet. Lia, on the other hand, has been gliding underwater since the summer in Grosse Pointe. So that week when we're at Tesco, I buy goggles and a set of earplugs for Nico. I'm hoping that the extra insulation against the elements will encourage him to be a little more adventurous.

I take Nico to the pool on his own, which he's very excited about — usually Lia and Shawn are there, but this time he gets Mommy to himself. I position his new goggles over his eyes and push the earplugs in, and we walk down the steps into the water together. I coax him to jump off the bottom step into my arms, and then encourage him to dunk his head under.

At first he isn't having it, shaking his head and whimpering, clinging to my shoulders. But finally I convince him that we'll do it at the same time, and I count, one two three, and we submerge together.

He comes up with a look of wonder on his face.

"Again, Mommy!" he says.

I count again and we bob down and up.

He is grinning his gap-toothed grin, and I am so chuffed that I finally figured out what would help him feel good in the water. We bob for a while, and then I ask if I can try swooshing him under the water like he's swimming. I put my hands around his chest and zoom him around, my little submarine. He comes up gasping and wiping at his face, begging for another go. "Again, Mommy! Again!" Ten more times, twenty, and he still isn't tired of the thrill.

Finally I put him on the bottom step and ask him to swim to me. "I'm so close, you just have to jump and I'll get you." He stands there, looking at me, fear and courage wrestling for supremacy, hugging himself (though not shivering, never shivering). And at last, he leaps, face scrunched, arms flapping, sinking until I snag him under the arms and pull him into a hug.

"You did it, Nico! Look at you!" I laugh in amazement that something so simple can be so intoxicating. How many billions of people have learned to swim, but here, now, I am watching this boy discover the wonder of moving through water. My heart wants to swallow him whole. "Wait till you show Daddy and Lia!"

Nico's wet face shines with pride. He plunges toward me many more times, and then he dashes over to the wading pool where he can bob and crawl and dive all on his own. I sit on the edge with my arms around my knees (though not shivering, never shivering) and bask in the joy he radiates.

The kids and I are lounging on the tile floor doing jigsaw puzzles while Shawn works out in the gym downstairs. I actually feel chillaxed — I'm not worrying about what else I have to do or itching to turn on my computer. Suddenly we hear loud drumming and cymbal crashes coming from outside. We go to the balcony and down below in the circular driveway is a lion-dancing troupe beginning their performance. They've arrived in two flatbed pickup trucks and everything is red and yellow — the flags decorating the trucks, the drums, the two shiny lion costumes trimmed with fur. We've seen these troupes driving around, and apparently they visit many of the large condo complexes during the week to bring luck for the New Year and rid the building of bad spirits.

Lia wants to run downstairs immediately, but Nico is nervous of the noise and the big lions. He hides behind my legs as we walk toward the condo entrance where the lions are cavorting. Each lion is danced by two people — one controlling the head and one bringing up the rear. Everyone has brought oranges to feed the lions, which they hold out in their hands for the dancers to take. The lions crouch down with the oranges under their costumes for a long time, and when they get up, they have peeled the oranges and arranged them into a New Year's greeting.

Then the lions head toward the parking garage, and their entourage follows. Lia's right in there at the head of the parade. They're going to the shrines next to the hillside to pay homage — one little Buddhist shrine and a larger Malaysian one next to it.

I love being in a place where it's so easy to celebrate Chinese New Year. Everything we need is in the markets and stores — lanterns and red envelopes and bamboo shoots tied in ribbons. You see decorations everywhere, in shops and homes and buildings. The kids' school has a party, and the city has a concert. In Canada, you have to make an effort to create your own celebration, and still it feels like a token. Here, everyone is celebrating, and you feel part of something larger.

Once again, our environment is a labyrinth, a support for the life we want to have. And my hybrid existence as a writing working mother is held up by daycare and school schedules, family routines, holidays, writing retreats, the needs of clients. Sometimes the structure is not strong enough, and I stumble into the daze of overwork or the strident need for time alone. But I keep returning to the labyrinth, adjusting the supports until they hold me securely again.

Our time in Penang turns out to be one of the most chillaxed periods of our life so far — certainly since the kids came along. Chinese New Year marks my turn away from hectic work to a more even pace. From our easy mornings getting the kids to school, to our always-clean apartment, to delicious meals out with friends, everything is humming along nicely. Shawn has made many friends playing Ultimate Frisbee. I love the hot weather, how it's simple and cheap to live here. Although we had planned to leave at the end of March, we extend our stay an extra month to take advantage of the lovely arrangement a little longer.

In fact, our plan is to return to Penang in September, after we visit our extended families in July and August. The kids will be able to finish out the school year that started in January, and we can move Lia to an international school or switch to homeschooling after that. We've only begun to sample the pleasures that Penang and South East Asia have to offer.

But all too soon, the end of April arrives, and our apartment folds itself back into a pile of suitcases and backpacks. The night before our flight to Singapore, Shawn has one last Ultimate game with his Penang team while Nico and I shop for warmer clothes for the next leg of our trip. May is springtime in Paris, but the weather will still be cooler than here.

The Ultimate team has arranged for us all to go to a food court as a farewell party. Lia insists on wearing her new skinny jeans even though it's sweltering. The group sprawls out on both sides of a long table, the sky dark, the fluorescent lights illuminating bottles of water and beer, plates of curry and satay sticks, piles of dim sum. Bedtime for the kids has long passed, but we stay for a protracted photo session cum good-bye, Lia and Nico on shoulders and balanced on hips for group shots, Shawn's teammates putting their arms around him, all of us trying to capture how we feel about leaving.

Flow Exercise: Life as a Prius

Thinking about all the different parts of my life, it's easy to feel like I'm being torn apart, pulled in many directions by the competing interests of art, family, and finances. Or like I'm one of those plate-spinners, trying to keep everything aloft at the same time by frantically running between them, dreading the crash that happens when any one area is neglected for too long. I start to think that I'm failing at everything.

But chopping my life up into pieces like that is a fallacy. I'm one person, not a Frankenstein mashup of writer, wife and mother, friend and coach and freelancer. I'm creating one indivisible life, and everything I am, everything I do, is contributing to that whole, not competing.

What if I imagined myself as a hybrid car that runs on gasoline and electricity?

There are times when I'm puttering around town, stopping and starting, poking along the back lanes and side streets. That's when I draw on the battery to keep me going. These are the times when I'm playing with my kids, sightseeing, doing yoga, reading a book, talking to a friend.

There are other times when I'm zooming along the highway, crossing long distances, making great time. That's when I start burning gasoline. These are the times when I'm writing and working, juggling clients and appointments, going to parties and networking events, setting and reaching goals.

Whatever I'm doing, my inner hybrid engine knows which energy source to draw on to keep me going, switching between them seamlessly. Maybe we could call those two energy sources yin and yang. They work in tandem to help me run efficiently.

Do you know the signs when your yin and yang drives are out of whack? Maybe your battery isn't getting recharged or your gas tank is running empty?

For me, I know I'm lacking in relaxed yin time when I'm cranky and forgetful, when I'm wired, anxious, and jumpy, when I snap at my family, and when I feel overwhelmed and have trouble sitting still or going to sleep.

It's more rare that I'm missing active yang time, but when I am (like after a vacation or an illness), I feel bloated and dopy. Life starts feeling meaningless. I lose confidence. I don't know what to do or where to start.

Does your hybrid engine need recalibrating? Try this. Go for a little trip using whatever energy you want to engage. So if you want more yang, take a zippy car ride at top speed, pedal your bike down a hill, or go for a run. If you want more yin, walk through a labyrinth, take a paddle in a canoe, or drive a slow winding scenic route.

While you're on this trip, invite ideas of how you can bring more of this energy into your life. What activities can you start or stop doing to feel more settled and in flow?

PART 4: EUROPE AND ONTARIO

14 Couchsurfing

Our flight to Paris leaves just after midnight, so we are entertaining the kids in the Singapore airport while we wait to board. This is not difficult to do in a place that boasts several nature gardens, a swimming pool, a movie theatre, and a napping room. But we don't have to go any further than the one-and-a-half storey slide in the basement of our terminal, which keeps Lia and Nico occupied for more than an hour as they careen down, whooping, and then dash back up the stairs. As our flight gets closer, I change them into their new warmer clothes, and they play horsey in a deserted waiting area, with Princess Lia riding on the stalwart Nico's back.

The two months we are spending in Europe this spring are the icing on the cake of our first travel year. Shawn and I have already made two trips there together, one in 1998 after I finished graduate school, and another in 2004 to celebrate Shawn's parents' fortieth anniversary. I got my first taste of jet lag on the hot streets outside Buckingham Palace, was charmed by the eminently civilized country of my husband's Dutch ancestors, and had a romantic whirlwind tour of Paris.

When we planned our Operation Hejira itinerary, we asked our-selves, what places can we absolutely not pass up? Where would we go if we only had one year instead of two or five? Malaysia fulfilled the tropical beach and Chinese cultural destination, Detroit was the un-missable chance to live near my sister and her family, and the Nether-lands was the heritage portion of the trip — the Old Country populated with relatives who hug us tightly and press us with drinks, sweets, and gifts.

Visiting the Netherlands will bring back memories of our twenty-something selves on our first backpacking trip, taking the high speed ferry across the channel from Harwich to Hoek van Holland, getting picked up very late by Shawn's dad's cousin Piet because the ferry lost one engine en route. I had picked up enough Dutch from lessons on tape to trade a few phrases with Shawn's *beppe*: I would say *"Heel mooi!"* and she would say, "Very nize!" We spent many hours in cafes and backyard patios and living rooms drinking tiny cups of strong cof-fee and chatting, then being toured around little towns and along ca-nals. I have a very special attachment to the place.

Since our round-the-world airline tickets require us to go through Paris, we've decided to spend a week there in a flat in the Batignolles neighbourhood and then rent a car and couchsurf through Normandy and Belgium. We've rented a vacation apartment on a farm just south of Amsterdam where we'll stay for another seven weeks before flying back to Canada in July. We are looking forward to really good wine, cheese, and pastries, and we can't wait to introduce Lia and Nico to their many aunts, uncles, and cousins. Living in Holland will be like coming back home.

On the Singapore Airlines flight to Paris, Lia and Nico fall asleep al-most immediately. I nap for a while too, wearing my hand-knit eye mask and wool socks. When I wake up, it's still dark, and to pass a few hours I watch a film called *The Vow* with Rachel McAdams and Channing Tatum. In the story, Rachel has severe memory loss after a car accident and forgets that she's married to Channing — he has to woo her all over again. A good airplane movie, just interesting enough to hold my attention. I appreciate the time to myself, which will be in shorter supply in the next few months since the kids will no longer be going to school.

At the end, the credits start rolling to familiar chiming chords — "Pictures of You" by The Cure — and almost before I know it I am crying, a full-on wrenching cry that grips my chest and floods out of my eyes. Gasping, heaving sobs from somewhere primal. Thank goodness it's dark and many people are asleep. "What is this about?" I ask myself, bewildered, and the answer comes instantly: "My mother." I don't understand, but I know. The music takes me back to high school and the words are of regret and longing, wanting to know someone truly and not just as they appear.

I have been calling my parents every week on my Sunday night, their Monday morning. They didn't ask me to, but I could tell they wanted me to. My mom's mental state has stabilized over the winter, thanks to a new psychiatrist and a new combination of medications. I still wanted to clear up a few things about Mom's journal entry to me last summer before I saw her again, so I finally sent her an email at the beginning of April. I told her that I was sorry she was sad about not seeing me more when she came to Ottawa to look after Lia and Nico, and that I hoped she would be more upfront with me about what she wanted in the future. I said that I thought some of our misunderstandings came from me not wanting to trust her with my thoughts and feelings because of her mania, but that now she was centred I thought we could have a good conversation.

I got a note back from Mom right away. She didn't feel up to talking about it in person, but she apologized for what she had written when she was manic. She said that she regretted hurting me and affecting our relationship. She wanted to keep the door open to share more of our feelings now that she was well.

I felt so relieved after this exchange, like I'd moved a big iceberg out of my way. I was free to look forward to seeing my parents in a few months without worrying about any awkwardness between us or having to pretend that everything was fine.

Now "Pictures of You" has triggered a physical release of all this worry, sadness, and desire for my mother. I don't try to figure it out, just let the tears take their course and then sit quietly in the dark, curled up in my airplane blanket, for a long time.

Our week in Paris has a strange duality to it. During the day, we wander slowly through the city, more like casual weekenders than tourists. The kids are not that impressed with the fancy museums and landmarks, but food and playgrounds are a big draw. On our first morning in the city, we head for the Eiffel Tower, but Lia is more obsessed with the raspberry tart we bought for our picnic on the Champ de Mars. Shawn and I sit on a park bench for an hour while the kids climb and slide and hang on the jungle gym. The lines to go up the Eiffel Tower are very long since one of the elevators is not working, so we decide to skip it and take a ride on a nearby carousel instead.

In the evenings, we go back to our little walk-up flat in Batignolles, put the kids to bed, and start working madly on our laptops. We are about to launch an online fundraising campaign for *Pilgrimage of Desire* to help pay for the design and editing costs. Shawn is assembling the footage that we shot in Penang to create the all-important fundraiser video. I am working with Michelle to put the final touches on the book preview, which includes the prologue and first chapter, and to set up the campaign page and website with all the copy and graphics.

After day trips to Montmartre and Canal St. Jacques, the moment comes to push the launch button on the fundraising campaign. I can't wait to show off the book to everyone I know, but at the same time there's a looming fear. What if the campaign fails? What if I make a public disgrace of myself? What if the project dies here for lack of funding? Is it worth the risk? Can I handle the thirty days of uncertainty, the stress of asking for help?

I take a deep breath, squeeze Shawn's hand, and click the button. Whatever happens, it will definitely be interesting.

Then I spend the next two hours until midnight obsessively refreshing the site. I don't want to publicize the campaign until a few contributions have come in to move us off the $0.00 balance, but I have emailed a few close friends and family. Still, nothing happens, and I go to bed agitated and nervous. "Amma, what's going on?" I ask.

"I want to show you how this campaign will unfold," She says. "You can't make it happen. You just put yourself out there and let it happen in your sleep."

Ah, that makes sense. This method requires less effort but more trust. I can try that. I hug my pillow and go to sleep.

The next morning, I wake up to happy results — two family members have given a total of $775! Now it's time to tell the world. Out go blog posts and emails and tweets. The fun is just beginning.

The time has come to leave Paris and drive through Normandy on our way to the Netherlands. On the train to Charles de Gaulle Airport, where we will pick up our rental car, I'm prattling to Shawn: *I love labyrinths. One of the most famous labyrinths is at the cathedral in Char-*

tres. Chartres is in France. I am in France! I could walk the labyrinth in Chartres! Wouldn't that be perfect for my book?

Shawn is more worried about making sure we get a good vehicle for the next seven weeks and navigating the highways than about visiting a labyrinth. But he says sure, we can drive through and check it out.

I do more research in my French guidebook. The Chartres labyrinth, being on the floor of the cathedral's nave, is usually covered in chairs. But on Fridays in the summer they take the chairs away so pilgrims can walk the labyrinth's path. Today is not Friday, but we can visit the cathedral and have lunch in Chartres anyway. It will still make a good story.

Our luggage is very heavy. We have two large suitcases, and even though they're on wheels, I can only pull one for short periods before I have to stop and rest. I've also got a heavy backpack and a purse and two kids to keep track of. We have a long walk from the train to the rental car counter. I sit and catch my breath and amuse the kids (reading and feeding always works) while Shawn takes his reservation to the attendant. There's a lot of conversation, and phone calls, and walks to the parking lot to check out various cars. Shawn is a car rental connoisseur, so I assume that he's trying to get the nicest vehicle he can.

Finally he comes over to tell me that, although he has prepaid extra for a car with automatic transmission, they don't have one on the lot. They want to send us back to their city centre location to get an automatic, which sounds like it will take a long time. We discuss the pros and cons of getting a car with manual transmission. Shawn is comfortable with a stick shift, and he'll be doing most, if not all, of the driving, so we decide not to make the trip for another car. Then there are more discussions about which upgraded model will compensate for the automatic we paid for. We finally settle on a roomy SUV with built-in satellite navigation.

Hours have passed by the time we load all of our bags into the trunk, install the car seats, and get everyone belted in. I punch in the address of our couchsurfing host. The satnav tells me that we will arrive in time for dinner if we drive straight there.

There goes my stopover in Chartres. Dammit. If this were just my trip, I would have planned it around visiting the labyrinth. But it's a family trip, and in planning around the family, I've forgotten to ask for what I want. Shawn has his heart set on seeing the sites of World War II, and we needed to book in with child-friendly couchsurfing hosts, and those items set the itinerary. By the time I remember Chartres, I've missed my chance.

Yes, I could call our host and arrange to arrive later, but honestly, between the cell phone connection and my fumbling French, talking to her last night wore me right out, and I'm not up to a repeat. Besides, when people are putting you up in their house for free, you don't treat the place like it's a hotel, arriving late at night just to collapse into bed. Conversation is the currency, and we need to ante up. I'm sad to give up my personal labyrinth pilgrimage, but hopefully the couchsurfing experience will compensate.

My hopes are not in vain. The satnav directs us through the French countryside to an old grey stone house. Sylvie and Nathalie are our hosts, a mother and daughter who have welcomed many travellers through the Couchsurfing.org website. We carry our luggage up the worn stone staircase to the second floor. They've created a custom guest room with a double loft bed over another double bed, so our whole family will fit comfortably. Lia and Nico climb the ladder to the high platform to discover a chest of toys.

We chat in the living room while Lia and Nico twirl and careen in the backyard after their day in the car. We mostly use English, even though I'm ready to try out my high school French — the women seem to gravitate to English so we can have more complicated conversations. I'm flabbergasted when they bring out gifts for the kids: art supplies and tiny toys, a flashlight shaped like a pig for Nico and some jewellery for Lia. They have lots of sightseeing advice for us: Nathalie works in a museum and has access to many brochures. We discuss Normandy and the war history and hear stories about their family's experience. We're up very late talking, drinking, and eating after the kids go to bed. There is unpasteurized cheese and fancy Belgian chocolate that they insist we try. I say yes to wine even though I'm tired because, heck, we're in France.

The next morning, we take our leave, promising Sylvie and Nathalie a postcard from Holland to add to their collection. Shawn wants to visit some of the old battlefields, and I need to catch up on some fundraiser work, so he drops me at McDonalds and I take advantage of the free Wi-Fi while he and the kids visit a site nearby.

Later we go together to Pointe du Hoc, an area of the D-Day assault that hasn't been restored to its pre-war condition. The bunkers and the craters created by the shelling are still there, overgrown with grass. The landscape is pockmarked with these hollows, and the kids treat them as an enormous playground, racing down the steep sides and back up again, playing hide and seek in the bunkers.

I think that we've been very lucky with our first couchsurfing gig to get such sociable, giving hosts, but if that's true then our luck follows us. Our next host, Antoine, is going to the opera the night that we arrive, so we try especially hard to arrive on time (and still fail, thanks to misguided satnav instructions that our host warned us about). Antoine is a grandfather, living alone, and he reminds me of my dad, so dapper and chatty. He gives us a quick tour of his colourful and eclectic house — he's surely something of an artist or at least an art appreciator. Then he leaves us to get dinner from the supplies in his fridge, strawberries and more cheese and crackers and sliced ham. Shawn and

I are a little astonished that he would turn over his house to our busy family of four, but such is the nature of the Couchsurfing community.

I've gotten a cold, which, on top of the travel and managing the kids and running the fundraiser, feels like one thing too much. I'm often up late writing email, composing updates and posting on Facebook and Twitter. I decide to run a promotion for Mother's Day and pledge to knit lace bookmarks for anyone who contributes over the weekend, and I have eight takers! We're a week in and we've raised almost a quarter of the goal. Not too shabby.

The next morning, I'm in the bathroom, showering, when I remember a song that my dad and I used to do at church when I was little. "As the rain and the snow come down from heaven, and water the earth, and bring forth its fruit, so shall be the word that you are speaking. It shall not return empty to you; it shall accomplish your desire — it will surely succeed." I get chills, thinking of this as a little divine message about the fundraiser — the word "desire" a blinking beacon — and cling to the promise that "it shall not return empty to you." I want my words to return full and overflowing, the words and stories I've sent out.

For our sightseeing that day, I locate another labyrinth that we can visit, just a short drive from Antoine's house. It may not be Chartres, but at least I won't have given up on my quest. But after driving the narrow hilly goat-track roads through green fields to reach the place, we discover that it is closed until after lunch. It's hard not to see this as a sign — but does it mean that walking a labyrinth just isn't that important? Or that I should keep trying?

Shawn quickly detours us to the town of Dieppe, a famous and tragic WWI landmark for Canadians. We stop in the visitor's centre for brochures about the doomed assault on the pebbled beaches. Pause for lunch (mussels for me, *croque monsieur* for the kids) before proceeding to the shore to get a glimpse of the high cliffs surrounding the town. Long interlude at the playground with a climbing structure shaped like a pirate ship. Then a short visit to the Canadian war cemetery, vivid green lawns contrasting white grave markers.

Antoine makes us dinner in his cramped kitchen — he and I talk in French for a long time while he chops and mixes and cooks. We talk about Canadian and French politics, our families, travel, and couchsurfing. I know my conjugations and agreement are horrible, but it doesn't seem to impede the conversation. Shawn is in the backyard with the kids, who are making good use of in the playhouse Antoine built for his grandchildren. We're having *crêpes*, *naturellement* — mushroom for the adults and ham and cheese for the kids. They taste divine, creamy and woodsy and crisp.

The next morning Antoine takes us to the town market. What a revelation. Row upon row of stalls with the most succulent food: cheese, fish, fresh berries and mushrooms. I buy an antique postcard and some strawberries, olives, and crackers to bring to our next hosts in Belgium. I suddenly have a yearning to live here in France so I can take time to enjoy all the marvellous food. Even the grocery store has wonderful wine, cheese, and pâté for a few euros.

During our final lunch, Shawn and I try to convey the depth of our thanks to Antoine for his hospitality, but he shakes his head. "When I couchsurfed in Turkey, in Bulgaria, Syria, and Israel, people said to me, 'It is not you who should thank us. You have given us a great gift.' And now that I host people myself, I know that it is true."

Flow Exercise: Creating in the Middle

In his book *Coaching the Artist Within*, Eric Maisel talks about the importance of learning to create in the middle of things. In other words, don't wait until you have perfect quiet time and space, but write and make art while the flurry of work and cooking and children and friends swirls around you. I was reading the book while on vacation with my in-laws and fifteen-month-old Lia who was teething, so I both appreciated and chafed against the advice.

On one hand, I thought, why should I have to settle for creating in the middle of things? Don't I deserve the cabin in the woods, long days of writing and contemplation, walks and naps and cups of tea?

On the other hand, if I waited for those times, I wouldn't get much done. I knew that creating in the middle of things, a little at a time, was a skill that would serve me well if I could develop it. So I persisted, writing morning pages while Lia napped, teaching myself to get up early, poking away at my novel. Sometimes the noise and mess made me crazy, but I practiced tuning it out. I wrote in the car while the kids whined, I wrote when the laundry and dishes howled, I wrote on lunch hours and in bustling coffee shops. Slowly, slowly, creating in the middle of things got easier.

On the face of it, creating and running the *Pilgrimage of Desire* fundraiser while actively travelling in Europe seemed crazy! I wouldn't have chosen to time things that way, but they seemed to converge of their own accord. But the good thing about travelling while fundraising was that I couldn't get too obsessed with the campaign. When I did work on promotion, I brought the delighted energy inspired by the events of each day. Creating in the middle of things has a certain charm, the way it brings all the parts of one's life together into a jumbled and dazzling whole.

What do you need to create in the middle of? A demanding day job, chronic illness, toddlers underfoot, aging parents, depression?

Are you embracing or resisting creating in the middle of your particular brand of chaos? How can you reconcile yourself to the importance of creating in the middle?

And what can you do today to practice being in touch with your art no matter what life looks like?

15 Closing the Circle

You don't see many fences in the Netherlands because the water-filled ditches keep the livestock contained. So you'll pass a picturesque green grass field with horses, and next to that sheep, and then cows, and no messy metal or wooden fencing between to interrupt the view.

There are proper bike paths everywhere, separated from the roads, with their own traffic signals and wide dual lanes. And because the country is flat and the weather temperate, it's easy to bike anywhere at any time, and most people do.

The flat land reclaimed from the ocean by dikes creates dramatic skyscapes: high clouds, brilliant colours, rolling storms. And the architecture of the houses is cozy, both modern and peasant-like. The scale of the place is so human. Roads, buildings, and cities seem to be right-sized, not towering or sprawling but compact and inviting.

And everything is groomed, tended, and decorated. Gardens are intricate and immaculate tableaus of flowers, greenery, and pathways. Curtains are woven lace, and front windows hold plants and ceramic adornments. Canals, cobblestone paths, and walking streets trace an inviting labyrinth for pedestrians. You have to look hard to find piles of garbage, neglected houses, or graffiti.

We are spending our first week in Holland with Shawn's cousin Anne and his wife Tiny Kloosterman, the couple who hosted Shawn twelve years ago when he visited for his *beppe*'s funeral. They live on a little cul-de-sac in a tall row house that backs onto a canal. When we pull up, Lia and Nico are delighted to see a trampoline on the lawn in the centre of the cul-de-sac.

After eight months away from family, it feels so good to hug Anne and Tiny and their son Wiebren, who is now a young man instead of a ten-year-old boy. Their smiles are generous and genuine. We get our luggage settled — Lia and Nico are sharing the guest room, and Shawn and I are in the master bedroom while Anne and Tiny sleep in the attic. We protest, but they won't hear of other arrangements.

Then it's coffee time. We relax into chairs around the patio table next to the canal, drinking strong dark coffee and nibbling *gebak* (pastries). I would be happy never to move from this spot. The conversation is wide-ranging, frank, and empathetic. They ask after all of our families, our careers, our travels. The Kloostermans have also taken many family trips together, and Tiny prepares meticulous albums with souvenirs, tickets, receipts, postcards, and photos.

Adeline, the Kloostermans' daughter, arrives the next day from her job in Belgium, just to see us! She's all grown up now, but I can still see the spunky girl in her. Lia and Nico assume ownership of the good-natured young people and tackle them with requests for piggy-backs, hide-and-seek, trampoline, and whatever other games they can wheedle. Somehow the kids start calling their cousin Wah-bren, and we adults pick it up to tease him. Seeing Wiebren and Adeline with Lia and Nico, I feel as though a circle has closed, since I might not be a mother if it weren't for that week that Shawn spent with his cousins.

And how can I describe how wonderful Anne and Tiny are? Maybe they have their shadow sides, maybe they raise their voices and speak in bitterness or anger sometimes, but I can't imagine it. I've never heard anything but fondness and interest. They anticipate our every need and desire. For instance, Shawn mentions that he loves *suikerbrood*, and Tiny comes home with a loaf for breakfast. Suikerbrood is divinity itself — tender white bread with lumps of crunchy caramelized sugar scattered throughout. Spread it with butter and you think you're in heaven. Even Wiebren is unusually attentive. I pick up my empty juice glass, look at it, and set it down again, and Wiebren immediately offers me a refill.

In the evenings, after the kids are in bed, we play games until late. There is much laughing as we snack on cubes of gouda and drink the Belgian beer Shawn brought with us. The Kloostermans are all very competitive and feign nastiness in their remarks to each other, although there is always that undercurrent of affection. We play a long hard-fought game of Risk, and Wiebren thinks he has things all sewn up, but Shawn steals the victory from him at the last minute.

I have to spend some time working, but not too much. Writing guest posts, composing email appeals, doing social media. I feel a little overwhelmed, but I can't go overboard with effort because our week with the Kloostermans is so precious that I can't bear to spend too much time on the computer. They are very understanding, asking about the campaign and making their own contribution.

Anne and Tiny take us out every day. We go for a ride in their open-topped motorboat through the waterways and under bridges to the marina, where we dock to eat ice cream and drink beer. Shawn goes with the kids to a charity soccer tournament in memory of a friend of Wiebren's who died of cancer some years before. We have lunch in a fishing village and ride the bumper cars at a little fair.

One day, we go to a street performers' festival in a small town nearby. There are acrobatic dancers and people performing magic tricks, a slack-wire artist, and a clown in an elaborate costume. We buy *frites* and *kibbeling* (fried fish) from the food trucks to eat as we watch. On one of the canals that criss-cross the town, there's a ride where you can climb into a clear inflated ball and be set adrift on the water. We've seen this in China, and Lia decides she wants to try, so we pay the five euros and off she goes. She isn't nervous at all, but clowns around inside the ball like a hamster, throwing herself about and bouncing off other balls until her turn is over and they reel her in on a line.

We make our way to the back lawn of a restaurant where we can sit and have a drink. Across the canal, there's an enthusiastic brass band playing on a barge. Looking at Tiny next to me, her cheeks high and round with smiling, I am visited by a thoroughly self-conscious happiness. I am blissed out to be sitting here in the sun with these people, drinking this wine, listening to this music and watching the kids play on the grass. I wish this could be the one moment of my entire life. Later, I join our children on the lawn, and we dance to the music and chase each other for tag. I keep poking at my happiness like a soap bubble, wondering whether it will pop now that I've seen it floating just above my head, but it persists, flexing but never breaking apart.

On our last day with the Kloostermans, we visit the grocery store to stock up for our new apartment — meatballs, cheese, chocolate sprinkles called *hagelslag,* and canned soup for my cold. We also go to the bank machine to withdraw enough euros to pay for our apartment in Alphen aan den Rijn. I haven't used my card in ages, and I only remember the mnemonic word that corresponds to my PIN and not the numbers themselves! I have to go home and Google an image of a keypad to figure out the code.

Saying good-bye to Anne and Tiny is awful. I nearly start crying, trying to convey to them the extent of my gratitude for making us welcome. Being with people who love us deeply has been overwhelming after so many months on our own. As we pull away, I can't understand why we're leaving. If we can live anywhere, why aren't we living in Sneek where we can see the Kloostermans all the time?

We drive from Friesland into Nord Holland on the Afsluitdijk, a causeway that stretches thirty kilometres through the sea like a high wire. For fifteen minutes, we travel the narrow strip of road, grass, and rock to its vanishing point on the horizon, and the view is good for my sad, pensive mood; it's comforting to watch the waves, the ships on the inland water, the simplicity of the asphalt stretching before and behind.

We chose to rent an apartment in Alphen aan den Rijn because it's central, close to the relatives and major cities we want to see, and because it was available, attractive, and reasonably priced. We also have cousins in town — we haven't met them, but they know we're coming. The apartment is on a farm just south of town, and we have to drive under the highway on a one-lane road, little more than a bike path, to reach it. We pass a nature preserve, and then turn left into the cement yard of a well-kept property. The owner is a cheerful, no-nonsense woman with short dark hair and a bunch of kids.

Our apartment has a large wooden verandah with patio furniture that overlooks a little slough and a field with black-and-white horses beyond it. There's a narrow bedroom with two single beds behind the kitchen for the kids, and a large loft upstairs with a queen-sized bed for Shawn and me. I start laughing when I walk into the shower room. The mirror has obviously been hung by a tall Dutch person because I can't see more than the top of my head in it. Our home for the next six weeks is all very clean, simple, and comfortable.

We eat our dinner on the verandah, watching swans in the slough glide by with their babies, and I am somewhat consoled at leaving Sneek. We have a good view of the bike and foot traffic on the little road — cars are a rarity. In the distance, we can see trains skimming by and airplanes approaching Schiphol Airport. We joke about being able to see every form of transportation just by sitting in one place.

We get right down to business in Alphen. I need to go full-steam on the fundraiser, and Shawn takes over the cooking and childcare so I can do that. The campaign has been going well but has plateaued in the middle as usually happens. I have lots of promotion to do if I want to succeed.

That Sunday, I arrange to do a virtual reading at our old church in Ottawa. I dial in early, and my friend Dwayne brings up the video call on his iPad. I am able to hear and watch much of the service — the Scripture readings, the sermon, the confession and absolution. He even brings me around during the passing of the peace so parishioners can greet my disembodied head on a tablet! I have been weepy with nostalgia all along, but this really does me in, saying hello to beloved friends and seeing my friend Sonia's new baby for the first time.

I'm flooded with a feeling of selfishness for leaving this community and becoming preoccupied with my own little creative project. Who cares about a dumb old book? Who am I that I think people want to read about my life? What I'm doing suddenly seems insignificant and bizarre.

After the service, they set up a projector and screen downstairs in the parish hall, and I read Chapter 5 of *Pilgrimage of Desire,* which is about God and church and the labyrinth. The small audience is very appreciative, and a few women tell me afterward that they identify with my experiences.

I am wrung out with tears and sweat afterward, my ears aching from wearing the headset for hours. Shawn and I take a walk down the road, past the farmyards and gardens, the kids racing ahead. I tell him about the feeling of selfishness and insignificance, and he chides me a little. "Don't downplay what you're doing. These people love you. They're excited to support your work. Let them."

I take a deep breath and try to let all the love in.

Our first week in Alphen, we have unseasonable blue-sky weather. While I work, Shawn takes the kids out — one day they visit the Kinderdijk to see the restored windmills. Another day they visit a farm, pet the animals and buy delicious fresh *vla*, a kind of yummy dairy custard. Then they go to a lake to swim.

I see the photos and hear the stories afterward. I try not to feel guilty or jealous for missing these outings because I'm writing and working. I tell myself that Shawn has long had this dream to show the kids around Holland, and they are all happy whether I'm there or not. I tell myself that this is my cost of doing business, that I used to do things with the kids while Shawn was at work, and that I need to suck it up and be okay with it. I mostly believe these things, but I wonder whether I will ever come to regret the trade-off — the missed opportunities that will never come again. But the fundraiser will end soon, and then I will relax and spend more time with my family. I remember the rhythm of Penang, the way busy periods alternated with idle ones, and remind myself to trust the cycle.

I've been having mini-moments of panic throughout, but the closer we come to the end of the campaign, the more anxious I get. With six days left, the total stands at $6,000. Getting to $10,000 seems impossible. In my journal, I write, "Amma. I'm scared. This is too much. I don't see how I'll meet my goal, and all this work will have been for no money. I can't write when I feel scared. My stomach is in knots." A friend asks what I'll do if I don't make it, and I start crying because the future without *Pilgrimage* looks bleak and meaningless. "I just want to write this book!" I sob to her. And I know I don't need the money to write the book, but if I can't sell it to the people who know and love me, what hope is there for it?

Shawn gives me pep talks multiple times a day, and he helps me record an update video with an honest and direct appeal. I have a few important guest posts going up in the last few days of the campaign, including one for the short story writer Sarah Selecky that I'm especially proud of. I have one last email to send to my friends and family. I won't give up until I've done everything I can do.

At 9:15 p.m. on the second-last day of the fundraiser, we are at $8,365. There's been a flurry of activity, tweets and email list subscriptions and campaign contributions since my guest post for Sarah Selecky went up. And I finally allow myself to believe that we're going to make it. From the gut-clenching anxiety, I've emerged into a place of deep pride in myself and the book. In my journal, I write, "I am in love with the crazy ride of this unfolding story of my life. I'm going to enjoy this, and I'm going to celebrate. Jump up and down. Call my parents. Take a day off. Or two. Start writing *Pilgrimage* again in earnest, this time knowing that its future is assured, that the money and audience is there like a labyrinth to support its creation."

The night that the fundraiser ends, I get caught up in the excitement of the last few hours, seeing my friends obsessively checking the total and tweeting or Facebooking about it, watching the final contributions come in. My friend Nate, who I met at the World Domination Summit last year, gives the exact amount we need to bring the total to a nice round ten thousand and his gesture is so touching and perfect.

I'm up late with phone calls and emails, but Shawn and I share a glass of wine on the verandah in the dark, listening to the rustling grass, the breath of horses, watching the headlights of bicycles zoom past. I'm already mentally preparing for writing the rest of *Pilgrimage*, and dealing with the twelve hundred messages in my inbox, and starting more contract work. I feel tired and homesick and nostalgic and a little sad and disoriented now that this huge undertaking is over.

But yes, we're going to do the book. And it's going to be good. I'm sure I'll feel better about it tomorrow.

Flow Exercise: The One Moment of Your Life

I have a very active mind, and I often find myself living in the past (mulling over failures and pining for lost joy) or in the future (spinning mad schemes and fretting over their outcome). It can feel good to let my thoughts run wild all over the place, like a kid tearing around a playground, but when I want relief from the dizziness and overwhelm, I bring myself back to the present.

I have a simple process I learned from Eckhart Tolle in *The Power of Now*, which is to get quiet inside and pretend that I have no past and no future, that I am just living this current moment for all eternity.

I found our time in Holland very intense because of the extremes of happiness and anxiety stirred up by our family visits and the fundraiser. And reining in my consciousness to the present helped me cope with that intensity. When a moment was so good that it was almost painful, like the afternoon we sat drinking wine and listening to music at the street festival, I allowed myself to forget that the moment would end and imagined instead that it would be my heaven, my forever.

When I was suffocating with worry that the fundraiser would fail or feeling overwhelmed by the many people, tasks, and emotions I had to handle, I closed my eyes, breathed, and asked myself whether I had any problems *right now*. And the answer was always no. I was safe, fed, and warm. My lungs were taking in oxygen and circulating it through my body. In the Netherlands, I was in a slow, beautiful environment, surrounded by kind people who loved me. Issues with money and career success and my children's development couldn't invade the present moment because they were all about the future. And even this moment, just sitting and breathing, could be a heaven.

When you are feeling dragged through past and future by your runaway thoughts, can you stop and draw a little box around this moment? Call it your eternity, a place without problems. Be a woman riding a bicycle, a man eating a sandwich, a writer holding a pen, until the end of time.

16 Anything Is Possible

"You can do most anything that means enough to you."
— Joe Hampson, "Is There Anybody Here," performed by Sharon, Lois & Bram

After the fundraiser, I am in a state of creative spent-ness. Not exactly exhausted, but empty. The motor won't start. If I could just stop altogether, I would, but I need to keep moving, or at least approximate moving. So I need to find the important stuff, do that, and find some ways to fill up fast.

I need a good book. A really good book that is not a memoir. I need to go out for dinner with Shawn. I need to plan the rest of our schedule here in Holland. I need to do yoga and go for walks. I need to go sightseeing in Amsterdam, go to the beach, go to Madurodam. I need to write postcards. I need to watch TV.

And I do. I devour *Blink and Caution* by Tim Wynn Jones. A cousin comes to watch Lia and Nico while Shawn and I celebrate our anniversary at a busy Italian restaurant and marvel that a year has passed since our final days in Ottawa. We arrange more family visits and schedule day trips to landmarks we don't want to miss. I send postcards to Sylvie and Nathalie in France and to Mariana in Penang. Shawn and I go to Amsterdam for the day, and I try once more to walk a labyrinth, but when we get to the spot where it's supposed to be, we can't find any lines on the paving stones. Thwarted again! We watch the Euro Cup, Netherlands against Denmark, and Lia gets right into it, excited by Shawn's passion for the game. (I sneak peeks at the novel I'm reading, and Lia says, "Mama, aren't you watching the game? We need more cheer-ers!")

One night, I push open the upstairs window to hear a virtuosic bird singing, and see mist rising off the *sloten*, and the sun glowing watermelon just above the horizon, and two large spiders building a web just to the right, and *meerkoet* in the water, and a few clutches of ducks flying by. Another moment to live in forever.

The fundraiser money lands in my bank account, and with it, more good news. A client wants to hire me to write a book for him. I've done some editing on his preliminary material, and now he'd like me to take his ideas and notes and give him a finished manuscript. I'm thrilled at the prospect — both of doing such an interesting job and getting paid for it. The timeline is tight and overlaps with *Pilgrimage*, but I don't want to lose the opportunity and the money. I figure I can do an hour or two on my memoir first thing, and then move to client work for the rest of the day.

Each morning, we have the kids sit down at the dining room table for an hour of schoolwork. Their school in Penang gave us stacks of worksheets so they could keep up while they were away. Occasionally, they sit happily, Nico drawing his letters and characters, Lia doing her science and Mandarin reading, but usually there's a lot of drama. One morning, Lia pitches a huge fit over her one page of English home-work, which she says is boring review and she's already done it. I am trying to get her to think creatively about how to make it interesting — write the letters backwards, write with her other hand, write upside down — but she isn't having any of it. She ends up finishing the page while crying hysterically (her way of making it less boring).

And I'm discombobulated about our plans for September. Shawn and I are now considering staying in Ontario for the fall. I haven't had much contract work this spring, and it's looking like we won't have the money to go back to Malaysia right away. I'm thinking that if I want to do a proper book launch for *Pilgrimage*, I need to be in North America. Also, this year away has actually strengthened our relation-ships with friends and family in Ontario, and there's a strong pull to be back in the arms of that community.

I'm feeling bad about Lia missing preschool graduation in Penang. I don't like breaking our promise that we would return. But it would cost us $6,000 for airfare, and we'd miss out on the contacts and net-working in Ontario for our work. We have to balance all of these fam-ily priorities: Mandarin, work, money, travel, simplicity. Hopefully, the solution will come to us.

I dive back into the *Pilgrimage* manuscript once I've had a little recov-ery time. The book needs to be done by the end of the summer so we can publish it before Christmas. That means I need to write one or two chapters a week, which is much quicker than anything I've done before. But I produced so much writing for the fundraiser that I'm in good shape for keeping up the pace. Right now, I'm working on the chapters about becoming a mother, and I'm surprised at how deep I need to go to tell these stories.

I write a little love letter to *Pilgrimage* in my journal:

"This is a special time for us. In the next six weeks, I will tease out all your words from the ether. I want to cherish this time with you. Everything I've done up to now, the planning and fundraising and dreaming, has been to create this space in which I can write you with joy, knowing that you have a home and an audience.

So how can we enjoy this time together? I am reminding myself that you are a pleasure to write, that the hours I spend at the keyboard are very enriching. You are a treat. You are a chocolate sundae with nuts and cherries and whipped cream. You are a warm bath with fragrant bubbles. You are a long walk in the sunshine with my family. You are strong sweet coffee and the sound of my best friend's voice. You are bright squooshy yarn waiting to be knit. You are the wash of waves on the beach.

Pilgrimage, let's have some angels join us in the writing. The Angel of Flow, who wears watered silk in shades of blue. The Angel of Love in pink spandex. The Angel of Poetry, black and white words dripping off her fingers. The Angel of Getting Your Shit Together, in tight jeans and a rock-and-roll T-shirt. The Angel of Truth and Beauty, who combines the grace of Venus with the mouth of a trucker. Together we're going to rock this manuscript. We're going to luxuriate in each other's presence. And we're going to write lots and lots of words. Alison xoxo"

How strange that Shawn has connections with all these people living in the Netherlands just because they share common ancestors, and now they are connected to me through marriage and to my children through adoption. And we have the freedom to strengthen those connections by visiting.

I've been thinking about why it was so important to Shawn and me that we form and nurture these global connections — why Shawn went to a teammate's housewarming party in George Town, why we invited Mariana and her son to Lia's birthday party, why we are spending many days in Holland sitting in people's living rooms and backyards. And I've concluded that we do these things because we believe that there's great value in knowing and loving people around the world, not just in our own city and country. We get pleasure from our conversations, the tangible and intangible gifts we offer each other. And our perspective on life is challenged and widened. What could have been remote and inconsequential becomes personal. We care more about the planet because we know more of its people intimately. Simply put, tending our global relationships feels meaningful, so we make it happen.

We joked with Anne and Tiny about the contradictions — here we were, the Canadian family spending a week with them, and yet they don't often get together with relatives who live close by (nor do we see all of our relatives in North America regularly.) There's something about our limited time in Holland, the urgency and specialness of our stay here, that drives us to connect.

We've been really touched by the help and hospitality we've received from the cousins who live in Alphen aan den Rijn. By great coincidence, they are related to Shawn on both sides — his mother's cousin Klaske married his father's cousin Jaap. Jaap and Klaske came to Canada at the time of our wedding, and we were thrilled that they could attend. Their three children live in Alphen with their families. We contacted their daughter Katja first, and right away she invited us over for dinner. She also put us in touch with some friends who were willing to babysit Lia and Nico a few mornings a week. And when we came to visit, they offered to loan us Katja's bicycle, which was large enough for Shawn and had a child's seat on the front and a trailer bike on the back. Shawn took the kids all over the countryside on that rig.

Today is Father's Day, and Shawn has offered to make pizza at Ed and Katja's house to reciprocate for several dinners they've served us.

After dinner, Lia and Nico watch their youngest, Amos, play Minecraft on a desktop computer in the dining room. The adults set up a game of Settlers of Catan (in Dutch it's called *De Kolonisten van Catan*) with the Knights and Cities expansion pack. Katja is a cutthroat Koloniste player, so we all have to have our wits about us.

Shawn and Katja trade barbs — he can't resist trying to get under her skin now that he's seen how much she cares about winning. Ed and I are just trying to stay in the game. In between turns, he teaches me some new Dutch phrases. *"Het spijt me"* means "I'm sorry," *"Het spijt me echt"* means "I'm really sorry," and *"Wil je me vergeven?"* means "Will you forgive me?"

I move the robber onto one of Shawn's resource tiles so he can't collect his grain anymore. "Hey!" he protests. "I'm your husband! Why are you picking on me?"

With my best Dutch inflection and emphasis, I bat my eyes and say to him, "Het spijt me echt. Wil je me vergeven?" Everyone laughs heartily.

It turns out that I was right to come after Shawn with the robber because he ends up winning the game. We finally head home at 11 p.m., and the kids fall asleep in the car. Just another special everyday family evening in Alphen.

One of our last visits is the most important. Shawn's uncle, Oom Enne, was diagnosed with cancer years ago. Then his wife, Tante Cor, also became ill and passed away. Oom Enne has been holding on, but they don't know for how much longer. It takes a few weeks, but Shawn arranges a visit through Oom Enne's daughter, who's been caring for him. Shawn is nervous about seeing him — he doesn't speak much English, and we've heard he's frail — but we can't let the chance go by.

We drive several hours on a Saturday morning to Gieten where Oom Enne still lives on his own in a single-story row house (the Dutch are so sensible with their modest, dense housing). I've packed lots of toys and activities for the kids so we can keep them calm while we visit. Oom Enne's daughter is there to greet us and bring us into the living room where Oom Enne is sitting, with a cannula delivering oxygen to his nose. His face softens and brightens as we come in and give him careful hugs.

At first we mostly talk to Oom Enne's daughter in English, slowly and loudly so Oom Enne can listen. She wants to hear all about our travels. The kids show off their charm for a few minutes and then get rowdy, so I move them to the table with books and colouring. We also take a little tour of the back yard. The last time we were here, in 1998, Oom Enne walked through his garden with me and pointed out the flowers. The fuchsias were beautiful, and I remember them because he told me their name in Dutch, pronounced *fuk-see-ya*, which made me giggle. This time he stays in his chair while we ooh and aah at the garden on our own.

Oom Enne's daughter has prepared a lunch of homemade soup and sandwiches. Then she leaves so we can have a little time with Oom Enne on our own. Now the conversation switches languages, and I get to hear Shawn practice his halting Dutch. But it is good — intimate and touching — to talk to our uncle directly.

Before we leave, we take some photos and then collect the leftover food and treats he insists we have for the road. As we take our leave, I try to forget that this is the final good-bye, but I can't, and my chest gets tight and my tongue tied. Our eyes have to do the talking.

And now we come to the perfect day in Holland, the day that I will talk about when people ask about the highlight of our trip. Saturday morning, June 30, we pack an overnight bag and are on the road by 7:30 a.m. We drive north, over the Afsluitdijk and through Leeuwarden to the ferry for the North Sea island of Ameland. Luckily the sun is out, so we change into shorts and sandals and take the 10:30 a.m. ferry for forty-two euros.

The crossing is just long enough for a snack of pizza and orange soda, and we disembark and join the great stream of people turning off the sidewalk and into the bike rental shop. For thirty euros, we hire two *kindertandems,* which have a shorter seat at the front for a child, and a taller one at the back for an adult.

With seats adjusted, we are off, first into the small town of Nes and then further on. Consulting our map, we decide to head to the next town over, Ballum, but somehow end up on the north beach instead. We are getting the hang of these double bikes pretty easily, and the kids are practiced at cycling now.

We ride by a bouncy castle, and Lia is very unhappy when we give it a pass and stop at the dunes instead.

"Isn't it nice here?" I say, spreading my arms to the glory of the place.

"It's not nice! I hate nature! I want to be in the city!" Lia shouts.

Shawn jollies her along, takes off her sandals and has her start running down the dunes, these tall soft sand hills. Mollified, she takes turns with Nico running and leaping down the dunes. We watch people flying kites on this long wide expanse of dusky sand feathering into the slate-coloured ocean.

We keep going, past a campground crowded so thick with tents that you can hardly see how people walk between them. Our tires dig into the dirt-and-shell path between the dunes, and the charm is overwhelming, our two bikes flying along next to each other, all of us pedalling and taking in the wind and sky and sand, ringing our bells. All of Hejira was for this moment.

When we arrive in Ballum, we choose a little café for lunch, and the kids find a wooden playhouse and pretend they are mom and baby. I drink *cassis* (blackberry soda) and eat a *nasischijf* (a disk of Indonesian rice, breaded and fried). Shawn orders a hamburger dressed like an *uitsmijter* (an open-faced meat and cheese sandwich with a fried egg on top) and he asks whether his hamburger comes with the special *frites* that the waiter described.

"Anything is possible," the waiter says with a smile in his crisp Dutch accent.

This becomes our catch phrase for the day.

After lunch, we continue on to the *vuurtoren* (lighthouse), then down to the beach again where men are playing volleyball with their feet ("Anything is possible"). The wind is strong and cool here at the western end of the island. We cycle through a section of pine forest, past little farms and houses, between the ocean and the dike covered in grazing sheep. We stop to watch kite surfers near the ferry terminal, and the bay is so shallow that it looks like people are walking on water in the distance ("Anything is possible"). By this time, my bum is very sore and my legs are burning with lactic acid.

Shawn falls asleep on the return ferry ride, but the kids, surprisingly, stay awake. Our cousin Elizabeth and her three children are waiting for us at the dock. How nice to have someone greet us when we arrive! We end the day at Elizabeth's house, the kids playing in the tree house, adults chatting in the backyard with beer and rosé wine. Elizabeth and her husband Wilfrid love to laugh and tease, and we talk about our families and what we did together on our previous visits (Elizabeth came to Canada when Shawn and I were in high school).

And this day, this is why I wanted Operation Hejira. Tandem biking on a Dutch island, running down the dunes, a visit with relatives. A day that proves anything is possible.

Flow Exercise: Love Letter

Writing a love letter to my work-in-progress is an idea I got from my first writing coach, Cynthia Morris. It's a great way to air all the emotions swirling around a project and bridge the distance between us, to re-establish what I first saw in the story and why it's important to me. Writing a letter reminds me that I'm not alone, but that the work has a life and spirit of its own, and I'm just the conduit.

If I'm angry about what the story is demanding from me or hurt by its seeming failures, I can get that off my chest. If I'm bored and forcing myself to work on the project, the letter helps me revive the romance and remember that things work better when I can follow the thread of desire.

What kind of letter can you write to your current creative project? Something coquettish and inviting, to get to know it better? An apology for neglect or not giving your best? Or do you need to break up with a Dear John letter? Every relationship has its own shape and trajectory, and you can serve yourself and the work by bringing it to light.

17 Hairpin Turn

"Some inventors have a goal in mind and work persistently toward it. Others stumble across solutions to problems they weren't trying to solve."
— Lemelson Center for the Study of Invention and Innovation, *Invention at Play*

I keep looking for the end of my book.

With the arrival of July, the first year of Operation Hejira is over, and I need a neat spot to wrap up the story of *Pilgrimage*. I could use the joyful airport reunion with Shawn's parents. They are waiting outside the arrival doors when we get off our overnight flight from Paris to Toronto, and they scoop us into their arms and the waiting minivan. We cut our time in Holland a little short so we could be home in time for his mother's seventieth birthday, and our first days in Ontario are rich in conversation and celebration. I feel closer to my parents-in-law than I ever have — they've been very excited to hear about our life and travels, and my mother-in-law tells me that my memoir and writings about depression this year really spoke to her.

We start looking for an apartment to rent in Hamilton, but before we get too far, Shawn's mom and dad suggest that we might stay at their house in Vineland, near St. Catharines. They'll be gone for much of the fall, first to Holland and then to Florida. We're using their large guest room downstairs, and house-sitting for them would be so much easier and cheaper than finding and setting up our own place. They live close enough to Hamilton that we could still visit friends there and go to our old church, St. Cuthbert's. The kids could go to the local public school.

I never thought I would be comfortable living in my in-laws' house, but we've gotten into a relaxed routine with them, having meals and coffee on the back deck, taking walks to Lake Ontario, but also spending time by ourselves working and reading. Mom does all of our laundry on Mondays, which is such a gift. I sometimes write at the library, and Shawn takes Lia and Nico to vacation Bible school at his brother's church for a week.

I could conclude *Pilgrimage* with our return to Grosse Pointe for a week's holiday with Melody and her family. A nice bookend to the beginning of Hejira, no? I take the opportunity to work on the Michigan section of the book, with the familiar environment jogging my memories. We revisit the Henry Ford museum, and the kids remember the Oscar Meyer hotdog whistles and rock candy they got from the gift shop last year. With her new swimming skills, Lia jumps off the diving board in the deep end at the local pool. Mel and I go to see the movie *Brave* at the community centre theatre, and I cry buckets when Merida and her mother are reunited.

I could end on the moment when I see my own mom and realize with relief that I've forgiven her. We are spending a week in a rented cottage next to my grandparents' place on Lake Dalrymple. The patter of gravel in the car's wheel wells on the cottage road takes me right back to childhood, the endless days that are mine to fill with cross-word puzzles and boat rides, catching frogs and waving sparklers.

I have my seatbelt off and my car door open before Shawn even shuts off the engine. Hugs are the first order of business. When I look at my parents, I feel dislocated — I haven't seen them in a year but they are so familiar: I know every cross-hatched wrinkle in my dad's smile, the flecks of green, blue, and brown in my mom's eyes. If I didn't have the stamps in my passport, I would have sworn I saw them yesterday, last week, last month. The familiarity feels dangerous, as though I could forget to visit them because I don't notice the time passing.

My mom looks so good — present and grounded, with light in her face. Her voice has the mix of joy and calm that tells me she's balanced, neither manic nor depressed. I'm glad to have the chance to talk again while we cook and do dishes, throw toys for grown-up puppy Rika, rock on the verandah settee. I'm still knitting the pair of socks I started on the airplane to Hong Kong, and she's making a multi-coloured blanket for my sister Joanna. Ordinary time.

I take my travel yoga mat to the deck of the boathouse and do the poses that I used to do on my Penang balcony. I miss the warmth, the view, the peace of our little apartment in Malaysia, but I'm comforted that we'll be back there again in January. I hope Lia doesn't lose much of her Mandarin.

The week is over too soon, but we're not saying good-bye for long — we'll be back at my parents' house in a few weeks, and Joanna has invited us all to Toronto for a weekend retreat in September. I'm really happy to be able to say yes, I'll be there. I'm making lots of other plans for the fall too: a fortieth birthday party for a college friend, a drive down to New Jersey to work on *Pilgrimage* with Michelle, a Deep Writing workshop at Omega with Eric Maisel, my coaching mentor. And another family Christmas, which feels really important after spending last year on our own in Kuala Lumpur.

Throughout July, I've been getting more and more behind on my two books, the travel memoir and the ghostwriting project. I've never tried to write two things at once, and now I find they are duking it out for space in my brain. When we go to Ottawa after our week at the cottage, it's even harder to work. We've got doctor and dentist appointments and many meet-ups with friends.

The four of us are sleeping together in yet another guest room, so it's hard to get up early, and I have no separate space to write. Moving houses every week with kids is not something I recommend. One week couchsurfing in Europe was fantastic; three weeks in Ontario has been manageable; but now we're on week five, our suitcases are a jumble, I'm behind on the laundry, and the kids have no regular routine. Not that it does much good to create guidelines for myself — we're moving because we have to, in order to see everyone we want to see. We'll just have to hang on until we head back to Vineland and get settled.

I am thrilled to discover that the documentary *I'm Fine, Thanks* is showing at the Ottawa International Film Festival during the week when we're in town. I backed the film during its record-breaking Kickstarter campaign, so I could have watched the download on my computer, but I'm much happier to see it at a public screening. The World Exchange Theatre is a short walk from our old house on Nepean Street.

I'm standing on the corner by the library, waiting to meet my cousin Joe so we can go to the show together, when a tourist approaches me.

"Excuse me, do you know this area well?" he asks.

Inward laugh to myself followed by a slow smile. "Yes. Yes, I do," I say.

I've walked every block of this downtown dozens of times, I want to say, often pushing a stroller or holding the hand of a child. I used to bring my little girl to story time at this library every Thursday morning. How many hundreds of books have I checked out and returned to this branch? And toward the end, how I ached to go somewhere new. Not to see the same shops and houses and office workers, not to know exactly where the nearest gym was (I sent the tourist to GoodLife Fitness on Queen Street, for the record).

I'm Fine, Thanks is a film about people who've done what we've done — questioned and rebelled against the societal script, chucked their jobs and houses to travel or volunteer or just live simply. The producer of the film, Adam Baker, took his wife and little daughter around Australia, New Zealand, and Thailand back in 2009, and their story was another inspiration for Operation Hejira.

And what a great film to watch in a crowd. Hearing the laughter when Johnny B. Truant talked about the banality of bread in crumb form. The gasp when the voiceover described how John Vogel and Nancy Sathre-Vogel cycled from Alaska to Argentina with their two boys. The tears when Victoria choked up about how she felt trapped in her life as an attorney, unable to spend the time she wanted to with her daughter.

I am struck early on by a short clip from director Grant Peelle's childhood, of his dad telling him to put the video camera down, that nobody wanted to watch all that footage he was taking. What's telling is not only the moment itself, but the fact that Grant remembered it and was able to find the clip decades later to include in the film. That tossed-off remark must have made a big impression.

As I work on *Pilgrimage*, the story of my relationship with my mother and her influence on my choices in life has loomed large in the narrative. Of course our parents just want the best for us, but they don't always know what that is. All the more important to question the expectations of those closest to us, which can send us furthest off course.

Another favourite moment of mine is the look on Karen Putz's face when she goes barefoot water-skiing. I guarantee that everyone in the theatre is thinking either "I want that!" or "Thank God I have that." It reminds me of our day on Ameland, riding tandem bikes along the dunes, when I couldn't wipe the ridiculous grin off my face.

Grant, the director, is there to introduce the film and answer questions afterward, but I don't get a chance to talk to him in person. As I'm leaving the theatre, I run into Jennifer, a coaching client of mine who lives in Ottawa. She and I worked together by phone while I was in Malaysia — she's a screenwriter who was suffocating in her government job. As we emerge into the theatre lobby, she tells me that she has just give her notice at work and will be spending the next year devoted to her film and writing projects. Jennifer's decision has been a long time coming, so how cool to learn about it after watching *I'm Fine, Thanks* (which she loved, by the way). We talk until the lobby has long cleared and share a couple of long, emotional hugs. I'm really touched to have played a small part in her emancipation.

"How was lunch?" I ask Shawn when I pick him up from his old office in Ottawa, where he spent a few hours visiting with his former coworkers. He gives me a cryptic look, and in an instant I know that something juicy happened.

"What?! Tell me!" We are only driving a few blocks to the coffee shop where I'm meeting a friend, but I'm dying to know.

His face is a jumble of awe, excitement, and chagrin, like the cat that swallowed the Pop Rocks. "You remember that job listing that I showed you for my company, the one for a research coordinator in Vancouver?"

I vaguely recall him mentioning it as an "in another lifetime" kind of thing.

"My old boss wants me to apply."

I can feel the involuntary smile of Pop-Rock-swallowing spreading across my face too. "Wow!" First there's the pride at Shawn being recognized as a great researcher and manager, the pleasure of being picked for something. Then there's the delicious door-opening fantasy of a what-if life in Vancouver. We've often talked about living there — Shawn has visited many times for work and loves the temperate climate, the city-sea-mountain combination. How easy it would be to pick up our suitcases and relocate there. There's a sizeable Chinese population, and the schools would be good. And Shawn would have meaningful work again, and a steady paycheque, which is the only way we could ever afford to live in such an expensive city.

When I ask, "Are you thinking about it?", I already know he's thinking about it. And I know he knows I'm thinking about it too. Even though we've just made all these plans to stay in Ontario for the fall and go back to Malaysia in January.

"I'll have to look into it more," he says.

"Wow," I say.

"I know," he says.

I take a mental snapshot. This could be the hairpin moment when everything changes. Again.

Workwise, things have not panned out for Shawn this year the way he had hoped. He did several contracts, but most of the work he was offered was the kind of thing he used to delegate to juniors. He's been wanting to do more project management and creative direction for research, but that kind of work isn't compatible with location independence.

Shawn certainly hasn't minded a reduced workload, unwinding after thirteen years of full-time school and career, enjoying naps and afternoons in the pool with the kids. But he's still young and ambitious, and he needs interesting, meaningful work as much as I do. This position in Vancouver as research coordinator for the Centre for Employment Excellence is a rare opportunity for him career-wise, as well as geographically, and we have to take it seriously even though it would cut short our Hejira travels far sooner than we had planned.

The West Coast is very tempting. I have some family there, including my cousin Simone, who has four teenage kids, and a few friends from university. There's skiing and hiking, sailing and kayaking. The city is close to Seattle and Portland, the Gulf Islands and Victoria. We wouldn't soon run out of places to explore.

But after the initial euphoric rush of a wonderful new option, I'm now drowning in something that feels like grief. Letting go of the many plans I had for our time in Ontario and kissing our return to Penang good-bye. What does it mean for Hejira? We had always planned to travel for at least two years, maybe up to five. We went through all that work of selling the house and our possessions — are we giving that up to settle down in suburbia again?

And the logistics are giving me kittens. Where should the kids go to school? Are we too late to enrol them in French or Mandarin immersion? How much can we pay in rent? What neighbourhood should we live in? How much of our stuff should we ship and when? How do I renegotiate my schedule for the books I'm writing? It's like I'm snorkelling along the sea floor, and I've flailed around and kicked up silt and sand that is obscuring my view.

After our week in Ottawa, we drive into the countryside past Perth, to the home of Madeline, my women's retreat leader and therapist from years before. Madeline and I have kept in touch, and when she offered her secluded home for house-sitting in August, I jumped on it, knowing that Shawn and I would be ready for a week on our own after all this visiting.

Madeline's property has an extended gravel driveway that ends at a large tree with several rope swings. Lia and Nico dash out of the car and climb up, shrieking and pushing each other. The front yard is mostly overgrown with tall wildflowers and thistles, except for two patches of garden and a little verge of shorn grass. Madeline is waiting inside for us, and after I claim my motherly hug, she makes us tea from the lemon verbena in her garden. We chat in the sitting room for a while, and then she heads out to meet her own daughter for summer visiting.

Madeline's Victorian chic farmhouse is a refuge where we can catch our breath. She keeps a colony of bees, and the children and I snuggle up with a children's book all about how the bees gather nectar, care for their young, and overwinter. One morning I step to the dining room window and lock eyes with a deer on the lawn until it turns to bound away.

Later that week, Shawn and I sit outside in Adirondack chairs, watching the sun set and the insects swarming in the dusky air.

"Tell me what excites you about employment research," I say, aware that I sound like a coach but needing to know that he has a good answer.

"It's the possibility of influencing policies and programs based on actual data," he says. "Doing research that could change the way employment practitioners do their work. I've thought more generically about ways to help job seekers, which is often very fragmented because you're just testing one idea. But here I would be helping one group of people be more effective in what they do."

I like what he says — it's specific, and it's in context with what he's done before. He's focusing on why his role in the process is meaningful to him.

"Do you want this job?" I ask. I'm looking him dead in the eye, as though the fate of our lives together hangs on what he says. Of course, it does.

He takes a moment, gazes at the tree line at the edge of Madeline's property. His eyes meet mine again.

"Yes. I want it."

His words carry the weight of a marriage proposal, a pregnancy announcement, an offer on a house.

Looks like we're going for it. And I think I just found the end of my book. Vancouver will be the epilogue.

Flow Exercise: The Path with Heart

It's one thing to make a decision between what you want and what you don't want. Choosing Operation Hejira was mainly about figuring out whether we could make it work, whether the risk was manageable. We *knew* we were going to pursue it if it proved possible. But how about when you're choosing between various good things, all of which you want? What do you do when the desire lines seem to diverge?

Poet and teacher David Whyte writes in *The Three Marriages* about the necessity of tending to your relationships with your partner, your work, and your self. These relationships are not competing but interconnected. Together they create a complex web of experience, support, and meaning in your life. Strengthening one can bolster the others. Neglecting one can weaken them all. So choosing between good paths involves a calculus of the heart. Which direction calls to you because it holds more good for all three of your marriages?

Vancouver was clearly beneficial for my marriage with Shawn because it would make him happy by serving his own marriage with his work and self. I could also see that Vancouver would be a good place to grow my marriage with writing and coaching, with the in-person opportunities that the city offered. And I knew it would challenge my marriage with myself by asking me to redesign my life yet again. Vancouver seemed to be the direction with the most heart, even though it meant the premature end of our world travels.

What desirable paths lie before you? Draw a map of their branchings and confluences. How would each route affect your marriage to your partner or family, your work, and your self? Don't think in terms of right and wrong choices, but in terms of where your heart tugs you. That's the direction of growth and healing.

PART 5: VANCOUVER

18 Life from Scratch

"What is my right path?" …

"All paths are the same; they end up in the same place. What is important is to ask yourself, 'Does this path have a heart?' If the answer is 'yes,' then that is the right path for you."

— Carlos Castaneda as quoted in *The Van Gogh Blues* by Eric Maisel

Shawn has decided that he wants the Vancouver job, but they haven't decided whether they want him. He needs to go through the application process, which means submitting his resume and doing an interview with his old boss in Ottawa and his potential manager in Vancouver. Shawn has done his homework, though, and he's got good experience doing employment research and lots of ideas for the new centre's initiatives. He even went to a conference of employment practitioners in BC last year to present some research findings. We think he has a good shot at success.

The weeks between deciding to go for the job and finding out the results of the competition are tense and uncertain. We are in limbo, unable to start making arrangements for Vancouver but unmotivated to do any more settling in Vineland until we know where we'll be. We are also worried about breaking the news of more change to the kids.

To bring down my anxiety, I start researching where we might live. Right now Vancouver is a confusing mass of neighbourhoods, and I don't know where we should look. I post a question in an online forum: "My husband is considering a job in Vancouver. His office would be in the Downtown Eastside. We have two kids who are entering Grade 1 and senior kindergarten. Which neighbourhoods should we look at that would allow us to live car-free with minimal commute time near good elementary schools?"

I get lots of good responses and learn that we probably don't want to be in the downtown area (City Centre, West End, Yaletown) because there are fewer schools, which are very full and possibly not as good, but we can look in the neighbourhoods close to downtown like Kitsilano and Mount Pleasant. Schools there will probably also be full at this time of year, but we may have a chance.

At last the telephone rings. Shawn takes the call behind closed doors in the study, and his parents and I sit nervously outside, trying to guess the outcome based on the tone of his voice. Finally he emerges, a stunned smile on his face.

"I got it," he says.

"Woohoo!" I shout and run over to kiss him. We break out shots of coffee liqueur to celebrate, and Shawn's mom teases me for being so giddy. The happiness has gone to my head — I am glad the uncertainty is over and that we got what we decided we wanted. The salary is really good, and there's a moving bonus we didn't expect. I know that the high will wear off, but right now I'm nursing it because this move is going to be a ton of work and stress, and I want to savour the good parts. We are going to be West Coasters.

Now we fly into action. There's a difficult decision to make about timing, because Shawn's employers want him to start work as soon as possible. But my aunt and uncle's anniversary party is coming up, along with my friend's fortieth birthday party and the retreat weekend in Toronto with my mom and sisters. I hate to miss these things, but I'm more scared that we could lose a chance to get the kids in a good school if we wait too long. So Shawn books airline tickets to Vancouver on the Wednesday after Labour Day.

We contact courier companies and figure out that we can ship some boxes of our essentials — clothes, kitchen supplies, pillows, our food processor and coffee grinder, Christmas decorations, toys and books. We haul out what was stored in my in-laws' basement and gradually assemble a pile of thirteen boxes to ship.

I email my cousin Simone to let her know we're coming, and she offers to have us stay with her family in North Vancouver while we look for a house. We're only too happy to say yes — not just to avoid paying for a hotel but because we'll have advice and company while we search and make decisions. And with four teenagers in the house and a trampoline in the backyard, Lia and Nico will have a ball. So funny that we just saw Simone and Keith and their kids in Ontario a few weeks ago, after reconnecting during the book fundraiser. We had no idea at the time that we'd be relocating to their end of the country!

On Labour Day Saturday, we go to my aunt and uncle's anniversary party. I'm happy that we can balance things out by seeing many of my domestic relatives after visiting the international ones. Lia and Nico join the packs of kids (my aunt and uncle have nine children and many grandchildren), tearing around the hall, hiding out with bowls of candy, and dancing up a sweat when the music comes on.

This is the last time I'll see my parents before we leave for Vancouver. They've brought some boxes of things I had stored at their house, like my cookbooks. We stand around by their trunk to say our goodbyes. I am doubly torn to leave my folks because I had thought we would have time together in the fall, but I console myself that we'll be back in a few months for Christmas.

So once again, almost exactly a year after we left for Hong Kong, we are packing up suitcases in my in-laws' basement, getting ready to fly away. This time we are taking as much checked baggage as we are allowed, filling huge duffel bags and backpacks with everything we can fit to avoid shipping it.

The kids are excited to be flying again so soon after our trip home from Paris, especially since they get to watch unlimited TV on the seat backs in front of them. The flight seems short compared to the intercontinental travel we've been doing lately. We arrive at the Vancouver airport, pick up an enormous rental SUV (great for hauling luggage and furniture), and drive to Simone's house.

Taking our first look at our new home city, we wind through south Vancouver, the residential neighbourhoods with their enormous leafy hedges and stately windows, then over the Burrard Bridge that spans False Creek, with marinas and water taxis below, across downtown with glassy condos and office towers, expensive shops and hotels, beneath Stanley Park's urban stand of rainforest trees, over Lion's Gate Bridge with its vista of mountains and ocean beyond, then up the slope of North Vancouver to a cul-de-sac of large homes built to take in the view of the city. I don't think we'll get tired of what Vancouver offers to the eye any time soon.

Simone's house is spacious and welcoming for our little family of four. We have just enough brain power to eat dinner and talk about our strategy for house-hunting the next day, and then we collapse in bed, felled by jet lag.

On Thursday, we sift through the online rental listings for two- and three- bedroom places in Kitsilano and Mount Pleasant and start to line up viewings. One house looks promising — a family in the television industry is moving back to Toronto and renting out their place. The decor and fixtures are lovely, but it's on a very busy street in a less walkable neighbourhood. We see a fifth-floor penthouse in a building on West Broadway that we like — small but gorgeous views of the mountains and a gym in the basement. We go south as far as Kerrisdale and tour an enormous apartment that is actually two suites joined together, but the layout is odd and hard to imagine furnishing from scratch, and the distance to downtown is a bit much.

House-hunting feels a little like vacation. We're out all day with the kids, walking through townhomes and apartments, trying to imagine our lives there, and then we mark time between appointments by hanging out at a playground, eating Pirate Pak kids' meals at White Spot, walking through the markets at Granville Island, and watching the boats and paddle boards in False Creek.

I post on Facebook that house-hunting is not so much about finding a place to live as it is deciding who we want to be. The neighbourhood and space we choose will determine our friends, our activities, the way we spend time together as a family. Do we go upscale or bohemian? Frugal or house-poor? Family friendly or resort enclave? Having so many good options can be intimidating and disorienting. Luckily we've been practicing knowing and following our desires, and we keep getting drawn back to Kitsilano, which feels human-scaled and garden-like, not too commercial or car-oriented. And all along the north edge is the beach on English Bay!

On Saturday, we hit the jackpot: the rear half of a duplex in Kitsilano, very close to two elementary schools, right across the street from a large park. I am enraptured the moment I step inside: hardwood floors, a gas fireplace, and built-in bookshelves grace the living room; the kitchen boasts a large butcher block island, gas range, stainless steel fridge, dishwasher, and lots of cupboard space; there's halogen lighting everywhere and glass doors facing south on to the back garden.

Up the smartly carpeted stairs, there are two bedrooms on the second floor and a full bath with shower and double sink. The third floor is the clincher, though — two adjoining rooms nestled under the sloping roof that will be perfect as the kids' domain, one room for toys and the other for sleeping.

The back garden has a single-car garage for storage, vines everywhere, a little patch of grass, and a fruit-bearing fig tree. The house is walking distance from the library and the community centre, not to mention a few blocks from the beach! And there's a playground in the park.

My heart is enthralled by this space. The rent is a little higher than we budgeted for, but the house is also miles better than anything else we've seen. I visited one of the nearby schools a few days earlier, and the administrator and principal were both very friendly and told me they did have space for our kids.

So I ask for a rental application, and we take it back to the car and fill it in immediately. I can see another family approaching to view the house and I feel the competition — *no, you can't have it, that's my house!* The kids are getting restless in the back seat but I know in my bones we need to jump on this house now, not think about it, not wait and see. I hand the application back in and hope that the fact that we have two children won't penalize us when compared to other renters. The rental agent says we'll know on Monday or Tuesday whether we've been approved.

While we wait, I turn to my laptop. With all the travel and house-hunting, I haven't been getting much work done — a phone call here, an hour of writing there. And creating in the middle of things is harder now than it was back in Holland. I can't let myself think about the books too much or else I'll sink under the weight of everything I have to do. I am just trying to focus on getting settled so I can return to work in earnest, but I have an ominous feeling that I'm not going to have the space and time to bounce back the way I did in Detroit and Penang. Some big emotions are waiting for me on the other side of this move.

Staying with Simone and her family is a godsend. Lia and Nico have lots of toys to play with, and they spend a lot of time on the trampoline, giggling and shouting while their cousins roughhouse with them. I have long talks with Simone in the kitchen about everything from family history to international living (they were in Chile for several years before coming to Vancouver).

Finally, late in the day on Monday we get word — we've been approved! I feel the joy down to my toes as a big piece of the puzzle falls into place. We sign the lease on Tuesday and find out that we can move in a week earlier than expected. At last we have the precious piece of paper and can get the school registration process started. Maybe the kids can be in class in a week!

Now we have to reverse the process we followed in Ottawa and re-acquire all the necessities to set up house. This buying spree stirs up a lot of emotions for me. I feel tired at the thought of finding everything we need — beds, dressers, couches, chairs, tables. Doing research and making decisions takes energy, and I'm hoping that intuition combined with serendipity will smooth the way.

I feel weighed down by the tangible reminder that our travelling days are over for now. Flying here and hunting for a place to live, I could still pretend that we were mobile and flexible. But buying furniture means staying put. I'm wondering whether we'll be able to hold on to elements of Operation Hejira, like the material simplicity and lighter schedule, or whether we'll get drawn into the lifestyle of play dates, afterschool activities, parent councils, and church commitments and end up right back where we started.

I dread being responsible for stuff again. Hopefully travelling light for a year has inoculated me against frivolous purchases. I remember my vow to buy second-hand as much as possible, and I'm determined to do most of our shopping through the online classified ads.

The purchase that irks me the most is buying toilet brushes. I never wanted to own another toilet brush. It's a concession to the fact that I'll be cleaning bathrooms again.

I feel sheepish that I made such a big deal of selling everything and now we have to re-buy a lot just a year later. Does that make me look like a hypocrite? I hope not — Hejira wasn't supposed to be about the superiority of the location-independent lifestyle, but about following our desires and embracing our values. Now that those desires and values have brought us to Vancouver, things may look different on the surface, but we're still the same people underneath.

And finally, I must admit, I feel excited at the chance to start from square one. We all love snuggling up together on lazy mornings, so I am determined to get a king-sized bed this time around. There's one listing for a luxury mattress and frame that looks good, so I reach out and am astonished to learn that the couple who own the bed are selling everything they own so they can travel! It's too, too perfect. In addition to the bed, David and Jessica offer us a parade of their belongings: a leather couch, a barbecue, a computer monitor, an automatic hot water heater (for making tea and coffee on demand, don't you know).

We also visit a place that sells used furniture from hotels, and I get the biggest surprise — a matching set of armchairs in the same fabric as an ottoman I once owned (the one I bought with the money from selling my first story for publication). I adore them, and they are exactly the right size for our living room. We also spot a dark wood dinette set with six chairs. Sold and sold. And another find at a thrift shop: a mahogany-coloured IKEA desk that is identical to the one I had in my writing studio for years. I close my eyes and say thank-you for these little signs, small comforts from my past in this new place.

I call the school administrator and get good news. They've accepted the kids' registration, and Lia and Nico can start on Wednesday. Shawn and I talk over the options and decide that we'd like to be in Kitsilano for the week, even though we can't move into our new house yet. That way we'll be close for school drop-off and pickup, and Shawn can take the bus to his new office. After spending most of the summer as other people's guests, we're more than ready to be on our own again. Shawn finds a cute garden suite on Airbnb, and we move in on Sunday.

After months away from school and other kids, Lia and Nico are quite keen to start again. They help me make their lunches the day before and we pack Nico's containers into his good old froggie lunch bag. The next morning they put on their favourite clothes, and I make them pose for a photo holding signs that say Kindergarten and Grade 1. On the walk to school, we are all bouncing with anticipation — the kids to meet their teachers and classmates, and me to have my first childfree day in ages.

The ruckus in the hallway is a little overwhelming, but we get the kids installed in their classrooms with little fuss. What a change from Nico crying and vomiting in Penang! Shawn and I are just about to leave the school grounds when a woman with curly salt-and-pepper hair and a ready smile approaches us.

"Hi! I'm Sheila," she says in a perky voice. "I noticed that you have an adopted Chinese daughter."

Before I have time to register that her comment is a little forward, Sheila explains that she also has an adopted Chinese daughter, who happens to be in Lia's class. Not only that, but Sheila's daughter Anna was born in Jiangxi, the same province as Lia. And to top it off, Sheila is the co-chair of Families with Children from China BC, an organization that connects adoptive families in the province.

In other words, we have just met the most helpful, friendly, and simpatico person we could possibly ask for. Welcome to Kitsilano.

A few days later, it's my thirty-ninth birthday, and I wake up with an oppressive feeling of dread. Maybe it's because we're still in limbo and waiting to move into our new home. Maybe it's because the garden suite where we're staying is dastardly cold, and I just want to huddle under the duvet. It's definitely because my little relocation reprieve is over and I'm supposed to start working on the books again, but I can't because the kids are home from school for a Professional Development day. There is no special breakfast and no latte.

Feeling a little pathetic, I invite myself over to visit some new friends. Heather and I were at grad school in Calgary together, and she and her husband Jeremy and their two kids have just moved here from Toronto. When we arrive, I discover that Jeremy has bought cupcakes for my birthday. Seeing them in their plastic holder, bearing stiff pink grocery-store icing, I suddenly want to cry. His gesture is so kind and feels so undeserved, and yet it means the world to me.

After our snack, we take the kids to the park and talk about writing — Jeremy is a children's book author and illustrator. We commiserate over deadlines and the challenges of working with kids around. Lia and Nico are happily worn out by the time we head home. I pull myself together enough to order Chinese food, which we eat outside in the garden. Then I take a hot bath and curl up in bed with some comfort reading, a young adult romance novel called *Lola and the Boy Next Door.*

Next year's birthday is bound to be better, but I see some difficult months ahead.

Flow Exercise: Exercise Your Desire

I was fascinated to watch as Shawn and I navigated the logistics of our move to Vancouver. We had to make many decisions in a short time, often with limited information. The process was a master class in divining our desires. We knew that the life we were designing would be stronger and more supportive if we built it on a foundation of what we wanted, not what the world told us we should want.

Here are the things that helped:

Clarity: We had examined the previous incarnations of our lives to determine what we loved about them, everything from living car-free to a short, active commute to having the kids attend a neighbourhood school. We knew that we valued local community, natural beauty, and a simple but inviting living space. So we were able to transplant that old lifestyle into a new environment because we understood its essential ingredients.

Intuition: We didn't always reason out what would be the best direction, but listened to our instinct and the leap of our hearts. The beach and a seawall bike ride downtown were siren songs for Shawn. Something about the shopping streets and the library in Kitsilano made me feel at home. The little blue duplex instantly trumped every other house and apartment we'd seen.

Signs: We noticed and shared the little markers that showed us we were on track and drew encouragement from them. The desk and chairs that matched the ones I used to own. The fact that one of Shawn's coworkers lived around the corner from the duplex we rented. Our friends offering us a Groupon for a car-sharing service.

Every day, you get a chance to exercise your desire muscle. Make a decision today using your own clarity, intuition, and reading of the signs. Whether it's ordering a meal, buying a notebook, or picking an evening outing, try to choose swiftly and fluidly without much rational thought, and see how the choice fits. If you're happy (or not), what have you learned about what you want that you can remember for next time?

19 An Avalanche of Problems

My story is supposed to be over. We sold our house and travelled the world, and then we moved to Vancouver. The end.

Except there's that saying: "Everything will be okay in the end. If it's not okay, it's not the end."

And despite my attempts to chin up and muddle through, life is most decidedly not okay. I finally admit this when I find myself walking to school in the rain, choking back sobs because I could run into another parent at any moment. The end of October is near, and once again my workday has been cut short at 2:30 p.m., just when I was starting to get into the groove. The afterschool program at the kids' school is full — we're on the waiting list but we probably won't get in before the new year. I thought I had found a babysitter, but just before she was supposed to start, she emailed to say she'd taken another job offer and couldn't do it after all.

The ghostwriting project I'm working on is due in early November, and there's no way I'm going to make the deadline. I haven't even finished Part 1, and there are still Parts 2 and 3 to go after that. I forfeit part of my fee for every week that I'm late (yes, I put that clause in the contract, so it's my own fault). But I've lost my motivation to catch up because it seems hopeless. And I haven't had a good writing session in so long, I've lost faith that I can get back into the flow. My heyday of productivity during the fundraiser is far away.

Everywhere I look, there are problems. Solving one seems futile because there are twenty others waiting in the wings. The lack of childcare and the late contract are just the beginning, along with the fact that we are haemorrhaging money to pay for all the furniture and housewares, and I won't earn anything until Part 1 of the book is finished. Then there's *Pilgrimage*, which looks like it's going to be delayed indefinitely since the manuscript isn't close to done. I haven't been able to bring myself to work on it since September; every time I think about it, I am flooded by sadness that Operation Hejira is over and shame that the book is going to be late. The house is a welter of chaos — how I miss Mariana and the way she would leave our sparse apartment shiny and neat.

Mornings are plain awful. I scramble to put together lunches that the kids will eat, frying rice, toasting quesadillas, grilling French toast, boiling pasta, scrounging fruit and snacks. They're constantly changing what they like or what they'll eat, and it drives me crazy trying to keep up. Fig Newtons are Lia's favourite thing ever for three days, and then she refuses to eat them ever again. Nico loves bananas at home but leaves them uneaten in his lunch bag. Every other day, Lia melts down in a volcanic tantrum because the tights she wants aren't clean or because she doesn't like flax seeds in her oatmeal.

And I am sick. Miserably, relentlessly sick. It started with a cold just after we moved into the new house. At first I wasn't worried; it made sense to me that I'd come down with something given the stress, the new germ pool, and the wet environment. I could handle a week. But then another cold followed on its heels. I should have just taken a week off, given myself permission to lie in bed, binge-watch *Girls,* and eat chicken soup. But I soldiered on because otherwise I would have gotten buried in the avalanche of problems.

One morning, I notice that my eye is really weepy. I keep going to the washroom and picking out goop with a tissue. By the end of the day, the lid is pink and swollen, the lashes gummed up. I put two and two together and realize that I have an eye infection. Conjunctivitis. Off I troop to the drop-in clinic for eye drops.

On top of all that, Halloween is almost here, and I am spending my evenings feverishly knitting two hats. Lia wants to be a black cat, and Nico wants to be a bat musketeer, so I found a pattern with ears and whiskers that will suit both purposes. Why am I knitting hats when I have so much to do?

So now I am walking to school tormented by the unceasing procession of all these catastrophes, dashing away my tears, keeping my head down and hidden under my hood, hoping no one says hello. But I can't avoid the crowded hallway, all the kindergarten and Grade 1 students and their parents clustered around lockers and doorways. (My parents rarely walked me to and from school — at five years old I was getting myself there and back twice a day. And look what we've become, all these hovering adults, clogging up the works.) There's so much noise, and I don't know where to stand out of the way, and I just want to get home so I can have a tidy little private breakdown.

When Nico bounces out of his classroom and takes my hand, we fight our way upstream to Lia's door. Sheila is waiting there for her daughter Anna, and I say *hello, how are you*, attempt to smile and nod and hope my eyes aren't too red. Sheila's been inviting us to adoption community events and parent council activities, but so far I've begged off. We have had Anna over for a play date that was thoroughly enjoyed by all three kids, but I can't manage much more until I get healthy and get a handle on this book. Regret grows thick in the back of my throat. I really hope Sheila doesn't give up on me before we've had a chance to become friends.

Once Lia has switched her shoes for boots and donned her jacket and backpack, we can make our exit. I wrangle the kids down the sidewalk, and as often happens, they're both harassing me about being hungry and needing snacks and wanting screen time the minute we get home.

"I don't have anything to eat in my pocket; you'll have to wait," I say, and you'd think this rational statement of fact would be the end of it, but no, they keep insisting they are starving for something to eat, thinking, I assume, that I can produce food out of thin air.

I am wrung out at the end of the ten-minute walk and fire up the computer to show them a movie as quickly as possible. Then I go upstairs to strip off my soaking wet clothes and cry in bed until Shawn comes home. I have no idea what we'll eat for dinner; everything is frozen.

Am I depressed? I look like I am. I have the hollowed-out desperation, the occasional catatonia. I wake to the weight of despondence on my chest. I work slowly and sporadically. I have little good to say to Shawn about how my day went. I get flashbacks of our life in Malaysia and Holland that pierce me with loss.

But I do not have the hopelessness. Despite the crying jag, I do believe underneath that things will get better — when I find childcare, when I finish this book, when I make some more friends. I do not have the vicious invective against myself. I do not call myself names or think I am worthless, but I am gentle and try to show myself care by taking baths and doing yoga and making homemade soup. I don't have complete anhedonia — I'm still reading books and enjoying concerts and some touching moments with the kids.

And I believe that how I am feeling is a normal reaction to my circumstances. Of course I feel grief. Of course I am overwhelmed. Although Vancouver is very good, and though its newness and beauty offers some of what we love about travelling, Vancouver is not an extension of Operation Hejira.

Vancouver is a new operation that doesn't have a codename yet.

On Halloween, Lia and Nico put on their knitted hats, which I finished late the night before. Lia has a black shirt and yoga pants, Nico black leggings and a shiny blue and silver musketeer tunic that my parents gave him. At school, I stay for the Halloween parade, watching the costumed children march past the parents lining the hallways, tickled to see my kids part of this happy mob and also fretting over how much of my workday I'm losing.

In the afternoon, I talk to Bridget. We are in the same time zone now, and I have regular sessions with her because I need the psychological support. We talk about the impending deadline for the book I'm ghostwriting, and I give her the whole loving picture of what a truly messed-up situation it is, with me feeling like I'm moving a mountain with a teaspoon.

She tells me that I am holding emotional space for my client's book, which takes a lot of energy. This could sound like gobbledegook, but I know what she means instantly. Not only am I putting words onto the page, but I am helping him create something real in the world: a movement, a change, a new way of being for the people who will read his book and be influenced by it. I'm breaking ground so my client can move forward, demonstrate his authority with tangible proof of what he knows and offers, and forging that new identity is not an easy thing.

Bridget's insight crumbles my brave façade. No wonder I'm struggling with what this work is costing me. Not to mention that my domestic overhead has tripled, and I only have half the working hours I did before. Just admitting what a huge task I'm undertaking with limited resources helps me feel more stable and give myself grace. And remembering that I am choosing to do this work, that I am not giving up because my client and the job and the money are important to me, is quietly liberating.

Then, over the weekend, a little miracle happens. I put a notice in the school newsletter that I was looking for afterschool care, and another mom at the school mentions that maybe she could babysit for me. Alex is the parent council rep for Nico's kindergarten class, and her daughter Martha is good buddies with Nico. At first I don't take her offer seriously. I mean, Alex already has three children, aged two, five, and eight. I can barely handle my own two kids; how would she manage five? And why would she want to?

But she mentions it the next day as well, so I drop by her house so we can talk details. Again, this is mostly me asking variations of, "Are you sure you want to do this?" and her saying yes. Alex and her family are from Scotland and don't have permanent residency yet, so babysitting will be a way for her to make a little money. Her household is loud and happy and energetic, much like ours, and there's no doubt that the kids would enjoy each other's company. So we settle on terms and it's official: I have afterschool childcare starting Monday.

On November 5, I reset the book schedule with my client. I won't be able to deliver the manuscript until the end of January. He takes it hard, saying that he's surprised, shocked, and unhappy. But amazingly, he wants to keep moving forward. I'm relieved that he doesn't want to fire me, but that he can get past my broken promise and keep working with me. The revised schedule gives me a sense of space and optimism that I haven't had in months.

My new tactic is to take my computer with me when I drop the kids at school, work at a coffee shop for an hour, and then move to the library. I do this one morning and finish over one thousand words, which feels like great progress, but as I'm powering down my laptop, I realize that I feel so awful, I need to see a doctor. I've had a really bad cough for a week, and now I am faint and a little feverish.

I check in at the drop-in clinic, feeling sheepish because there's not much wrong with me. What if it's just a virus? But there's only a thirty-minute wait, so I decide to stay. The doctor is very nice. I tell her that I've had a cold for a month. She listens to me breathe and hears crackling at the bottom of my lungs. She doesn't call it pneumonia, but she gives me antibiotics and an inhaler. So there was something wrong after all. Good to know.

The antibiotics help, but ten days later, I feel as bad as before. My breathing is shallow so as not to disturb what feels like a deep pool of fluid in my lungs. I have coughing fits that leave me doubled over, gasping for air and holding my ribs. I go back to the clinic and get another round of stronger antibiotics, which finally clears up the fever and body ache but leaves the congestion in my chest.

Each morning, I drag myself out of bed as though it's a pit of mud. I feel like my mind is only firing on half its neurons, and it's all I can do to make breakfast and lunches and assemble paperwork and get Lia and Nico ready for school, all at the same time. The kids insist on asking me questions while I'm busy turning my lungs inside out, as though they don't notice I can't reply, and one time I'm so stressed that I roar at Nico, "I can't talk when I'm coughing!" Another time he depresses the last few puffs from my inhaler, and I shout at him again, "Leave that alone! I need that!" The medicated vapour is my only hope of keeping the fits subdued.

In mid-December, I am still coughing so much that I have to leave a coffee shop only an hour into my morning writing session. The regulars in this place must hate when I walk in, having to listen to the wheezing hack every thirty seconds. I'm so hopeful each time that I've gotten my lungs clear, bought a few minutes of peace, but then the tickle starts again, a crinkling in my chest, and I'm hunched over, stomach muscles aching, bringing up gobs of phlegm.

One night I catch Shawn watching the latest episode of *Boardwalk Empire* without me.

"What are you doing?" I ask. "You keep acting like I'm not even here." I reel off examples of this pattern of benign neglect, the way he spends hours on the computer playing train simulation games or falls asleep on the couch right after dinner. Some nights we hardly talk. It reminds me of the way he avoided me during our residence days, when I was depressed.

Now I pester him until he finally admits what's going on.

"I'm really happy here," he says. I know this is true. I've never heard him talk so excitedly about his job before, and he is constantly going into raptures about biking home from work along the sea wall, or running in Pacific Spirit Park, or taking walks at the beach. He's always loved the mild temperatures of spring and fall, and now he has them all year round: the thermometer has rarely dipped below freezing here and we've only had one day of snow.

"And?" I ask.

"I'm afraid that if we talk about you being unhappy ... I don't know what I might have to do to make you feel better."

Ah, so that's it. He thinks that if he looks too closely at what I'm going through, we might have to leave Vancouver. And that makes me really sad, that right now he can't trust me to consider his happiness when I'm trying to make myself happy, that his fear is trumping his love for me at the moment. But I know how he feels. He was struggling last summer in Detroit, sad to have left Ottawa and anxious to get overseas. And mostly I ignored that struggle, because I didn't share it and didn't want anything to kill my buzz.

I get that he can't take care of me right now, that I need to step up and take care of myself. But that doesn't mean it doesn't hurt.

And finally, we aren't flying home for Christmas. Not only would the tickets cost money we don't have, but my energy level is not up to travelling. I'm just starting to get some momentum on my client's book, and if I can catch up over the holidays, I might be okay. The kids are disappointed — heck, we're all disappointed. The consolation is that we'll see Simone and her family on Boxing Day, and Sheila has invited us for their big Christmas Eve gathering.

The decision to stay in Vancouver is confirmed when I develop yet another sore throat during the kids' final week of school. Flying would have been torture. As it is, I can hardly keep it together for a special evening outing with Colin and Tracy Burns, our friends from Penang. They're in town for ten days with Colin's family before they head to Big White for a few weeks of skiing. I've arranged for us to meet at a restaurant in Chinatown and then tour the Sun Yat Sen Garden as part of the Winter Solstice celebration. I watch everyone else eat spring rolls, wonton, and crispy beef while I drink hot tea and try not to swallow too much. Seeing our Australian friends on our own turf is somewhat bizarre, but I'm glad that we've been able to stay in touch and preserve a little piece of our travelling life.

The next morning, Saturday, it becomes clear that I have more than a scratchy throat. My temperature has climbed overnight, and I feel too faint to get off the couch. What I thought was a burn from a piece of hot pizza or an overly vigorous brushing of my teeth is turning into dozens of sores on my swollen gums. I remember that Nico brought home a notice about a classmate with a case of hand, foot, and mouth disease. Looks like this is more than a simple cold or flu — I've got a nasty virus and I'll just have to ride it out.

Ten days, it takes. Ten days spent horizontal in sweats and fatigue, napping and reading and watching *Glee* and trying not to moan myself into oblivion. Poor Shawn is left with cooking and childcare for the whole holiday. I feel so bad for the kids, who are mostly trapped in the house, cranky and bored. We have to cancel our visits with Simone and Sheila. I can't eat anything solid or drink anything hot — I can't even brush my teeth because the bristles provoke shooting pain. I lose a noticeable amount of weight and never do manage to send out the Christmas cards. And my hopes of getting caught up on the book are shot. Forget writing, I can barely make a grocery list.

I give up.

Flow Exercise: Tonglen

I'll admit it: part of me believed that Operation Hejira meant I would never suffer again. I was secretly betting that I'd reached enlightenment, that I'd cracked the code for happiness even in the midst of challenges. But life in Vancouver got hard and stayed that way. I kept hoping the problems would resolve quickly, but they didn't. My body was giving me messages that I didn't want to hear about grief and change.

What I know now is that this period in my life was not a sign of failure. It was not a punishment. It was just a turn of the labyrinth. Another spiral deeper into myself and what I'm here to learn.

I know I'm not the only writer or artist who has felt busy, disoriented, and smothered, whether negotiating a big life change or not. If you're there now, will you do this exercise with me? (Bridget gave me this to help me regain my footing — it's based on a type of Buddhist meditation called *tonglen*, which means giving and receiving.)

Close your eyes and imagine everyone around the world who is wobbly and wants to get grounded, who is tired and wants a break, who is lonely and wants to be seen. Reach out to all of those people and wish them peace and ease and connection from the bottom of your swirly, overwhelmed heart.

And then, imagine that all of us are sending that peace and ease and connection back to you. I am doing that right now. I am beaming you the rock-solidness of the mountains, and the nimble current of whitewater, and an enormous West Coast hug.

20 You Can't Bake a Cake Without a Cake Pan

"It is easier to enhance creativity by changing conditions in the environment than by trying to make people think more creatively."
— Mihaly Csikszentmihalyi, *Creativity: Flow and the Psychology of Discovery and Invention*

The holiday virus has reduced me to a helpless babe. Square one. Unable even to feed myself or walk around. Sapped of any strength or recovery I'd made in the fall. Momentum on the ghostwriting project has ground to a halt, and precious extra weeks are slipping through my hands. Happy New Year indeed. I could put on a diaper and pose as 2013.

In early January, I go to a one-day New Year's retreat on Bainbridge Island, Washington with Jen Louden, an author who teaches about the challenges of caring for oneself while also serving the world.

The theme of the retreat is Savoring Your Heart's Whispers, and one of the questions Jen asks us is, "What is your name right now?" Because I feel like I have lost all solidity, I don't want a human name — I want an elemental name. I've been reading Alan Lightman's book *Mr g: A Novel About the Creation*, and Joni Mitchell is always in my mind, so the name that comes to me is Stardust. The word speaks of the unformed, the diffuse. I am in a place of pure potential, ancient and full of light. At least, that's how I feel. Back at the beginning.

Jen's teaching encourages me to go back to my long-ago study of the heroine's journey. Everyone knows the hero's journey of Joseph Campbell, which is the prototype for everything from the Gilgamesh epic to *Moby-Dick* to Harry Potter. But when I was writing my bullying novel, I discovered the counterpart, the story of the heroine, whose journey takes a different shape. While the hero's tale traces a linear arc from start to finish, the heroine's is circular and episodic, like a spiral or labyrinth.

The hero is content at the beginning of his story until his perfect life is disrupted by a call to adventure. But the heroine starts out miserable, having awakened from the illusion of her perfect life to realize that she has no power. In this framework, I have to peg the opening of my story to the moment I admitted I was depressed. My life looked good, with a husband and a corporate job and lots of friends and family. But I felt trapped, not only by my circumstances but by my patterns of behaviour — the way I put others first and denied myself the creative life I craved.

Whereas the hero progresses by defeating ever larger opponents, the heroine descends into the underworld and is stripped of every weapon until she stands defenceless. In the years of therapy and healing, I've surrendered my arsenal of martyrdom, appeasement, silence, guilt, workaholism, the denial of my own desire. I've laid my marriage on the line. I've put down my childfree shield, which I thought I needed to protect me from the compulsion for self-sacrifice. I've shed the ego-stroking and material supports: the job, the house, the furniture.

The hero wins the reward at this point, but the heroine has merely reached the eye of the storm. Everything seems calm, which lulls her into a false sense of security. But the loss of her weapons wasn't the true ordeal, only the preparation. All along I've been thinking that Operation Hejira was the end of my struggles, the reward for the work of paring back my psyche to the bone. But it has only been an interlude, a restorative pause so I can catch my breath before this journey's climax.

But here, where the hero returns home in triumph for one last battle, the heroine faces a total reversal. Suddenly, all is lost — a virtual or physical death. The grief I harboured in my lungs this fall tells the truth: Operation Hejira is gone, and I am bereft.

At last I understand that I am not at the beginning of my story, nor at the end. I am entering Act III, when everything comes together. And my determination kicks in — the same determination that saw me through depression in the first place, its wild and desperate quality mellowed to steady assurance. I want to show that laying down all my defences was worth it, that I can face adversity and find a different way through with help from others and devotion to myself. I need to remember that having a rough time doesn't mean I'm a bad person or that I haven't learned anything. I'm just getting the chance to rise to a new challenge. The time has come to gather support. The heroine knows that she cannot be reborn alone. She needs people and places to hold her up.

I know exactly what I support I want. I want to write in a group, in a space outside my house.

When I'm sad and tired and the house is messy, I need to exert a lot of willpower to work instead of reading or watching TV. But when I'm out, especially when I'm with others who are working alongside me, I have so much more focus and flow.

I first discovered write-ins during National Novel Writing Month in Ottawa, when people working on their books would gather in a coffee shop or food court and support each other just with their silent, typing presence. I organized a write-in at Raw Sugar Cafe for my last birthday before Hejira, and it was so delicious to feel the creative hum in the room as people scribbled in their notebooks and typed on their laptops.

Now I get on the Internet and search Meetup.com for writing groups. I don't want critique or discussion or teaching — too much potential for comparison and hurt feelings, walking the minefield of feedback. I just want writing. And I find the perfect thing: Just Write Vancouver. They have a Saturday morning event in East Vancouver every week, which doesn't really work for my schedule. But Shannon, the organizer, is open to people starting new groups, which is ideal for me because I can pick the time and place. I go to a Tuesday evening event in Yaletown to try it out and meet Shannon, and I'm thrilled with the possibilities (not to mention the words I write that night). I return to Kitsilano and scope out the best spot in my neighbourhood, a bright, quiet coffee shop with a few long tables and lots of electrical outlets. The January resolution energy seems to inspire the membership, and within a few weeks we're drawing over a dozen people to write side by side on Thursday nights.

But I want more. I want a coworking space where I can work every day. Coffee shops aren't going to cut it long term — I can't bring my lunch, and I can't leave my computer to go to the bathroom, and they're often too crowded and noisy. There are a few coworking spaces in downtown Vancouver, and I book trial days at all of them. One is funky and affordable, but all the members are men; another is impersonal (I don't get a tour, and I have to ask where the bathroom is); the last is large and noisy. And all are a bus ride away from Kitsilano. But at least being out looking gives me a sense of excitement and purpose. And more words written.

Then I meet with Mitchell, a web designer who is opening a new coworking office in Kitsilano. It turns out that we live practically on the same block! He had been coworking downtown but didn't like the commute and decided to start his own space — he's just signed the lease on a suite near Burrard Bridge. I really enjoy talking to Mitchell, who is also a dad to a six-month-old girl and enjoys travel, camping, and good food. He seems like someone I'd love to have as a friend — enthusiastic and hard-working and thoughtful. I hope he gets his enterprise off the ground because it's the closest fit to my criteria — small and sociable and close by.

I also find another kind of support in the form of an online self-portrait photography course. I've been watching people post selfies on Facebook and Instagram for years without the slightest inclination to join them. But then Melody asks me to share some photos of what life looks like in Vancouver. Shawn did most of the family blogging and photo-sharing while we travelling, but that's dropped off now that he's gone back to work. And I find the downloading, editing, exporting, and uploading from our point-and-shoot camera too daunting. But when Melody asks, I decide to figure out how to use Shawn's iPod Touch to upload straight to the web.

First I share a photo of our back alley as seen from my office window. Then one of my new green bicycle and me in my bike helmet. A few of the kids — Lia skipping rope on the way to school and Nico cutting his crepes into the shape of Shel Silverstein's Missing Piece.

After the torrent of online activity for my fundraiser, the fall had shocked me into silence. Whenever I tried to blog or tweet, or even write in my journal, I found myself stopped, the words smothered. I couldn't even see inside myself — the view was smoky and obscured.

But now, posting grainy photos on Facebook, I feel seen again. I can see myself. I have a new way to tell the story of me.

So I sign up for Vivienne McMaster's self-portrait class, Be Your Own Beloved. Maybe doing a course for something so simple betrays a lack of self-confidence; why don't I just take more photos on my own? But I want the scaffolding of daily prompts, encouraging direction, little technological tips, and comments from the other participants. Posting my pictures in a group for a shared purpose feels more meaningful and more nurturing than taking random shots on my own. And I don't need to look beyond my own desire to see this is a good thing to do: Vivienne's photo prompt email is the first thing on my mind when I wake up. Taking and sharing my photo is often the brightest part of my day.

So this little creative outlet makes me happier because I feel more whole. There is my face with its dimples and shaded cheekbones and dark eyes. There are my slippers on the mat next to Lia's pink rain boots. There is the spiderweb scar on my hand, the flute of my collarbone. I'm real. I deserve to be photographed. I deserve to be loved.

Between Just Write meetups and coworking days and lots of decaf lattes in coffee shops and the kids finally getting into the afterschool program, it happens. I mean, I make it happen. I write and edit and check and review, and I deliver a fifty-thousand-word book to my client in mid-February. He is delighted. He sends me flowers, I send him wine. The mountain has been moved.

To celebrate, I order my very first smartphone. I've had mixed feelings about the constant distraction that seems to go along with smartphones, but after using Shawn's iPod Touch for a few months, for photos and audiobooks and even an exercise program, I believe the usefulness outweighs the dangers. I'll finally have my calendar, my address book, and a map always with me instead of having to remember to look things up before I go out. I can keep a shopping list and use a budgeting program. Another little support structure.

I also go on retreat. I haven't had an overnight writing getaway since Penang, almost a year ago. Shawn was away for five days in January, so it's easy to ask for a reciprocal weekend off, and I find a shared room for rent on Airbnb in a stately old home on Arbutus Ridge. I know I'm in recovery, so I don't expect myself to jump on *Pilgrimage* at top speed. Instead I nap and watch *Pitch Perfect*, knit and write in my journal.

When I finally do re-read my unfinished manuscript, I have mixed feelings. Yes, it's good, but I wrote it when I was in the centre of the labyrinth, and my excitement and starry-eyed wonder belong there, in the time of respite and stillness called *illumination*. I will need to finish the book soon if I want to preserve the aura of that place, because I have begun my journey out again, plunged into the challenge of *union*. There's so much uncertainty and turbulence as I pull together everything I've done and been.

I had pictured spending a few days a week on *Pilgrimage* now that the ghostwriting project is done, but my client has more things for me to write: postcards, emails, web pages, and quizzes. Another client wants me to write an ebook, package her workshop materials, and do the copy for a technology website. Between them they want to book all my time from March until July. Crikey. I don't see how I can say no because the money and experience would be really valuable. The one comfort is that Mitchell has opened his coworking space, Suite Genius, in a beautiful stylish sky-lit room that I can bike to from home in ten minutes. When I see it, my heart reaches up to shake me and says, "I want to work here!" I can just picture the quiet productive days, the company, the routine. If I join, I know I can get lots done and start making up the financial shortfall from last year. So in March I join Suite Genius and sign on for all the client work I can get.

Part of me despairs and rebels at having to postpone my own project even further, but I'm still too depleted to hold more space for *Pilgrimage*. At the beginning, I was writing the book while I was living it, celebrating it. My spirits were high, and I was delighted to put my experience into words. But now I feel like I'm writing a memorial, an obituary.

I'm still grieving the end of Hejira because life was easier on Hejira. Writing was easier. I miss all the places where I worked on *Pilgrimage*: at the Grosse Pointe library, on the airplane, next to the pool, in the car driving through the Dutch countryside.

Resting was easier. I miss Thursdays with my sister Melody, and the quiet mornings with Shawn in Penang when the kids were at school. I miss empty weekends and long hours travelling with nothing to do. I miss napping and yoga and swimming.

Holding my home lightly was easier. Not easy, but easier. I miss being able to fit all of our dishes and pots in one dish rack. I miss having half-empty closets and drawers. I miss Mariana coming twice a week. I miss the butter chicken and grilled fish and *nasi goreng*.

Now everything feels hard. Handling the kids and keeping the house going is hard. Someone is always whining or shouting or crying or fighting. There's so much to remember: home reading, gymnastics clothes, library books, permission slips, hot lunch fees, pyjama days, and dentist appointments. The laundry never ends. Dinner is relentless.

Keeping our spending in check is hard. The price of soup and pasta in the grocery store makes me gasp. A cookie at a coffee shop is more than a whole meal in Penang. I used to go days without pulling out my credit card and now it smokes from overuse.

Writing is hard. *Pilgrimage* and I need to be born again into this new life, this busy, expensive, urban life far away from our families, where we are no longer travellers.

But no matter where I am, or how hard life is, or how far away I seem from writing, I hold fast to this truth: I am still a writer, and *Pilgrimage* is still my book.

Flow Exercise: Your Heroine's Journey

I learned about the feminine counterpart to the hero's journey from Victoria Lynn Schmidt. In her book *45 Master Characters,* she describes the nine stages that track the heroine from the illusion of a perfect world through the gates of judgment to the moment when all is lost, then back through rebirth and return. She writes, "Many women realize they're living a life filled with other people's goals and ambitions. They have no sense of what they truly want deep down inside until their world comes crashing down around them and they're forced to reexamine everything."

In addition to helping me with my fiction writing, these nine stages give me a way of making sense of my life and understanding how far I've come. The heroine's journey showed me that the painful awakening to depression and the stripping-away of my coping mechanisms were necessary steps in my story. I also gained strength to gather myself for the next stage when I saw how close I was to the end of this cycle of my narrative.

Where are you in your heroine's journey? (Both men and women can have a heroine's journey, just as both men and women can have a hero's journey.) Can you point to the inciting incident when you woke up to your unhappiness? Have you been shedding your weapons and defences? Have you encountered the eye of the storm? Have you experienced a death? Have you gathered support and come back to claim a new life? What's the impact of knowing where you are in your story?

21 Labyrinth of Light

Spring in Vancouver is a concerto of colour that goes on for weeks. Purple and yellow crocuses emerge on our back lawn in February. Snowdrops follow, crouched under hedges that stayed green and leafy all winter. I've known the word *rhododendron* for a long time, but I've never connected it with the torrid pink and magenta buds that light up all over garden shrubs. Magnolias were just brown-and-green leaves in a Martha Stewart magazine until now, when the pink and white alien flowers whirl open on bare branches. And the smell. I walk to school to pick up the kids, inhaling like a paint-huffing junkie, and still I can't get all the fragrance into my nose fast enough. Every yard gives off a different note, like walking down a perfume counter. And then come the cherry blossoms, velvet curls sprouting above our heads and transforming the streetscape with great dust clouds of light.

Spring in Ottawa only seemed to last a few days, barely giving the tulips a chance to emerge before turning up the heat for summer. Spring in Malaysia didn't exist. But spring in Vancouver is a virtuosic performance that lifts my mood with a flurry of cherry blossom snow.

And spring in Vancouver also means skiing during Spring Break. Shawn and I have rarely been skiing since the kids came along, but we think they're old enough to try, and it seems a crime not to when there are so many world-class mountains nearby. Back in January we visited Colin and Tracy at Big White near Kelowna, and the kids had their first lessons on rented equipment. They seemed ready and willing, so we bought second-hand skis and boots and registered them for a weeklong ski camp at Grouse Mountain.

I am aware of the contradiction between my fussing over needing to work and paying off our debt and the decision to drop hundreds of bucks on ski equipment, passes, and lessons. I haven't forgotten the agony of the stereo system and how I resented it for forcing me to work more and write less. But I also haven't forgotten the imperative of Hejira, which is to seize opportunities when they come to do things that fill us with joy.

The night before ski lessons, I am even more organized than usual. There's a checklist on my smartphone of everything we need, from snacks to parking pass to lip balm. The kids' bags and lunches are packed, and I figured out the schedule for our 7:15 a.m. departure time. I am thrilled to have arranged a week off work.

We drive over Lion's Gate Bridge in the pink morning light, get suited up, and do our goofy heel-toe walk in ski boots to the Sky Ride. I drop the kids with their instructors and head up the mountain alone for my first time on the slopes in ages. A decade since I last skied? How did that happen?

The lifts have just opened, and the runs are pristine. I give myself permission to take it slow, stick to the easy hills until I get my mountain legs back. Standing at the top of a river of white between banks of trees, my chest expands to take in the air and the view of rocky peaks like sharp grey and white coral. Wind and joy on the descent make it hard to catch my breath.

Back at the top of the mountain, I take a self-portrait that reflects the camera in my pink ski goggles. I laugh to think that the ski hills of British Columbia would have been a luxurious and expensive March Break trip if we lived in Ontario, and now they are in our own back-yard. I remember our weekend trip to the island of Koh Lipe when I had the same feeling.

Shawn takes a few days off work himself, and on Thursday we ski together, giddy as high schoolers, holding hands on the lift. On Friday, we drop the kids off and go for a walk along the shore at Burrard Inlet in the warm spring light, which reminds me of our mornings alone together in Penang.

I know Shawn is relieved that I am finally perking up and starting to fall in love with Vancouver the way he has. I had to navigate my unhappiness on my own and find the supports I needed, and he's here to meet me on the other side. I now count his withdrawal during my struggle as something of a gift because it helped me step up for myself. Sometimes a partner's limitations serve you as much as their generosity.

Writing sessions for *Pilgrimage* in March and April have ranged from discouraging to excruciating. The first Thursday in May, at a Just Write meetup, I declare that I will not leave until I have written at least one paragraph. I do, but it takes three hours. The manuscript has been like a solid sheet of ice, cold and unyielding. Prizing in that one paragraph bloodies my fingernails. I torment myself with thoughts that the book will never open to me again, that I will have to walk away leaving it half-formed.

The next week, though, as I re-read Chapter 10 yet again, my heart warms with love for the words, for the person I'd been when I lived and wrote those scenes. They are good. I want to add to them. I test the ice with my foot, and just like that it gives way, breaking apart to fluid water underneath. I insert a sentence. I reshape a paragraph from my journal and place it in. A new paragraph appears, spontaneous and playful. I am writing!

After ninety minutes, I have one thousand new words in Chapter 10. I float home on a wave of relief. Suddenly I can imagine working on the book in the mornings, finishing a few chapters on a writing retreat. *Pilgrimage* has let me in again. The difference between the book from one week to the next is so palpable, I feel like a buzzing, menacing electric fence around the text has suddenly been switched off. Why? Maybe because of the spring weather and the flowers. Maybe because of the love letter I wrote. Maybe because I've been biking to work. Maybe because I sat with the book every Thursday night. Maybe because enough time has passed.

The current running through the electric fence was emotion: grief, disappointment, nostalgia, and shame, a potent mix that had to be acknowledged and allowed to pass through my body and my heart until the juice ran out and the charge dropped. My heroine's journey is moving into rebirth in time with spring.

I work steadily on the book through June and July, and in August, I pack for a trip to Hollyhock Retreat Centre on Cortes Island. I'm going to a Deep Writing workshop with Eric Maisel. I missed him last fall at Omega, but now he's coming to BC, and I'll be there as a fortieth birthday present to myself.

I doubt I could come up with a more idyllic vacation for myself than Deep Writing at Hollyhock. The property overlooks an ocean bay that teems with bioluminescence after the sun sets. Gourmet vegetarian meals are served — meals that I do not need to lift a finger or spare a thought to prepare. I can read, sleep, and write whenever I want to. I get up early to work on my book and then go to yoga class.

And I am taught daily by my foremost creative mentor. In his slow, assured cadence, Eric reminds us that we do not need to entertain thoughts that don't serve us, even if they are true. We can err on the side of our own opinion and decide to prove the exception when we are seized by doubt and discouragement. We can make our own meaning, writing not for fame or money or accolades, but just because the process of writing matters to us.

Our small band of writers begins the retreat making small talk about where we live and how old our kids are, and these conversations spin wider and deeper, into threads of ideas and feelings that connect us close. On our last night, another writer and I become engrossed in discussion about family and travel over dinner, and we carry our talk to the hot tubs overlooking the ocean, and then into the ocean itself, on bare feet over rocks and logs, the bioluminescence in the water mirroring the stars overhead. I add these little creatures, dinoflagellates, to my list of the many ways stardust has appeared to me this year.

On Labour Day weekend, our family goes for a cycling outing. Shawn and I have created makeshift tandems by attaching trailer bikes for the kids to the backs of our own bikes. I throw sunscreen and water bottles into my front basket, and we head up a steep road toward Pacific Spirit Park. Lia fusses that the forest will be too dark and scary, but when we arrive and embark on our hike, she's darting ahead on the path, inspecting ferns, and gazing up at half-burned mossed-over tree trunks. "I love the smell here," Shawn says, and I breathe it in, green and ancient and mouldering.

We bike on afterward, down the hill to a little café by the beach where we buy banana popsicles. The sun pours caramel onto the sand,

and we take off our shoes to watch while the kids scamper like goats, kicking and spinning and falling over, Lia riding Nico's back the way she did at the airport in Singapore.

Another memory hits me, and I turn to Shawn.

"This is Ameland," I say. "The tandem bikes. Riding through the forest. Playing in the sand at the beach. Eating at the café. We have all of it here, any time we want. Anything is possible."

Shawn squeezes my hand as though he had planned this all along and I've just clued in now. The labyrinth twists, and we think we're somewhere new, going in a different direction, but our desires persist, helping us create what we love all over again.

Our second fall in Vancouver is a breeze compared to our first. We settle in to a good morning routine, adding in time for Chinese homework now that the whole family is going to Mandarin lessons on Saturday mornings. We find a neighbourhood church that feels like home. I start organizing all-day writing meetups at my coworking space every other month. We host a bunch of old college friends for Thanksgiving dinner and cook our very first turkey.

In December, for Winter Solstice, we go to Chinatown for the lantern festival. It's exactly a year since we met Colin and Tracy here for dinner, when I came down with the terrible Christmas virus that had me in bed for ten days. This year we meet up with our friend Sheila, her husband Don, and their daughter Anna, carrying homemade paper lanterns in a cheerful, motley procession to Sun Yat Sen Garden.

At the end of the evening, we take the kids home on the bus and put them to bed. It's tempting to cozy up with Shawn on the dark, chilly night, but I'm heading out again to Granville Island, where the Solstice festival has created a Labyrinth of Light. All those times on our trip, in France and the Netherlands, I had tried to visit labyrinths and failed. This time I know in my bones that I must go. The labyrinth is more than a metaphor; it's a physical journey that my body needs to experience.

When I arrive, the room is in shadows, and the path of the labyrinth is illuminated by flickering candles in paper bags. Something about the place seems very familiar, like I have been here before. Droning chant music plays in the background, and a few people off to the side add the voices of singing bowls. I pause to get my bearings, read the instructions, and take a few photos before I enter the labyrinth.

Walking slowly feels awkward. I have to fight the urge to turn around and see whether I'm holding anyone up. I want to savour the experience, but I don't want to frustrate the people behind me.

I'm reflecting on all that has happened since I last walked a labyrinth at a retreat centre in Arnprior, Ontario on my thirty-fourth birthday. My parents were there, and I walked with one-year-old Lia in a sling. In the six years since, we had adopted another child, left Ottawa, travelled for a year, and resettled in Vancouver.

I feel that this is the moment that marks my transition away from Operation Hejira. I need to say good-bye once and for all. I begin the litany in my head.

Good-bye, Ottawa. The canal, the Parliament buildings, our neighbourhood streets where we pushed our stroller.

Good-bye, Nepean Street. The sunny kitchen, my writing desk in the loft, the alphabet animals in the kids' bedroom.

Good-bye, all my stuff. The books, the artwork, the bedroom set, and the pink recliner.

I feel a surge of emotion, and the tears start, so I know I'm on the right track.

Good-bye, Detroit. Meeting cousins at the playground, making dinner in my sister's kitchen.

Good-bye, Malaysia. The view of the ocean, the afternoon swimming, never being cold.

Good-bye, Holland. The flat green fields, coffee in sitting rooms, games of Kolonisten.

Good-bye, Ontario. Snowy winter, friends and family, childhood haunts.

When I arrive in the centre of the labyrinth, I am full-on bawling. I have no tissues, so I wipe my snotty nose and teary face on my sweatshirt sleeve. My eyes are tight closed (because, as my favourite yoga teacher says, that way no one can see you), and I stand there, trying not to take up too much space so people can get by me.

"Amma, this is a marker," I pray silently. "I'm leaving Operation Hejira here, at this spot. I'm carrying on with life in Vancouver, *Pilgrimage*, and all that." I can imagine Her smiling, resting a hand on my head in blessing. We will always find each other in the labyrinth.

When I'm feeling calm and complete, I venture out again. As I walk, I think about this city, everything to enjoy here, starting with this Solstice festival. I think about the spring flowers, my coworking office, the parents and kids at school, the concerts that Shawn and I go to. I think about walking to the beach in the evening and swimming at Kitsilano Pool. I think about how the hard times make the easier times possible, and the easier times make the hard times more meaningful. By the time I leave the labyrinth, I have a big grin on my face.

Not long after, I discover why the Labyrinth of Light seemed so familiar. I had found a photo of it when we were living in Penang and used it to illustrate one of my posts about depression. I had hardly noticed that the labyrinth was created by the Solstice festival in Vancouver, and I certainly never imagined that I would be living there and walk it myself.

In the grand scheme of world history, the fact that I got depressed, took a trip, and wrote a book about it isn't that important. And there were many moments while I was writing when I thought, "Who's going to care about this story? Anyone could have done what I did."

And that, I think, is partly why the story matters. Because it's not exotic and sensational. I'm not unusual or extraordinary. I'm just a woman who decided to stop trying to be a good girl and go after what she wanted. A woman who realized that she could do more for the world by being herself.

Just before we adopted Lia, I read Elizabeth Gilbert's book *Eat, Pray, Love*, which is also about a woman who got depressed, took a trip, and wrote a book about it. Reading that book was like being injected with a radioactive tracer that lit up all the desire centres of my body. My feet wanted to travel, my mouth wanted to eat fresh pasta, my throat wanted to write, my spine wanted to do yoga, my belly wanted to make love on a tropical island (and, unlike Gilbert's, my arms wanted to cradle a baby). She's gotten a lot of flack for writing that book: people say that she was cheating because she financed it with a publisher's advance, that she was only playing tourist, that the book is inferior because it isn't hard-hitting journalism like her previous work.

But I don't care because I didn't read *Eat, Pray, Love* as an artifact of literature. I read it like a map of where I could go. I loved how she chose her destinations of Italy, India, and Indonesia based on personal connections to the language, the food, and the spiritual practice. I admired her chutzpah in raising the money she needed. And I was impressed by the faith she had in herself, that she would live a story worth telling, that she would discover her heroine's journey on the way.

Sometimes we can imagine and go where no one has gone before. And sometimes we need the faint track on the ground ahead, the reassurance that others wanted to veer off the pavement and had the resolve to do so, and that everything worked out okay in the end. Sometimes we need the ancient geometric lines of a labyrinth that we can surrender to, knowing they will lead through all their turning to the centre and back again.

And here is the end of this pilgrimage of desire. I will have others. Some I haven't told you about. But this one ends in Vancouver, between the beach and the mountains. I am okay. I am more than okay. I have the happiness of a good story of my life, and I have many brain waves of pleasure too. I have good company as I walk my desire lines and labyrinths. And I have the marvellous game of writing to play for the rest of my days.

Afterword

I wrote *Pilgrimage of Desire* for all those who feel trapped in a life that doesn't let them practice their creativity in a way that feeds their soul, for those who have so much to express but have boxed themselves in with rules and responsibilities.

If that's you, I'd love to continue the conversation that this book has started. To help you take your next steps on the road of hope, I created a workbook with all of the Flow Exercises available for free at gresik.ca/books/pilgrimage-of-desire.

My pilgrimage is that much more meaningful in the companionship of others. So please come to www.gresik.ca to share your own stories, questions, and insights.

Further Reading

Martha Beck, "The Formula for Happiness" at marthabeck.com. I also recommend her books *Finding Your Own North Star* and *Steering by Starlight* for discovering your desires and going after them.

David D. Burns, *Feeling Good* and *The Feeling Good Handbook*. Burns provides a thorough and accessible introduction to working with depressive thoughts in order to improve your mood.

Julia Cameron, *The Artist's Way*. If you are just beginning to explore your creative desires or returning to them after some time away, Cameron's program of journalling and artist's dates is a fun and effective way to do that.

Carol P. Christ, *Diving Deep and Surfacing*. My thesis supervisor, Aritha, assigned me this book of literary criticism about women's spiritual quests back in grad school, which reminds me that I have been engaged with the heroine's journey for a long time.

Mihalyi Csikszentmihalyi, *Flow* and *Creativity*. Through his research, Csikszentmihalyi gives us a detailed portrait of the flow state and compelling insights on how to cultivate it.

Neil Fiore, *The Now Habit* and *Awaken Your Strongest Self*. Fiore's work is especially useful for people in recovery who need gentle strategies for getting things done.

Byron Katie, *Loving What Is*. The Work of Byron Katie is a simple yet transformative series of questions about the truth of one's thoughts. The videos at Katie's website, thework.com, give you a look at the process in action.

Sue Monk Kidd, *The Dance of the Dissident Daughter*. A writer who got her start at the inspirational magazine *Guideposts*, Kidd tells the surprising story of her journey from Christian tradition to the sacred feminine.

Eric Maisel, *The Van Gogh Blues, Rethinking Depression*, and *Coaching the Artist Within*. As a coach, writer, and teacher, Maisel has developed a comprehensive body of work on the creative life. His website is ericmaisel.com.

Michael Meade, "Myth Makes Things Whole" at mosaicvoices.org. Meade is a mythologist and the author of *Fate and Destiny*.

Justine Musk, "Service Is an Act of Leadership" at justinemusk.com. Musk writes fiction, and her website is for creative badasses.

Victoria Lynn Schmidt, *45 Master Characters*. Schmidt's book contains a well-developed exploration of the masculine and feminine journeys.

David Schnarch, *Passionate Marriage* and *Intimacy & Desire*. Schnarch has a nuanced and egalitarian approach to strengthening relationships, and his books are filled with satisfying stories of conflict and reconciliation.

Eckhart Tolle, *The Power of Now*. Tolle shares simple teachings about transcending the ego and finding inner peace, inspired by his experience of depression and the spiritual awakening he had at age twenty-nine.

Bethany Webster, "Why It's Crucial for Women to Heal the Mother Wound" at womboflight.com. Webster is a writer and speaker who calls herself a midwife of the heart. Her work is focused on supporting women in living out their truth with self-love.

David Whyte, *The Three Marriages*. Beautifully woven with literature, life, and nature, this is a wise book about how our selves, our work, and our relationships intertwine. I also love Whyte's audio recordings of his poetry and teaching, especially *A Great Invitation* and *Pilgrim*.

Author's Note

I did not know when I started *Pilgrimage of Desire* that I would write about my mother the way I have. I didn't set out to tell stories and expose secret thoughts that might hurt her and others in my family. And yet, the book required certain revelations in order to keep its integrity. I had to go to the very roots of my depression and recovery so that what I wrote was true and whole.

What I did know was that I wanted my parents' blessing on this book. I did my best to win that blessing by talking to them from the beginning and showing them drafts throughout. The difficult chapters I read aloud over video calls and listened to their reactions. We had tearful and difficult discussions that we otherwise might never have had.

Would I still have written and published *Pilgrimage of Desire* if my parents hadn't approved? I don't know. I'm grateful I didn't have to find out. I know other authors keep their writing process private and publish their work in spite of the risk to their relationships, and I respect that choice too. But I wanted to involve my family, and I was able to, so I did.

The hardest conversation happened in August 2012, the summer after we returned from Operation Hejira. While Shawn and I were considering our move to Vancouver, we stayed at my parents' house for a few days. We'd already seen them at the cottage, so the visit felt relaxed and comfortable despite the close quarters in their empty-nester's bungalow.

One night, my parents and I sat down in the living room, and I took a deep breath before starting "the talk" that had been hanging over our heads.

"I'm sorry I don't have more of the book ready for you to look at," I said. "I want to write about what happened with our journal last summer, Mom, and we haven't talked about that yet."

The look on my mom's face was utter consternation, weary and wounded. I waited for her to put her feelings into words.

"Was I that bad of a mother?" she asked with despair, and oh, that pierced me. Because the last thing I want anyone to think — anyone, but especially her — is that I am judging her performance as a parent. What matters to me is not so much her successes and shortcomings as the glorious fact that she is *my* mother. My deep compassion for her is not cancelled out by a frank acknowledgement of how her mothering has shaped me. She is the mother I needed as a child and the mother I need still. By not giving me everything I wanted, she left me something to give myself. Longings unsatisfied, needs unmet, business unfinished, so I could undertake my pilgrimage of desire.

I have deliberately left out the parts of my mother's story that don't intersect with mine. I will leave those things for her to tell when and if she chooses.

The upshot of all these conversations is that we are good. I love my mother and father, and they know that, and they love me. Parts of the book are still painful for them to read. But they believe in the book's purpose, and that means the world to me.

Acknowledgements

I am so thankful for the people who gave their time, money, creativity, and emotional support to shepherd this book along.

Michelle Farinella brought me to tears in the Portland Airport with her vision of what *Pilgrimage of Desire* could be, and she helped me realize that vision through her gorgeous design and unflagging encouragement. Brenda Leifso gave me insightful and poetic editing direction for making this book the best version of itself. Jan Westendorp shared her valuable publishing and printing expertise. Many people gave vital early feedback on the manuscript, particularly Lori-Ann Claerhout and Niya Christine.

I received 157 contributions to the Indiegogo campaign for *Pilgrimage of Desire,* and I treasure the excitement and enthusiasm of the contributors every bit as much as their money. These backers stepped out to make a commitment to the book, and their faith carried me through to completion. Thanks especially to Mark and Joelle Belletrutti, Kevin and Jacquie DeRaaf, Janice Falls, Joanna Gresik, Rick and Brenda Gresik, Keith and Simone Harris-Lowe, and Maile Topliff.

Much gratitude to everyone who appears in this book and all those whose love, friendship, and hospitality played a part in making Operation Hejira such a wonderful experience.

Last and deepest thanks go to my family, who were all generous and full of grace in this whole process. Mom and Dad, your unconditional delight in me is the greatest gift. Melody, Joanna, and Ben, I cherish each of you and your honesty and devotion to staying connected. Lia and Nico, how could I ever put all my love and gratefulness to you into a single sentence? I would need a whole library full of books! Shawn, thank you for your belief in this project and in my ability to pull it off. I couldn't have done any of this without you, and I wouldn't want to.

About the Author

Alison Gresik is a writer and creativity coach. Her debut short story collection, *Brick and Mortar*, was nominated for the Ottawa Book Award in 2001.

Raised in Kingston, Ontario, Alison is a graduate of Redeemer University College and holds an MA in Creative Writing from the University of Calgary. She has published stories in the journals *Descant*, *Grain*, and *IMAGE* and in the anthology *The Company We Keep*.

Alison trained with Eric Maisel and the Creativity Coaching Association and started her coaching business in 2010. She works particularly with writers and artists who are prone to depression. Her website is www.gresik.ca.

Alison lives in Vancouver, BC with her husband Shawn and their two children. But you already knew that!

Permissions

16497404R00164

Printed in Great Britain
by Amazon